BUYING ANTIQUES

A Beginner's Guide to English Antiques

BUYING ANTIQUES

A Beginner's Guide to English Antiques

by

A. W. COYSH and J. KING

FREDERICK A. PRAEGER, *Publishers*

NEW YORK · WASHINGTON

BOOKS THAT MATTER

Published in the United States of America in 1968
by Frederick A. Praeger, Inc., Publishers
111 Fourth Avenue, New York, N.Y. 10003

Library of Congress Catalog Card Number: 68-14155

Printed in Great Britain

CONTENTS

5

LIST OF ILLUSTRATIONS

PLATES

7

LINE DRAWINGS

FOREWORD

MOST books on antiques assume that the reader has some knowledge of the subject. This book makes no such assumption. It has been written for the interested amateur and for this reason should prove useful in helping him to identify works of art and in directing his attention to some of the main points to be considered when buying antiques in sale-room or shop. The prices at auction given at the end of the book give some indication of price ranges as at 1967.

Arthur G. Negus

ACKNOWLEDGMENTS

WE are greatly indebted to Arthur Negus, Bernard Price, and Paul and Ken Smith who read the manuscript of this book and offered many helpful suggestions, and also to the many saleroom contacts who have helped us with information about prices; also to John Bone for the drawings, to Michael Wagen who took the photographs, and to the BBC for permission to use them.

A. W. COYSH
J. KING

CHAPTER ONE

BUYING ANTIQUES

W HAT is an antique? To all intents and purposes, any useful or decorative object produced by artists or craftsmen is regarded by the trade as an antique provided it is more than 100 years old. This is the period generally recognized by antique dealers though most organizers of antique fairs will only accept furniture made before 1830. The object must be sufficiently esteemed and sought-after to have value, and it may be coveted for various reasons—its beauty, craftsmanship, rarity or curiosity.

It is not wise to assume that all the goods for sale in shops which bear the sign 'Antiques' must be over 100 years old. Many shops and dealers sell items made during the last 100 years if they have a special interest for the antique-buying public—reproductions, *art nouveau* and late Victorian articles eighty or ninety years old which will become antique relatively soon and for this reason are attractive to people who are buying as a form of investment.

It is possible, even in a relatively short period, to develop a 'sense' about antiques: mistakes will certainly be made but confidence will soon grow, particularly if a special study is made of one field. If, for example, it is decided to concentrate on porcelain, or even porcelain of one period or of one maker, then knowledge and experience will accumulate relatively quickly, and you will soon feel able to back your own judgment and to buy with confidence.

What are the main fields? Among the most popular is silver, though much of this is expensive and beyond the price the average person can afford. Sheffield plate, however, can still be obtained quite reasonably. So can some furniture, especially that of the early and mid-Victorian periods and, surprisingly enough, some quite old pieces of oak and country-made furniture. Glass is a difficult subject. There is so little to be seen in a piece of glass which helps the collector to date it—and it can easily be copied. Nor is it easy for the beginner to recognize faked glassware.

Pottery is of wide interest and remains one of the most rewarding fields for the collector. It has always been cheaper than porcelain, because it was made in large quantities for those who could not afford the finer wares. In fact, poorer folk often demanded earthenware designs similar to the porcelain ones used by the wealthy. They also created a form of cottage art that delightfully reflects many of the sports, manners and customs of the time.

As a result of this demand, fine craftsmen appeared in the potteries: men like Ralph and Enoch Wood. Much of their work, particularly their figures, attracted a good deal of attention and was bought by people well up in the social scale. Later, there was also a considerable middle-class market for pottery, and manufacturers such as Spode turned out beautiful dinner-sets in simply decorated transfer ware.

Prints and paintings provide another profitable hunting-ground. Armed with a few essential facts and a discriminating personal taste, even the amateur can build up a small collection which will increase in value and provide constant pleasure.

Some people have no urge to 'collect' but enjoy having beautiful things around them in their homes—good antique furniture, a few fine pieces of decorative glass or porcelain, the odd print or painting. Fair enough. They will enhance the look of any room and bring themselves and their friends much real enjoyment.

But let us begin at the beginning. What is the best way to set about buying antiques? If you know absolutely nothing, the obvious thing to do is to go to a reputable antique dealer, tell him what you want and ask him to help you. Very often he will be willing to give you a written guarantee that the article you buy is a genuine piece of a certain period, style and date. You will obviously have to pay more than you might have to for a similar article in a saleroom because you are paying for his judgment and experience and he also has to make a fair profit. But until you feel you can rely on your own judgment this may well be the wisest thing to do. On the other hand, you will obviously be a little less likely to pick up a real bargain in this way than by hunting around secondhand stores and junk shops.

Then there are the public auctions, sometimes held in a sale-room, sometimes in a private house when the executors of an estate decide to dispose of the contents. It is possible to learn a great deal from these sales, particularly about current values, even without actually buying. But if the intention is to buy, it is wise to avoid being carried away by the excitement. Decide in advance the maximum price you are prepared to pay *before the bidding starts*. Resist any temptation to go higher or you may well regret it afterwards. On the other hand, never be afraid of bidding firmly and making your presence felt.

Auctioneers can no longer put the onus on the buyer to decide whether their description of an object is accurate or not. The Misrepresentation Act now provides a clear remedy for anyone who has been misled by a false catalogue description. The buyer has the right to revoke a contract within a reasonable period irrespective of whether the description was made in good faith or not. Nevertheless, check everything very thoroughly and do remember that some repairs are invisible to the naked eye. If you intend to buy a particularly expensive item it is always advisable to have it thoroughly checked in advance by an expert. For example, a skilfully repaired piece of porcelain must be examined under ultra-violet radiation to reveal the hidden damage. Well-executed repairs to furniture are often done with old wood and can only be detected by the most experienced eye. Most auctioneers will respect your caution and will readily agree to a detailed inspection, but it must normally be carried out during the time when the objects are on view to the public. Inspection of this kind would rarely be allowed during the actual sale. So it is wise to view as early as possible in case you need to consult an expert or look up the reference books.

Attending auction sales is a time-consuming business: it may be necessary to wait several hours before the particular item you are interested in comes 'under the hammer'. It is worth remembering that most auctioneers average from sixty to 100 lots an hour. Check with the firm responsible : they know their auction-eers. If you want to leave the saleroom for a time, it is possible to work out from the catalogue roughly when the item which interests you will be sold. If you find it impossible to attend a sale but can manage to view the lots at some other time to decide what you want to buy, ask one of the saleroom staff to bid for you, telling him the price you are prepared to pay for any given lot. It is usual to give him a gratuity for this service : about one shilling in the pound would be reasonable on most purchases, though obviously it should be a little more on a very cheap item. Finally, it is a mistake to be in a hurry to buy. Buying is an art in itself. Have a good look round, and compare the quality, con-dition and price of what the shops have to offer before making a final decision. A real lover of antiques never gives up the search; he keeps looking for what he wants. The very article may come in to an antique shop from a private house or a saleroom at any hour of any day and, if it is a 'good buy', it will soon have gone again.

A good motto for the inexperienced is 'if in doubt, leave it alone'. To recognize a real bargain needs knowledge and experi-ence, but the possibility that a real 'discovery' may one day be made always adds interest and excitement to the search.

1. Oyster-shell veneering on a William and Mary chest

2. *Part of the back of a Victorian papier mâché chair with mother-of-pearl inlay*

FURNITURE

ONE of the greatest pleasures for those who are developing an interest in antiques comes from the detective work involved in 'placing' an article. When was it made? Where was it made? Who made it?

How does an auctioneer decide on the descriptions he will issue in his sale catalogue? The 'Sheraton mahogany bow-fronted side-board' and the 'William IV oval cake-dish, pierced and chased, by Charles Fox, London 1835, 22½ oz', for example. Many sale-rooms employ experts who advise on such things. We aim to help the amateur to identify items and to understand some of the descriptions he will inevitably meet in the antique shop or the auction room.

The first problem is to decide roughly when an article was made; in other words, the period to which it belongs. The period time-table for antiques in Britain on the next page is closely related to the reigning British Sovereigns. It covers the seventeenth, eighteenth and nineteenth centuries and refers particularly to furniture. In earlier Tudor times, furnishings were sparse and very utilitarian in design, consisting almost entirely of trestle tables, stools, beds and chests made of oak: carving was very simple. Items of this kind are rare.

In Stuart times, however, the demand for furniture increased and craftsmen began to develop wood-turning as a means of embellishment; carving began to lose favour. Screws had not been invented at this time, so parts were secured by mortice and tenon joints held together by wooden pins or dowels. This was joinery as distinct from cabinet-making. Hinges and lock plates were of iron. The early Stuart furniture of the reigns of James I and

Period Time Table for Antiques in Britain	Reigning Sovereign	French Influences on British Styles
ELIZABETHAN 1600	ELIZABETH	
JACOBEAN (Conventionally used for antiques of the reigns of James I and Charles I)	JAMES I 1603-1625	
	CHARLES I 1625-1649	
CROMWELLIAN or COMMONWEALTH, 1649-1659 RESTORATION	CHARLES II 1649-1685	LOUIS XIV 1643-1715 A period distinguished by the pomp which surrounded Versailles. Large ornate furniture, often gilded
	JAMES II 1685-1688	
WILLIAM and MARY QUEEN ANNE Period of Dutch Influence 1700	WILLIAM AND MARY 1689-1702	
	QUEEN ANNE 1702-1714	
	GEORGE I 1714-1727	LOUIS XV 1715-1774 A more delicate 'rococo' style of decoration and inlay but very intricate. Some influence on Chippendale
THE GEORGIAN PERIOD was noted for its designers, especially of furniture. These men gave their names to styles which are widely recognized. (See Fig. 3)	GEORGE II 1727-1760	
————————1800	GEORGE III 1760-1820	LOUIS XVI 1774-1793 Simpler and more delicate forms
The term 'REGENCY' is used for the period from 1800 to 1830.	THE REGENCY 1811-1820	EMPIRE to about 1830 During the Directoire period, after the French Revolution, a new style developed in imitation of the styles of early Greece and Rome. Empire furniture was strong, massive and decorated with gilt bronze mounts. Greatly influenced British Regency style.
	GEORGE IV 1820-1830	
	WILLIAM IV 1830-1837	
VICTORIAN	VICTORIA 1837-1901	
1900		

EDWARD VII
1901-1910

Figure 1   THE ANTIQUE PERIODS

Charles I is commonly referred to as Jacobean. Then came the Civil War and the furniture made in Cromwellian or Commonwealth times between 1649 and 1660 became plainer, in keeping with the puritanical philosophy of the day. In the Restoration period which followed in the reign of Charles II, the pendulum swung back. New designs emerge: the spiral twist and woven cane seats and backs are seen in chairs, and the 'grandfather' or long-case clock appears for the first time.

The William and Mary and Queen Anne periods produced what is generally regarded as some of the finest English furniture. By now the craftsmen were taking a great pride in the finish of an article and were paying much more attention to overall balance of design. Veneering and inlay work flourished and carving had almost been forgotten. Furniture in these periods was often small—a highly desirable quality today.

As George I came to the throne, furniture-making was becoming more of an art than a craft and designs became more elegant with no loss of strength. The cabinet-maker was coming into his own. This process developed throughout the Georgian period, reaching its height in the reign of George III.

The term 'Regency' in the strict sense covers the years from 1811 to 1820 but as far as antiques and architecture are concerned it is used to cover the three decades from 1800 to 1830, a period which saw a complete change in furniture design. It became more decorative and was greatly influenced by the new 'Empire' style in France which, in turn, was inspired by the designs of ancient Greece and Egypt.

By 1830, the use of machinery for making furniture was increasing and the number of first-class craftsmen steadily declined. In wealthier Victorian times the size of furniture often seems to reflect social status. Carving returned with a vengeance and was often pretentious, fussy and ornate. Much of the grace that had been achieved in the previous hundred years was lost. There were, nevertheless, some distinctive styles in domestic furniture which emerged as a result of the great emphasis placed on comfort. The framework of the armchair and sofa had to lend itself to the padding of the arms and backs. Outlines became rounded and square backs disappeared. Over the same period veneering and inlay virtually disappeared and ornamentation was restricted to the carving of solid wood, usually mahogany, rosewood or walnut. In general, metal handles on furniture were giving way to wooden ones.

In the Edwardian period which followed, some of the vulgarity of the previous hundred years seems to have been recognized and the cabinet-makers spent much of the time copying—often quite well—the eighteenth-century designs of Sheraton. This is why the words 'Sheraton-style china cabinet' so often appears in auction sale catalogues; many were made in Edwardian times.

Materials readily available for making furniture varied from period to period and fashions also played a part. Some timbers were cut from our own British trees, others were imported from all parts of the world. Only those people closely associated with the antique furniture trade, or who work constantly with timber of all kinds, are likely to be able to recognize the many woods that have been employed over the years. But most people can soon learn to identify those which have been widely used.

The earliest furniture was made of oak drawn mainly from the woodlands which, in Tudor and Stuart times, extended more widely over the lowland areas of Britain than they do now. It is a coarse-grained, heavy wood noted for its strength. It has a great colour range but over the years develops a fine natural sheen or patina from polishing and constant use. It also darkens with age and is less subject to woodworm than many other woods. In late Stuart times, a good deal of oak was either japanned or else coated with several layers of varnish and then polished. This protected the oak which was otherwise liable to warp from changes of humidity and temperature.

Towards the end of the seventeenth century, in Restoration times, walnut became very popular for making solid furniture. Much of it came from England—a pale brown wood with dark veining—but the severe winter of 1709 destroyed many walnut trees and supplies had to be supplemented by considerable imports from France. Walnut had advantages over oak; the closer grain enabled craftsmen to produce a smoother finish to their work; moreover walnut is slightly softer and lighter than oak and the varied direction of grain makes it easier to work. It soon became so much in demand that supplies were insufficient and craftsmen began to use veneers of walnut, thin sheets of the wood glued to a carcase made of a cheaper and often softer wood, such as pine. In the early part of the eighteenth century France stopped her exports of walnut and supplies of a darker walnut from the eastern U.S.A. were brought in. The very definite whirled graining of some walnut was used to advantage. This oyster-shell veneering was very popular during the William and Mary period (Plate 1). The growth rings in each of the pieces of applied veneer look very like the concentric circular layers seen on oyster shells. Plain walnut furniture of the early eighteenth century was often decorated with patterns made from different coloured woods and set into the piece. This is known as inlay: an example is shown in Plate 3. This method of decorating furniture grew in popularity as the years passed and reached perfection in French furniture (Plate 4).

In the early eighteenth century a new imported wood was being tried—mahogany. *The Book of Trees* (1852) tells the story of how it came into use.

> A London physician of the name of Gibbon had a brother the captain of a West India ship. On his return to England he had several logs of mahogany on board his vessel for the purpose of ballast, and as his brother was at that time employed in a building project, he made him a present of the wood, supposing it might be useful; his carpenter, however, cast it on one side, observing that it was of too hard a nature to be worked. Some time after, Mrs Gibbon being in want of a box to hold candles, the cabinet-maker was directed to make it of this same wood; he, in his turn, made the same objection as the carpenter, and declared that it spoilt his tools. Being urged, however, to make another trial, he at length succeeded; and when the box was polished, the beautiful colour of its grain was so apparent and novel, that it became an object of great curiosity, and attracted the notice, among others, of the Duchess of Buckingham, for whom a bureau was made of the same material.

By about 1730, much fine-quality mahogany was being brought into Britain, mainly from Jamaica. It has a rich, reddish-brown colour and a fine, straight grain and is an extremely strong wood for making veneers. Its fineness of grain made it particularly well-suited to the highly-polished surfaces which were being demanded, while the size of the trees provided wide boards especially suitable for tabletops. In early Georgian times it was used for making solid furniture, and replaced walnut as the chief wood. By the reign of George III it was being used for fine veneering.

As the supplies of mahogany from Jamaica began to run out, new sources were tapped in San Domingo and Cuba. This wood is known in the trade as Spanish mahogany. Still later, supplies came from Honduras but this timber, which grows on the flat, marshy coastlands, is lighter and looser in texture than the timber from the mountainous West Indian islands, though easier to work. The trained eye can distinguish between the various types of mahogany.

From about 1760, the light, golden-coloured satinwood which, as its name suggests, has a sheen like satin, gradually came into fashion. Some came from the West Indies, some from the East Indies. Both varieties were used for all forms of inlay decoration. Satinwood was also widely used for cross-banding since the light colour made an agreeable contrast to the reddish browns of mahogany.

Rosewood—a deep brown wood with definite darker stripes running through it—first came in towards the end of the seventeenth century but lent itself particularly to the flamboyant furniture of the Regency period, when it was widely used for solid work and veneering. It continued to find favour in Victorian times. Rosewood gets its name from the pleasing, fragrant aroma it gives off while being worked.

Zebra wood, used mainly between 1780 and 1820, is rather similar to rosewood in appearance, but the contrast between the stripes and the ground colour is stronger.

Ebony is a hard, black wood usually used for inlay work or for smaller pieces of furniture, though some was used for larger pieces during the late seventeenth century. Softer, close-grained woods were often stained black or 'ebonized' to represent ebony, but they can usually be detected by their lighter weight.

Woods such as ash, beech, yew, elm and chestnut were used a great deal during the seventeenth, eighteenth and nineteenth

	Antique Period	Favourite Woods	Some Innovations
SEVENTEENTH CENTURY 1600 — 1650 — 1700 —	ELIZABETHAN		
	JACOBEAN	OAK	
	COMMONWEALTH		Veneering begins
	RESTORATION		The earliest marquetry
	WILLIAM and MARY	WALNUT	Japanning started (1688)
EIGHTEENTH CENTURY 1750 —	QUEEN ANNE		Cabriole legs appear First imports of mahogany
	GEORGIAN	MAHOGANY	
		SATINWOOD	'Paper Ware' patented 1772—leading to *Papiermâché*
19th CENTURY 1800 — 1850 — 1900 —	GEORGIAN (REGENCY)	ROSEWOOD	
	VICTORIAN	MAHOGANY and ROSEWOOD	Revival of interest in rosewood about 1850

Figure 2   THE FAVOURITE WOODS FOR FURNITURE MAKING

centuries as they rather resembled oak in general appearance but were easier to work. These woods were used particularly by country craftsmen but they are prone to woodworm. You will find, however, that woodworm detracts little from the value of really good early country furniture.

Another material was used from the second half of the eighteenth century as an alternative to wood for making furniture, particularly smaller items such as tea caddies, spill holders and trays. This is now generally known as *papier mâché*, though an early form invented by Henry Clay in 1772 should strictly be referred to as paperware.

Papier mâché was made from layers of rags or paper soaked in an adhesive mixture of such materials as flour, size or glue. The pulped paper was then pressed into a metal mould, a layer at a time, and baked. The final product could be worked like wood and was so strong that even chairs could be made from it. The surface was covered with black lacquer, which was then polished by hand. *Papier mâché* articles were usually decorated with coloured or gilded floral designs or landscapes. A number of pieces were inlaid with mother-of-pearl (Plate 2). It is generally agreed that some of the best-quality *papier mâché* was made by Jennens and Bettridge between about 1820 and 1850, but only a few pieces bear a maker's name.

The quality of antique furniture depends on its design, the quality of the wood, and the standard of the workmanship. The finest pieces tend to be associated with the name of a designer, a craftsman, or a particular workshop which settled for nothing but the best. During the eighteenth century, designs were not protected by copyright and they could therefore be copied freely. As a result, a number of well-known 'styles' were established, based on the work of the best designers. Anyone developing an interest in antiques must aim to recognize these, although the actual work of the best designers and craftsmen is beyond the means of the average person buying for the home.

In the eighteenth and early nineteenth century the style of many pieces was set by one of the designers of the period—men such as William Kent, Thomas Chippendale, Robert Adam, George Hepplewhite, Thomas Sheraton and Thomas Hope. Their designs became widely popular because they were published in book form and could be copied by fine cabinet makers and by small firms all over the country.

Kent, who spent some time in Italy studying painting, was not only a furniture designer but artist, architect and landscape designer as well. His furniture in the 1730s was solid in appearance with cabriole legs and much decoration with acanthus leaves and gilding. He also used carved eagles and dolphins. Some of his designs were published in 1744 in a book by Vardy called *Designs of Inigo Jones and Kent*.

Chippendale was a Yorkshireman whose father was a carpenter, but it is known that by the time he was thirty years of age he was married and working in London. He took a shop in Long Acre and later acquired premises in St Martin's Lane. Although he already had an established business reputation as a maker of furniture, his real influence dates from 1754 when he issued 150 designs in *The Gentleman and Cabinet-maker's Director*, some of which were by cabinet-makers who worked for him. Chippendale had a fine eye for proportion and adapted many of the earlier and heavy Georgian designs to produce furniture—mainly in mahogany—which was lighter and more graceful but at the same time just as strong. His tables and chairs often have ball and claw feet on cabriole legs. His chairs often have carved splats and the line of the top rail is usually curved or broken. Many people regard Chippendale as the finest of all furniture designers; contemporary cabinet-makers who used his designs to make their own pieces were responsible for the wide range of furniture known as 'Chippendale'.

Before Chippendale died in 1779 a new style was beginning to establish itself. This was associated with the name of Robert Adam, son of a Scottish architect. He did not make furniture himself but used his architectural training and skill (which had been greatly influenced by travel in Italy and France) to initiate designs derived from classical styles. The trend away from the heaviness of early Georgian furniture started by Chippendale was carried much further by Adam. Everything became lighter and more elegant, the ornamentation had a new delicate beauty and in due course the material used changed from mahogany to lighter

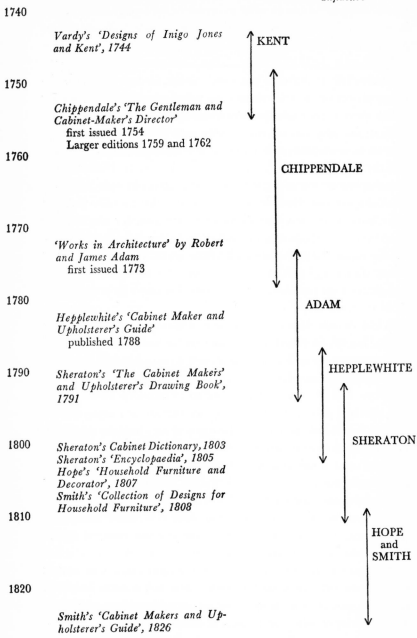

Publication of Design Books

Years of Greatest Influence

1740

Vardy's 'Designs of Inigo Jones and Kent', 1744

KENT

1750

Chippendale's 'The Gentleman and Cabinet-Maker's Director'
first issued 1754
Larger editions 1759 and 1762

1760

CHIPPENDALE

1770

'Works in Architecture' by Robert and James Adam
first issued 1773

1780

ADAM

Hepplewhite's 'Cabinet Maker and Upholsterer's Guide'
published 1788

1790

Sheraton's 'The Cabinet Makers' and Upholsterer's Drawing Book', *1791*

HEPPLEWHITE

1800

Sheraton's Cabinet Dictionary, 1803
Sheraton's 'Encyclopaedia', 1805
Hope's 'Household Furniture and Decorator', 1807
Smith's 'Collection of Designs for Household Furniture', 1808

SHERATON

1810

HOPE
and
SMITH

1820

Smith's 'Cabinet Makers and Upholsterer's Guide', 1826

1830

Figure 3   CABINET-MAKERS AND DESIGNERS OF THE
GEORGIAN PERIOD

woods such as beech painted in white or soft greens and blues. Adam's designs were issued in *Works in Architecture* which was prepared in collaboration with his brother, James, and started publication in 1773.

Meanwhile, a well-known cabinet-maker, George Hepplewhite, was working on his own designs in a London workshop, designs which were to gain little popularity in his lifetime. They were not particularly original; he was mainly interested in making chairs and these were based on Chippendale's designs with the splats and the legs fined down to produce a lighter style. He loved the graceful line and made great use of the curve, introducing oval, heart-shaped and shield-shaped backs. He died in 1786 but two years later his widow published his *Cabinet-maker and Upholsterers' Guide* which ran through three editions in a few years. This is when Hepplewhite's influence really began and it continued until roughly 1800. It is interesting to note that he was the first designer to use the Prince of Wales' feathers as a decorative motif on furniture.

While Robert Adam was still alive, a third influence came into play. Thomas Sheraton who, although he had some training as a cabinet-maker, had no workshop of his own, brought out some fine new designs in *The Cabinet-maker and Upholsterers' Drawing Book* in 1791. His designs tend to be 'straight and narrow'. He damned Chippendale's work as out-of-date and reacted against the use of the curve. There is a severe look about Sheraton chairs when compared with earlier designs. But he rejoiced in detail and much Sheraton furniture has fine veneering with satinwood and sycamore, and beautiful inlay work using satinwood, tulipwood and many other carefully-chosen materials.

Sheraton followed his first book with a *Cabinet Dictionary* (1803) and a *Cabinet-maker, Upholsterer, and General Artists Encyclopaedia* (1805). He died in 1806.

Already the influence of the French Empire style was having its effect on this side of the Channel, based as it was on the earlier styles of Greece and Rome and on the antiquities of Egypt. Thomas Hope, who came from a Dutch banking family, had travelled widely in Mediterranean countries. This, and his friendship with the French architect, Percier, led him to work on classical styles for the fashionable English market. In 1807, his *House-hold Furniture and Decoration* was published. Later, the Regency style became even more complicated : both Gothic and Oriental influences can be seen in the famous Brighton Pavilion. Unfortunately, many of Hope's designs for furniture paid too little attention to comfort and homeliness to satisfy many ordinary people. To meet the popular demand, they were often modified by the men who had to make and sell their goods. George Smith, a London furniture-maker, did this on a considerable scale and issued his own collection of designs for *Household Furniture and Interior Decoration* in 1808. He was certainly influenced by Hope but he also studied the work of Augustus Charles Pugin, the architect, who was anxious to revive the Gothic style. George Smith's second book, *The Cabinet-makers' and Upholsterers' Guide* published in 1826, reveals the influence of Pugin's ideas.

BUYING FURNITURE

Much of the fine furniture made by early craftsmen has lasted for generations and is now keenly sought. It often commands prices as high as those paid for articles made of precious metals such as silver. The value, of course, lies in the workmanship and because the basic material used in furniture—mainly wood—is relatively cheap, it is a field in which there is a great deal of faking and open reproduction of earlier styles. Moreover, since furniture suffers greatly from wear and tear, comparatively little old furniture is in its original state : most pieces have had repair work of some kind done to them. This is why the expert studies pieces with such great care. He will probably start by making a quick assessment at a glance but before he will commit himself to a certain identification he will open cupboards, pull out drawers, look carefully at handles and hinges and scrutinize the piece in detail and from every angle.

What does one need to know about antique furniture? The period during which it was made, the 'style', and the type of wood used. When this identification has been made it should be possible to assess its value, which will depend to a great extent on the craftsmanship and the condition. It is also helpful to know

Figure 4   CHAIR BACKS

(a) Caning, carving and spiral twist (Stuart, second half seventeenth century)
(b) Solid Splat (Queen Anne and early Georgian)
(c) Ladder Back (Chippendale, mid-eighteenth century)
(d) Wheel Back (Hepplewhite, late eighteenth century)
(e) Gothick (Chippendale, mid-eighteenth century)
(f) Ribband Back (Chippendale, mid-eighteenth century)

Figure 5   MORE CHAIR BACKS

(a) Chinese (Chippendale, mid-eighteenth century)
(b) Shield Back (Hepplewhite, late eighteenth century)
(c) Stuffed Oval (Adam, late eighteenth century)
(d) Prince of Wales Plumes (Hepplewhite, late eighteenth century)
(e) Sheraton (late eighteenth century)
(f) Balloon Back (Victorian, mid-nineteenth century)

how articles have been made because methods of construction varied according to the practice of the time and the tools available to the craftsmen.

The amount of furniture actually made by the great designers and cabinet-makers of the eighteenth century, or by the craftsmen and apprentices in their workshops, must be very small indeed, thought it is very occasionally possible to identify a piece when it is signed. It was their designs which were significant and the circulation of their design books, which were used by small firms all over the country, led to the wide popularity of their styles. Much of this early furniture consists of so-called 'country-made' pieces. Wealthier people could afford the expensive work turned out by the finest craftsmen using the very best materials but this was beyond the means of many country people, who, instead, bought from small carpenters who tried to be in the fashion by copying the work of the London designers. Country-made pieces are noted for their simplicity and lack the finish of the finer pieces. The woods used were very often cheaper and there was relatively little carving, partly because this took time and added to the cost, and partly because country craftsmen seldom had the skill to do this kind of work. Nevertheless, much country furniture is good and attractive and may often be obtained at a reasonable price.

The homes of the wealthy in the eighteenth and nineteenth centuries were larger than houses are today and furniture, too, tended to be larger. Small antique pieces which will fit readily into the modern home are therefore in greater demand and are consequently more expensive. Bureaux, chests of drawers and side tables are usually much less desirable if they are more than about 3 ft wide.

Because of the demand for small furniture, many larger pieces have been cut down and reassembled. This should be watched for. If a suspect piece has drawers, look for the marks where the handles may originally have been attached. If the drawer front has been cut down, the handles will have been moved inwards to retain the balance. Look also at the drawer runners, which should show considerable signs of wear in an old piece of furniture as the result of years of pushing and pulling out. Made up tables are relatively common. These may well have legs from one period married to the top from another.

Victorian furniture, which a few years ago was in little de-demand, is now commanding quite high prices. Much of it is full of character and can look charming in the right setting. Given time to seek out the right pieces, it is certainly possible to furnish a home with nineteenth-century furniture for little more than it would cost to equip it with the modern, mass-produced article. Even good-quality Edwardian furniture is increasing in price: in a 1966 auction sale a mahogany display cabinet, banded in satinwood, fetched £122. But this was not an 'antique'. We now consider a number of articles which are older but still relatively inexpensive.

Tables

These are always useful for a variety of purposes, and there is a wide selection to choose from. It is fair to say that, on the whole, the heavier a table is, the cheaper it is. For this reason, quite early country-made oak tables are worth looking for, especially the seventeenth-century, Jacobean-style, gate-legged table which was still made in large numbers well into the eighteenth century. Look for tenon and mortice joints with dowel pins. In early oak furniture the dowel pins are usually irregular in shape—never exactly circular. The turned legs of an old table will differ very slightly if you examine them closely, unlike the precision machine-made examples current today. The stretchers will normally show signs of wear where people have rested their feet on them but they should nevertheless show a good patina. Prices of such tables, however, are rising rapidly. Round tables with single pillars and three legs are commoner and cheaper. They have been made at all periods, especially in oak and mahogany. The single pillars allow more seating and more knee room. These tables usually tilt: there is a catch below the top which, when released, allows the top to be tipped up vertically so that the table may be placed against a wall. If the tops are large, this looks rather ugly; consequently, sought-after examples tend to be small. The pillars of these tables are usually turned, though some are fluted or writhen

3. *Sunburst inlay commonly used in the reign of George I*

4. *Marquetry work on a nineteenth-century French desk, using tulipwood, kingwood and satinwood*

5. *Dowelling on early oak furniture*

6. *Split-pin used to secure a drawer handle*

Figure 6   CHAIR LEGS AND FEET

Legs: *(a)* Turned; *(b)* Cabriole; *(c)* Moulded; *(d)* Tapered; *(e)* Sabre;
(f) Turned and Fluted
Feet: *(g)* Pad; *(h)* Hoof; *(i)* Scroll; *(j)* Claw and Ball; *(k)* Spade or Peg

c

Figure 7 FURNITURE MOUNTS AND SUPPORTS

Mounts: *(a)* Axe Drop (mid-seventeenth century); *(b)* Swan Neck with shaped pierced plate (early eighteenth century); *(c)* Pear Drop (late seventeenth century); *(d)* Swan Neck (Queen Anne); *(e)* Lion Mask (Regency); *(f)* Pierced back plate with Chinese influence (mid-eighteenth century); *(g)* Neo-classical (Adam); *(h)* Prince of Wales plumes (late eighteenth century); *(i)* French Rococo (mid-eighteenth century)
Supports: *(j)* Ball; *(k)* Bun; *(l)* Ogee; *(m)* Bracket; *(n)* Splayed Bracket

(twisted). The legs may vary from the sabre of the Regency period to the legs with 'knees' of the Victorian period. In general, the more definite the 'knee' the later in Victoria's reign the table was made.

Two- or three-pillar dining tables are much sought after but are generally expensive. Many Victorian dining tables had extra leaves which were fastened into place with brass clips at the sides.

Several other types of table of the Victorian period are attractive and have many uses. Small card tables were often made which would either stand against a wall or open out to a green baize top measuring about 3 ft by 3 ft 6 in. They were often made in pairs, one of which had a plain polished interior which could be used as a tea table.

Pembroke tables have flaps hanging on each of the longer sides which can be opened up to form quite a large dining table. They usually have a long shallow drawer at one end, the other end having a matching 'dummy' drawer.

Sofa tables were a direct invention of the Regency period, and were so-called because of their normal position in the house— behind the sofa which stood in the middle of the room. These tables have a flap which drops on each of the two shorter sides. Usually the long side contains drawers. However, there are sometimes two drawers to one side with 'dummy' drawers on the back; sometimes one drawer and a 'dummy' on each side. Unfortunately, many such tables in Victorian times were rather heavy and clumsy.

Sutherland tables are reputed to have been named after the Duchess of Sutherland who popularized the design during the Victorian period. These are small flap tables normally about 3 ft long by 2 ft wide when in the open position. The flaps are supported by legs which pull out in the same way as a gate-leg table and when folded down they take up very little room. They are usually quite low and are ideal tables for coffee or cards.

Wine tables were often placed around a room within comfortable reach of easy-chairs so that books or drinks could be placed on them. They are sometimes known as pedestal or tripod tables and, as these names imply, they had a single column leg with a small round top, usually 1 ft to 2 ft in diameter and three feet.

Chairs

Dining-room chairs were made in sets—as they are today—and are valued as such. A set of six matching chairs might, for example, fetch £80, whereas as single chairs they might only be worth about £5 or £6 each. Some early Victorian dining-room chairs can be very attractive. Following the Regency period in 1830, most chairs retained the broad yoke-rail back which extended beyond the uprights which were joined lower down by a narrower horizontal splat, nearly always carved. The front legs were straight and either turned or fluted. The seats were padded. Within a few years the broad yoke-rail began to disappear and chairs were made in which the uprights and the back follow a continuous curve which became more pronounced as the years passed. By 1845, the full-blown balloon-back chair was common.

Mother and Father chairs were very popular during the Victorian period. Father chairs are the large, upholstered, easy chairs with arms; the Mother chair is a smaller matching chair, often without arms. They can be bought separately and matched later, as many of the designs were standard.

The frames of these delightful chairs are usually made of mahogany, rosewood or beech. Examine beech pieces with great care. Beech is a softer and cheaper wood very subject to woodworm. Check that the joints are sound, paying particular attention to the point where the back legs join the chair and the point where the arms of the 'Father' chair join. The upholstery is often 'button-backed'. If you buy these chairs intending to have them re-upholstered, remember that labour alone on such a job can cost from £8 to £12 per chair.

Victorian sofas were the equivalent of the modern settee. These varied enormously in size and, as a rule, it is safe to say that the larger they are the more comfortable they are likely to be. The small salon-type sofa with a very upright back may have been suitable for the postures of the period, but is hardly so for relaxing. Watch out for those which have been cut down from large settees, a slice having been taken from the middle and the two ends rejoined.

Chests of Drawers

Victorian chests of drawers are usually very large; they seemed to believe in the old saying 'the bigger the better'. The craftsmanship was superb and the woods excellent. If you are lucky enough to find a smaller one, you will have a nice-looking, durable piece of furniture. Many had bow fronts which give a graceful appearance. Unfortunately, the Victorians were very fond of large wooden handles which project into the room and are a constant cause of bumps and bruises. These have often been removed and replaced by brass drop handles.

It is useful to know that in most eighteenth-century furniture made before 1730 the grain in the wood in the bottom of the drawer runs from back to front. From 1730 to 1830, it was made to run from side to side and from about 1810 a rounded beading was usually inserted along each inside bottom edge of the drawers so that dust would not collect in the crevices.

Desks

Most Victorian desks and bureaux were so large that they are seldom suitable for the small modern home, but from this period come some of the most delightful small or ladies' desks, generally known as davenports. The name derives from the fact that the first customer to order one from Gillow of Lancaster was a Captain Davenport. They had a great appeal to ladies of late Regency and Victorian days, who were great writers of notes, letters and formal invitations. The whole of one side of a davenport is usually devoted to drawers, with compartments inside for storing stationery and writing materials. Those with good interior fittings are worth more money. Davenports are very useful pieces of furniture: they are not only small and decorative but contain a great deal of valuable storage space.

'What Nots'

These normally consist of four turned posts, usually on castors, which support a series of shelves and sometimes a shallow drawer.

They were used for ornaments, photographs and knick-knacks and first appeared in Regency times. In Victorian days, few houses were without them. They can still be bought quite reasonably if, indeed you have any desire for one. They can be very useful as display units or magazine stands or, if you are lucky enough to find one large enough, strong enough and low enough, as a television table.

Mirrors

Mirrors are an essential part of any home and antique mirrors are usually most attractive. The mirrored glass is generally referred to as the plate. Most frames are of wood, though there are some in ceramic frames and occasionally in a metal frame. In some early mirrors the reflecting part was made of highly polished metal.

In the second half of the seventeenth century in Britain mirrors were usually rectangular and relatively small, as no technique had been discovered for mirroring large sheets of glass. The workshop which first suceeded in doing so was the Duke of Buckingham's Glass Works, Vauxhall, London. In the early eighteenth century this opened up a new range of possibilities for the mirror-maker and extremely large mirrors were often made, sometimes covering large portions of a wall. The glass or plate in such early mirrors is usually quite thin. The thickness of a mirror glass can be determined by holding a pointed object against the surface of the glass and noting the distance between the point and the reflection of the point. Most old plate has discoloured over the years and has a distinct blue-green or grey-green tinge and a mottled effect which gives a mildewed appearance. Bevelled glass in mirrors was popular during the reign of Queen Anne. Because the glass was so thin the bevels are usually broad and shallow. It was often set in plain wooden frames veneered with strips of walnut and edged with gilded plaster work (Plate 11). The most important part of an old mirror is, of course, the frame, though it is always more valuable if it contains the original plate in reasonably good condition. Carved wood gilded frames appear to be the most popular and heading the list are those designed by Chippendale in the Chinese taste. Gilt frames were plentiful during the nineteenth century but were cheaply made of plaster shaped to look like carved wood and then gilded. It is sometimes difficult to distinguish between gilded wood and plaster. To do so, take a pin and press it slowly but firmly into a high point of relief in the frame. Then, holding the pin by its head, slowly pull. If the pin comes out with little or no effort it is plaster; if it needs a little tug to remove it, then it is wood. Do remember, however, that most of the plaster work was built up on a wooden base, so try the pin test in several different places.

Many carved wood picture frames today pose as mirror frames. Among these is a particular type of carved wood frame which was very common in Italy during the late eighteenth and early nineteenth century. These, though desirable, are not as valuable as those made in this country. They can be distinguished by their florid, curling carved leaves; they are light in weight for their size and the gilding has a distinctly green tinge.

In the eighteenth century, a plaster-like substance made of a mixture of chalk and size was used for decorating woodwork. This is known as gesso work and it is often difficult for an amateur to distinguish between this and nineteenth-century plaster work. In gesso, the 'plaster' is very thin; in plaster work it is completely solid.

Many early mirrors have candles fitted to them. This served two purposes. The candles illuminated the face of the person using the mirror and the light was reflected by the mirror into the room.

During the William and Mary period, mirrors were usually mounted in thick rectangular frames veneered with tortoiseshell. Early Georgian mirrors had simple wooden frames veneered with walnut and wall mirrors were also set in flat-shaped wooden plaques which were decorated with delicate, gilded scrolls of gesso.

During the Regency period, circular convex mirrors were popular. These were decorated with small, gilded, wooden balls round the interior rim of the bulky, round, wooden frame and were often surmounted by a gilded and carved wooden eagle. It is said that these were often hung above a sideboard or serving table at the end of a dining-room so that a butler could keep an

eye on the requirements of the diners without actually facing them
Modern reproductions of this type of mirror abound.

Here are some of the types of mirror you may come across in
shops or auction rooms.

A Cheval glass was a long, narrow mirror supported on a stand
in such a way that the mirror can be tilted to give a full-length
view.

A Mantel mirror or overmantel consisted of a single, large
mirror or sometimes a series of mirrors fixed to the wall above
the fireplace. They were an essential item of home furnishing in
Georgian and Victorian times.

A Pier Glass was a mirror hung on the wall between windows,
with a side table matching the frame standing beneath.

Toilet or dressing mirrors were swinging mirrors supported
between two uprights on a base which rather resembled a small
bureau with little drawers for trinkets etc. They first appeared
during the late seventeenth century and were made right through
Georgian times. Sheraton dressing mirrors are still extremely
popular and command quite high prices with their delicate, often
shield-shaped mirrors and their shallow, three-drawer box-stands.
These have been reproduced time and time again. When buying
a toilet mirror, look for repaired or replaced uprights: these are
the parts most likely to have been broken.

THE CARE OF FURNITURE

It is easy in the sudden burst of enthusiasm which so often
comes with a new purchase to start on a cleaning or repairing
operation without sufficient consideration of what the result of
such action may be. It is useful, therefore, to sound a note of
warning in order to focus attention on the condition of what you
may hope to buy and to give a word of advice on how best to
treat the antiques you do buy.

It can generally be said that minor repairs to furniture detract
little from its value provided they have been done expertly by a
skilled craftsman. Nor does the presence of a few woodworm
holes, particularly in an unseen place, completely ruin a piece,
provided the damage has not gone too far and the piece has been,

7. *Dovetailing on the drawer of a Queen Anne chest*

8. *Cross-banding on the edge of a Queen Anne chest*

9. Interior of an early Georgian drawer showing the grain of the base board running from front to back

10. Interior of a drawer in a Sheraton washstand and dressing-table

11. The corner of a Queen Anne dressing-mirror. The walnut veneer has been applied in sections; note the gesso edge and the marking on the mirror plate

12. A typical Georgian silver hallmark

Maker's Mark   Lion Passant   Date Letter   Leopard's Head Crowned

13. A touchmark on late eighteenth-century London pewter

or can be, properly treated. However, if the activity has been so great that the wood in any place has become soft and spongy, leave the piece alone unless it is so desirable as to warrant an expensive repair.

It is unwise to get out the wax furniture polish in order to give a piece of furniture a high sheen. Years of use have probably given it a natural patina and this can easily be lost beneath a greasy film. Nothing beats old-fashioned 'elbow grease'. It is surprising how quickly an apparently dull surface on old furniture will respond to a good rub with a soft cloth.

Veneered furniture needs special care because under certain conditions the veneer 'lifts' or 'bubbles'. This is most likely to happen if the furniture is exposed to strong sunlight near a window, or if it is left in centrally-heated rooms without humidifiers. Heat from either source can also cause warping, which will cost a great deal of money to put right. So if you have central heating, think twice before investing in expensive, veneered furniture.

Some solid furniture, especially oak, can be cleaned by washing it gently with a damp cloth which has been soaked in warm water to which a little vinegar has been added. It can then be polished with a cloth on which a few drops of raw linseed oil have been sprinkled. Never have anything to do with varnish. Some furniture has been treated with varnish but such pieces are of little interest to the antique collector even if the price is low. It is true that varnish can be removed but it is a lengthy and expensive process which also involves repolishing and the resulting surface bears no comparison with the patina acquired by age.

CHAPTER THREE

CLOCKS, WATCHES AND BAROMETERS

OLD clocks can look very attractive in the modern home, but without some knowledge of the working of clocks they are tricky things to buy, particularly at auction sales. Although they may look sound and appear to be in working order, it is difficult for the amateur to tell whether parts of the movement have been replaced or modernized. If they have, such clocks are much less valuable than a genuine clock in its original condition. A clock or watch which is not in working order is seldom a good buy : the cost of repairs can be very high. To appreciate the value of old clocks it is essential to understand the various movements that have been used and developed over the centuries. This will come with experience and personal study. As with all antiques there is more to it than meets the eye.

Most old clocks fall into one of the following groups : lantern, bracket, long case, mantel, and ormolu.

Lantern Clocks

These are so called because they are similar in shape to an old lantern. They were originally made during the early seventeenth century but have been much copied. They were of brass and have a large bell above the working parts. Some of these were called 'bird-cage clocks' as the shape was similar to that of a bird cage. Another word used is 'Cromwellian'. There were doors on each side to give access to the movement.

Bracket Clocks

Bracket clocks were so called because they rested on brackets mounted on the wall, though very few exist today with their original brackets. They are usually much larger than modern clocks and the more desirable ones have pull winds. This was a cord with an ivory or wooden knob which, when pulled, wound the mechanism. Bracket clocks usually had a wooden case with brass or ormolu mounts, with a carrying handle at the top. The sides were often of fretted metal panels backed with coloured silk. Bracket clocks were common in late Georgian and Regency times.

Long-Case Clocks

The first long-case clocks in this country were made in the seventeenth century and they were still being made by country craftsmen when Victoria came to the throne. It is not surprising therefore that there is hardly an antique shop in the country without a long case or 'grandfather' clock for sale. Although large numbers were made, many of them are of little value. Those that fetch high prices are either very early examples, or were made by one of the few select clockmakers such as Thomas Tompion or Daniel Quare, whose workmanship was of the very highest quality. Most of these worked in London, so grandfather clocks made in the provinces are less likely to be of great value. As a general rule, old long-case clocks should have brass dials ten inches or less in diameter in order to have interest for the serious collector. Old clocks with single hands (i.e. the hour hand) are interesting. Many people dismiss them as having a hand missing but it is usually possible to tell by looking at the arbor or axle on which the hand is mounted to see whether there has ever been provision for another hand. One-handed clocks were made throughout the seventeenth century.

Clocks with painted dials (usually on wood or iron) followed the etched and silvered brass dials of the mid-seventeenth century. More often than not they are of no great value.

The style of the wooden cases usually corresponds to the style of furniture of the period and, as with furniture, the smaller the clock the greater the demand and the more valuable it is likely to be. 'Grandmother' clocks, which are less than 6 ft in height, are much easier to accommodate in the modern home than the very large grandfather clocks.

When buying an old grandfather clock, make sure that it has not been rehoused in a new case as this detracts greatly from its value. Good-quality clocks sometimes have a brass plate decorated with an etched design at the back of the clock movement. When the lead weights are enclosed in a copper sheath it is often a sign of quality manufacture.

It is important that all pendulum clocks should be placed on a level surface in a position where the pendulum swings exactly the same distance from the vertical on both sides. Slight variations from such a position will cause the clock to gain or lose, or even to stop.

Mantel clocks

These clocks as their name implies, stood on the mantelshelf. They were first in use during the mid-seventeenth century and, like bracket clocks, were popular because they could be moved easily from place to place without upsetting the delicate balance of the pendulum. In Regency and Victorian times, mantel clocks were made with matching side pieces—decorative ornaments which matched the style of the clock and which stood on either side of it. The whole set was known as a *garniture-de-cheminée* and often included candlesticks, urns or vases: most of the side pieces have by now been detached from the clock sets and disposed of separately.

Ormolu clocks

Ormolu is gilded brass or bronze, and clocks encased in this material are known as ormolu clocks. They usually rest on a base from which rise decorative mounts with figures or animals, all of the same material. These clocks were made in large numbers in France during the Empire period and are greatly valued. They are usually wound from the face. Many of them have small porcelain plaques inset, decorated with colourful scenes in enamel. These were generally referred to as Sèvres plaques, though most of them were certainly not made there.

Owing to the popularity of French ormolu clocks in the nineteenth century, manufacturers in England and France began to flood the market with cheap copies made from the soft base metal known as spelter, which was moulded and then covered with a thin layer of gilt. They can easily be recognized as they are relatively light in weight. The metal bends easily and is soft when filed. Moreover, the gilt often bubbled, leaving small blisters.

Watches

Old silver and gold watches are often found among family heirlooms. Few of them are of any great value unless, of course, they were made by famous makers. Even fine old Georgian silver pocket watches are little sought after and rarely fetch more than a few pounds. Many dealers still break these watches up and keep only the silver case to be sold for its value as scrap. It is worth remembering that these watches in good working order can be mounted on stands and used as clocks.

Barometers

Barometers appear to have been invented about the middle of the seventeenth century. A simple laboratory barometer consisted of a long glass tube with the open lower end immersed in a dish of mercury. Variations in the atmospheric pressure on the surface of the mercury in the dish forced the level in the tube to go up or down. The changes in level were measured against a scale placed at the side of the tube and this gave some guide to weather conditions.

It was from this simple piece of apparatus that stick or cistern barometers, as they are called, developed, and they were still popular well into the nineteenth century. But perhaps the best known and most attractive of all forms of barometer is the 'banjo' type in which the yard-long length of glass tube is curled about itself, eliminating the need for a long and often cumbersome case, and making it possible to have a circular dial. In the banjo barometer, a thermometer is usually included in the upright part of the case.

Unlike clocks which tend to be judged largely on the quality of their movements, barometers are judged on the quality of their case. Some of our great cabinet-makers have designed barometer cases. Many Victorian barometers with plain unveneered cases, often of oak, can today be bought quite cheaply.

THE CARE OF CLOCKS AND BAROMETERS

Unless these are handled with great care on the journey from the saleroom or shop to your home, considerable damage can be done. Never move any pendulum clock without first removing the pendulum otherwise the delicate mechanism may be damaged. Always keep barometers upright, particularly the stick barometers, to prevent bubbles of air from entering the column of mercury. Above all, avoid jolting both clocks and barometers. Pack them round with soft materials when they are being transported and avoid rough routes if possible.

Ormolu clocks are often found to be dirty, but they can be cleaned provided the works are removed. Gently apply a mixture of equal parts of ammonia and water with a toothbrush—but do this in the open air because ammonia fumes can be overpowering. Wear rubber gloves to avoid staining the hands. The gold is revived incredibly quickly and once the tarnish has been removed the article should be washed thoroughly under running water and then thoroughly dried. The solution must not be allowed to touch anything but the ormolu : it will bleach woodwork and discolour enamel. Ormolu frames of mirrors may be cleaned in the same way, provided the mirror is removed before the operation.

SILVER AND SHEFFIELD PLATE

SILVER has been used since the Middle Ages. Fortunately, it is easier to date and identify than furniture or porcelain since every British piece must, by law, have passed through an assay office to be assayed or tested. The assay office then marks the silver with its hall or assay mark (the name hallmark is commonly used for the assay mark because, in London, it is made in the Goldsmiths' and Silversmiths' Hall). The word 'hallmark' is now generally used to include several other marks that are made by the assay office at the same time, which enables us to learn a great deal about any particular piece of silver. On each piece of silver it should normally be possible to find four marks stamped on the metal, sometimes five (see Plate 12). These are:

1. The *Hallmark*, or town mark, which indicates where the piece was assayed. For London, the hallmark is a leopard's head. This has been used since 1478, except for the years 1697 to 1719 when a particularly high standard of silver was introduced to stop silversmiths melting down silver coins of the realm. This is known as the Britannia period and a figure of Britannia was used as the mark. Between 1478 and 1821, the leopard's head bore a crown, after 1821 it was uncrowned. Britannia silver is still used today, mainly for presentation pieces.

In addition to the London Assay Office at Goldsmiths' Hall there are, or have been, assay offices in Birmingham, Chester, Dublin, Edinburgh, Exeter (1701-1883), Glasgow, Newcastle (1702-1884), Sheffield, York (1559-1857) and Norwich (1565-1702). Each has its own town mark.

2. The *Maker's Mark* consists in most cases of the initial of the silversmith who made the piece, though in Victorian times the

mark was sometimes that of the firm which commissioned or sponsored the work. Most of the famous silversmiths worked in London and some identification handbooks list their initials and dates.

3. The *Date Letter* records the year when the piece was hall-marked at an assay office. It consists of a single letter of the alphabet in a particular style of print and shape of shield. These vary with each assay office, so it is first essential to identify the town where the piece was assayed. It is then possible to date the piece by referring to one of the many handbooks of marks.

4. The *Standard Mark*, which normally indicates that the silver is of sterling quality, is a lion *passant* (walking with the right forepaw raised). The only exception was during the Britannia period from 1697 to 1719, when a lion's head erased (the head and mane only) was the standard mark for the higher quality silver. The lion *passant* was not used on Scottish and Irish silver.

5. The *Sovereign's Head* is seen on silver assayed between 1784 and 1890. It indicates that the duty levied on silver during this period had been duly paid. Very small pieces were not liable to this duty.

Continental and foreign silver is imported into Britain and it is illegal for a dealer to sell such a piece as sterling silver unless it has been re-assayed on entry into this country. Any dealer selling a piece of foreign silver (which is usually of a lower standard than our own) which does not bear an English hallmark in addition to any mark of its country of origin is committing on offence if he sells it as sterling silver. The English hallmark will show if the silver is up to standard and also the year in which it entered this country. It is undoubtedly desirable that we should safeguard standards but it is sometimes sad to find that a piece of period foreign silver has had to be disfigured by the application of a modern English hallmark.

As with furniture, silver had its fashionable craftsmen whose names have become well known because of the high quality of their work. Each of these famous silversmiths had a flair and style of his own. Experts who constantly see and handle silver get so accustomed to the 'feel' of pieces made by these craftsmen that they can often identify the maker without reference to the mark.

14. *Acanthus leaf decoration on a Georgian silver sauce tureen*

15. *Classical decoration around the base of a George III butter dish*

16. Pineapple finial on the lid of a silver sauce tureen

17. Cauliflower knop on cover of silver dish

Most of the great names come from the eighteenth century. Perhaps the most famous is Paul de Lamerie who registered his work (LA with a crown above) in 1712. For some time after 1720 he continued to work in Britannia standard silver after the compulsory quality had dropped to sterling standard. His later work is noted for its figure engraving and applied decoration. By 1732, de Lamerie was using his second mark (PL with a crown above) on work made of the harder sterling standard silver.

Hester Bateman, whose work is particularly popular in the USA today, took over her husband's small business when he died and registered her mark (HB in script) in 1774. Her work was noted for its beaded borders, particularly on the edges of spoons and tableware, and on teapots, cream jugs etc. and also for delicate piercing and a lively, bright-cut engraving which was designed to catch the light to give a sparkling appearance. Her sons joined her in the expanding business and became quality silversmiths in their own right. Her son Peter worked with his brother Jonathan (PBIB recorded in 1790), Jonathan's wife Ann (PBAB recorded 1791) and her son William (PBWB recorded 1805). It is worth noting that a lesser-known silversmith used the initials HB in script: so do not confuse this with the Hester Bateman mark.

Paul Storr was a fine silversmith who brought to his craft his own version of the classical revival. He first worked on his own in 1793 (Mark: PS or P.S.) and had his own workshop just off Piccadilly between 1795 and 1807, where he soon gained a great reputation. He executed commissions for the firm of Rundell & Bridge who were appointed Jewellers, Gold and Silversmiths to the Crown in 1797. He joined the company in 1807 as their chief craftsman and his influence on the whole workshop must have been considerable. His great skill lay in his special ability to combine simplicity of line with an appearance of extravagance. Yet his designs never impeded usefulness.

BUYING SILVER

If you intend to buy silver or Sheffield plate it is obviously essential to be able to distinguish between them and also to be able to distinguish between Sheffield plate and more modern

D

electro-plated articles. It is important, therefore, to equip yourself for the job. You would be well advised to set out with a nail file, a caustic pencil (which can be bought at any chemist's shop), a small *Troy*-weight spring balance for weighing the silver, a magnifying glass and a book of hallmarks. Some auctioneers will lend prospective buyers a balance on viewing days before sales of silver. It is pointless to weigh silver on kitchen scales which register Avoirdupois weight.

First, examine the hallmark. If it is difficult or impossible to decipher, then the piece is worth a good deal less than it would be if the hallmark were clear. So beware of indistinct hallmarks.

If you are examing a piece made in more than one part, a tankard with a lid for example, see that each part has a hallmark and that these marks match. Any piece which does not bear a hallmark should, by law, be taken to an assay office where it will be assayed and marked with the year in which it has been declared. This renders the whole article valueless as a period piece. So always ensure that what you buy is fully and clearly marked. Faking was often done during the nineteenth century by taking a rather unimportant object such as a small plate, cutting out the hallmark and inserting this with the aid of silver solder into the base of a more important-looking but more modern piece. This act renders the piece valueless except, of course, for the price it would fetch per ounce as scrap silver.

Large silver pieces sometimes bore the initials of their owners and these may have been subsequently removed by grinding and polishing out before sale. It is possible that their removal may have worn away the silver to almost paper thinness. To find out, you should place your hand on one side of the object and run a finger nail gently over the suspect area, watching the other side. If the silver is thin you will easily see the movement of your finger nail under the metal.

During the reign of Queen Victoria it became fashionable to have a good deal of decoration on silver and, in order to be in the fashion, many owners of early silver sent their pieces to local silversmiths to have decoration added. This was widely done with tea services. Auction catalogues often draw attention to such pieces. A recent item read: 'George II baluster half-pint mug later chased with flowers and scrolls in Victorian times'. This mug would be worth considerably less than if it had been in its original state. In the antique trade, any silver decorated after the original assay date is valued roughly from the date of decoration.

Remember always that silver tarnishes quickly and can become so discoloured that it may look almost like pewter, so do not be put off by appearances. But do beware of repairs. These are often found where handles, feet, lids or spouts join the main body of the article and if the repairs have been done skilfully they may not be easily visible. If you are in doubt, breathe on the suspect part. Soldering will show up as being of a different texture where the condensation from your breath gathers on the surface.

Watch also for wear. This is very common on cutlery. It was often cleaned with an abrasive powder which quickly wore away the bowls of spoons and prongs of forks until the edges became quite sharp. Dents in silver articles, on the other hand, are not so serious : a good silversmith can usually rectify such damage for a relatively small sum.

A final important warning : if you have any doubt as to whether an item though hallmarked, is silver, a simple test can be made. With the permission of the owner find a part of the object which is not normally visible. Then gently file a portion of the surface with a nail file to remove any dirt or plating. Next, moisten the surface and gently rub the cleaned area with a caustic pencil. If the surface remains clear, then it is fairly certain that the object is silver (or gold). If the object is not silver the moistened area will turn black.

It may sometimes be desirable to take a copy of a hallmark for later study. It is possible to do this by placing a piece of fairly thin paper over the mark and rubbing it with a piece of cobbler's wax (heel ball).

Most fine old silver is very expensive. However, it is still possible to buy representative pieces from most of the Georgian periods which, though small and light in weight, have a charm of their own and at the same time lead to an appreciation of the work of early craftsmen.

Silver has always taken pride of place among collectable items, not because it is any more beautiful than porcelain or glass, nor because it is worth more or less money, but simply because it is so readily standardized in price that buying and selling become less of a gamble. For many years, silver has been bought and sold by its Troy weight and dealers refer to a silver purchase as having cost them so many shillings an ounce. The more beautiful and rare the piece the more shillings per ounce are paid for it. The lowest value is that of scrap silver. This is usually a few shillings under daily prices of silver and is quoted in the Press. It is usually somewhere in the region of 10s per ounce. But weight in itself is a dangerous criterion, so do not think that because someone has paid £8 an ounce for a George III silver teapot-stand weighing six ounces, making a total of £48, you would be safe in paying £160 for one weighing twenty ounces. This stand may contain more silver but the quality of workmanship may be poorer, so you must adjust your price per ounce accordingly, only paying shall we say, £6 an ounce. On the other hand, a particularly fine and delicate teapot-stand weighing only three ounces may well be worth £10 an ounce. This is possibly one reason why the buying of silver by the ounce is losing favour and more and more people are buying purely on the value of the item's merit. In the end, it is simply a question of deciding how much the article is worth to you.

Most items of silver which fall within the lower price range are either very small or are modern reproductions of older items. Here are some of the less expensive items which may be of interest.

Bon-bon dishes

In the Victorian period, these were often delightfully decorated but because they are usually small and light they can still be bought quite cheaply. They look decorative when scattered around a room but are often difficult to clean because of their decoration.

Caddy spoons

These are widely collected and, because of this, usually cost a lot of money for the amount of silver they contain. They allowed the creative imagination of the silversmith to run riot and so appear in the strangest forms and shapes. One of the most sought-after forms is the 'jockey cap', with the peak of the cap forming the spoon handle. Others were made in the shape of leaves, birds and occasionally fish. There are many Continental caddy spoons, particularly Dutch, and these are usually very much cheaper. But unless you intend to make a collection for display there is little point in buying more than two or three for general use, perhaps in antique tea caddies.

a   b   c   d   e

Figure 8   STYLES OF DECORATION ON CUTLERY

(a) Fiddle and Thread; *(b)* King's Pattern; *(c)* Rat's Tail; *(d)* Feather Edge; *(e)* Bright Cut

Cutlery

Buying antique silver cutlery can be a very expensive business. On the other hand, it is a field in which the keen collector can prove himself. With a keen eye and considerable patience, complete sets of cutlery can be assembled over a period of time from odd items for very little money. This is particularly so if you decide to collect a style known as 'fiddle pattern', as for some reason this is at present out of fashion. Other patterns include the King's pattern, reeded edge, rat's tail, feathered, and bright cut. Perhaps the most popular are the bright cut and King's pattern. Sometimes unscrupulous dealers will file away the steps of the fiddle in an attempt to bring spoons into fashion. If you are trying to accumulate a set of matching cutlery, remember to carry a sample with you at all times and do not pay high prices for fish knives and forks. For some reason they are not in great demand and should, therefore, be cheaper.

Knives are always a problem. Few silver-bladed knives exist or, in fact, were ever made. Most good knives of the Georgian and Victorian periods had steel blades with hollow, silver handles. The blades were set into the handles with pitch. These are almost invariably loose and are quite difficult to reset so that they will stand up to the stresses and strains of a solid steak. But steel-bladed knives with bone or ivory handles can be bought quite cheaply. They look well with period silver and are strong, sharp and serviceable. They have one great disadvantage, however; they were made before stainless steel had been invented and rust quickly. The housewife will have to be prepared to clean them regularly with an abrasive.

Sets of coffee, tea or egg spoons are fairly common, particularly those of the late Georgian or Victorian periods. They are often found in sets of six or twelve, sometimes still in their presentation cases. Apart from their obvious usefulness in the home, they make attractive gifts.

Do not buy spoons or forks which have worn thin at the tips. They dent and split easily and, as we have pointed out, the edges are often sharp and dangerous. Beware, too, of handles which have been snapped and re-soldered, leaving them weak.

Any cutlery which has pitch-filled handles should never be placed in hot water; to do so will almost certainly loosen them. If they are dented or damaged in any way it is a very costly business to restore them.

Mustard pots

Mustard pots were not always included in cruets and were often made as separate items. Large, decorated-lidded mustard pots with blue glass liners are much sought after and command high prices for their weight. Later smaller and flimsier editions, however, are not so much in demand and can therefore be bought relatively cheaply. Beware of any vessel that has been used for salt and has black spotting on it : this is caused by a chemical action on the silver and is difficult to remove. Blue glass liners should be carefully checked to make sure they fit correctly and can be readily removed. Where they are missing or broken, modern blue glass liners can usually be found or made to replace them.

Napkin rings

These can be found in a great variety of shapes, sizes and designs and do not cost a great deal. Most of them will bear the initials of the original owner engraved in a suitable cartouche. Before buying one, make sure that the silver is thick enough for the initials to be removed if you so wish.

Wine labels

These small labels or tags were suspended by fine chains from the necks of decanters to identify the contents. They were very common in late Georgian and Victorian times. Their shape varies from the straightforward rectangle (slightly bent or curved to allow it to hug the decanter) to the very charming leaf-shaped labels decorated with bunches of grapes and foliage. Although there are collectors of wine labels, quite early Georgian specimens can still be picked up for a few pounds and they enhance the appearance of decanters on any sideboard. Smaller labels, similar in type, were used to identify sauces in cruet bottles.

It is worth noting that Oriental silver, although slowly beginning to creep into fashion, is not yet in great demand and can be bought very reasonably indeed; it is often as cheap as silver plate.

SHEFFIELD PLATE

In the 1740s, an important discovery was made by a Sheffield cutler, Thomas Bolsover, which was to have far-reaching effects on the silver trade. It is said that while he was repairing the handle of a knife he touched some copper with heated silver. To his surprise, he found that the two metals had fused together. He then found that the metals could be hammered or rolled as though they were one. He soon realized the possibilities of this discovery; durable articles could now be made that would look exactly like silver but which would use relatively little of the precious metal which was, in any case, in very short supply. Sheffield plate had been born. Bolsover started by making small articles with the new material—snuff boxes, knife handles, thimbles and buttons. Within a few years, other manufacturers had entered the field. They were more ambitious and produced tea and coffee pots, urns, candlesticks and many other articles. The lower cost opened up a large new market. Expensive articles of silver had been symbols of status. The new Sheffield plate was comparatively inexpensive and enjoyed enormous popularity; fine-looking tableware became available to people who could never have afforded to buy real silverware. The industry flourished. By 1762, Sheffield plate was also being made in Birmingham by Matthew Boulton, an enterprising businessman who, in partnership with John Fothergill, founded the Soho Manufactory.

In the early years, the makers of Sheffield plate used their initials to mark their wares. After 1784, the law enabled them to use a symbol or trade mark—a bell, crossed arrows, a pipe, a fish or a ram's head, for example—though there was no legal commitment for makers to do so as there was in the case of silver. In the eighteenth century, many important makers marked their goods with their name and trade mark, but in the early nineteenth century the name was often dropped and the trade mark used alone. Sometimes a crown was used in addition to the maker's mark. This was intended to signify that the piece was of good quality. Nevertheless, much good quality Sheffield plate was completely unmarked.

Sometimes the surface layer of silver on Sheffield plate wears away with cleaning and the red colour of the copper below it shows through; which is one of the ways of identifying Sheffield plate. It was, however, a problem that concerned the makers. In 1830, Samuel Roberts patented a new invention designed to overcome this defect, and within a few years he was using an alloy of copper, nickel and zinc known as German silver (later to be called nickel silver) instead of copper. If the silver layer became worn this 'white alloy' was less obvious than the red copper when exposed.

Within a few years a new discovery led to the final decline of the Sheffield plate industry. In the 1840s, it was found that a thin layer of silver could be deposited on a base metal 'by electric agency'. So began the manufacture of electro-plate. Electroplated nickel silver (E.P.N.S.) could be produced very cheaply and largely replaced Sheffield plate. These goods can easily be recognized because they are so soft: they are often dented and the thin coating of silver is usually worn by cleaning, leaving dull grey streaks. The only plated ware of real value to the antique collector is Sheffield plate.

BUYING SHEFFIELD PLATE

Do not be too concerned if constant polishing has worn away some of the silver coating from the Sheffield plate you wish to buy. If the wear is slight it does not detract seriously from the value of the piece. If no copper shows, find an edge of the article and pull a finger nail across it. If it is made of Sheffield plate it should be possible to feel a small lip when the silver was hammered over to conceal the edge of the copper. There are several other points to look for which may help with identification and the assessment of value.

Remember that all round objects in Sheffield plate have a seam where the sheet was joined. This runs vertically through the body and is usually found beneath the handle. It may not be obvious but it can be detected by breathing on the surface; the resulting condensation will usually show up the line of the join.

On the more important objects, the manufacturers inserted a solid silver plaque into the side. This was to enable the owners to have their initials engraved without copper showing through. It can be detected by using the condensation test, which will show up the irregular outline of the plaque.

Many articles which were made in silverware were also made in Sheffield plate, though we have never come across any old Sheffield plate cutlery. The work of some eighteenth-century craftsmen is, therefore, still well within the range of the more modest budget.

Sheffield-plated teapots, coffee pots, milk and cream jugs can still be purchased today for less than £25, but if you are buying tea or coffee pots make sure that they are well tinned inside. This tinning was done to prevent the copper from tarnishing and can be recognized by its matt, dark grey appearance. These everyday items can be just as attractive, just as serviceable, and just as antique as some of their silver equivalents.

Wine coasters in Sheffield plate are common. It is obviously desirable to buy them in pairs or in fours, but this is more expensive than buying an odd one and waiting until you find its companions. Designs were repeated many times and the search may well be fruitful. In many cases the green baize will be missing from the base. If so, it is wise to replace it in order to avoid scratching polished surfaces.

Galleried trays (trays which have a wall round the edge) can be bought more cheaply than other types of tray, since the wall considerably limits the number of items than can be placed on them.

THE CARE OF SILVER AND SHEFFIELD PLATE

The most important part of any piece of silver is its hallmark: by this it is dated and identified. Unfortunately, silver tarnishes when exposed to the air and therefore needs frequent cleaning. Unless great care is taken when polishing, a hallmark may be damaged or even removed. Abrasives—even gentle ones such as jewellers' rouge—should be used very sparingly, if at all. The best way to keep silver clean and shining is to wash it regularly in warm, soapy water. The famous silversmith, Paul de Lamerie, sent cleaning instructions with the items he made. 'Clean it now and then with only warm water and soap with a sponge. Then wash it in clean water and dry it well with a soft linen cloth. Keep it in a dry place for damp will spoil it.'

Silver will remain bright for long periods if kept in an airtight display cabinet. If it is being stored for any length of time, it should be wrapped in baize or acid-free tissue paper and removed periodically for washing. Very badly tarnished silver, which has become really black, should be taken to a silversmith for cleaning.

Do not touch silver with the bare fingers more than is absolutely essential, as the small amount of acid on the skin will leave a definite mark on its surface. This applies particularly to silver coins in mint condition. On no account should damaged silver be soldered except by an expert who will use silver solder. Dents in silver should also be removed by an expert. Amateurs who attempt to do so more often than not stretch the metal, making the damage permanent. When cleaning silver candlesticks which are not solid, avoid twisting them round in the duster : this eventually results in the silver itself becoming twisted.

Plate should receive exactly the same care and treatment as silver. Constant use of abrasives will remove the thin surface layer and expose the baser metal beneath.

CHAPTER FIVE

NON-PRECIOUS METALS

Brass and Copper

IN general, brass and copper have never achieved a high value in the antique trade, with a few notable exceptions. Very old brass and copper pieces of the fourteenth, fifteenth and sixteenth centuries are worth substantial sums because of their rarity but, on the whole, brass and copper articles from the eighteenth century onwards are worth comparatively little. Yet people who collect these metals value them highly and tend to disbelieve those in the trade who regard their treasures as little more than interesting collections of curios. Many copper and brass articles end up in country inns and cottages. They seem to need a homely setting and go well with dark oak beams.

The vogue for collecting old horse brasses created a certain demand for these but the flood of mass-produced modern copies and the never-ending task of cleaning has tended to push them out of favour again. Nevertheless, some people are still keen and it is worth noting some of the characteristics of old horse brasses. Remember that a genuine antique brass was fitted to the horse's harness and should show signs of wear on the underside, a smooth polish resulting from constant movement against the leather strap on which it hung. This should be particularly obvious on the buckle-shaped loop by which it was attached. These old brasses usually had two small studs on the underside by which the brass was held in a vice when it was cut by the craftsmen. Occasionally they bear a date. The best period for horse brasses was between about 1800 and 1875. After that they were stamped out by machine. Modern reproductions which have been moulded are usually rough and have a narrower hanging-loop.

There is still a certain demand for old brass candlesticks, and old copper and brass cooking utensils are still bought, sometimes for use but more often for home decoration. Old copper jelly moulds of the Victorian period and copper coal scuttles, particularly those of helmet shape, sell well. Some early pierced brass fireside equipment is well worth looking for, since it was designed by great furniture designers such as Hepplewhite and Sheraton and is most attractive. The old fire rests make good door stops, and old brass trivets are often very useful in the modern hearth. There is even a demand among interior decorators for old brass bedsteads which, a few years ago, could be seen on rubbish dumps or blocking gaps in farm hedges.

Brass candlesticks are today cast in the same shapes and forms as they were during the eighteenth century. The only discernible difference in many cases are the brazing marks. Early candlesticks of the period around 1700 were made in two halves which were then brazed together leaving the stem hollow, a useful saving of metal. The foot, which was cast separately, was then brazed to the stem. Old candlesticks have had their edges and mouldings softened by years of cleaning.

Very few great craftsmen worked in either copper or brass. It is worth remembering that late Victorian brass often shows a registration mark which makes it possible to decide the year in which the particular design was introduced.

Bronze

Unlike copper and brass, bronze has always been a popular material with artists and craftsmen. The price of objects of quality in this metal is high. Because of its serviceability and its lasting finish, bronze was often used for works of art which were to be exposed to the elements. The Italians used it a great deal for statuary and for crucibles, mortars and pestles and they often partially gilded it. It was widely used for cast decoration, clocks, candlesticks, candelabra etc, and during the eighteenth century became *the* metal in which artists cast their sculptures. It was also very popular during the French Regency period. A good deal of spelter masquerades as bronze : it is worthless, although it sometimes fetches unreasonable sums in London antique markets which are so affected by the whims and fashions of the interior decorators.

Iron

This has never been a popular metal for artistic work for the obvious reason that it rusts very quickly and therefore does not last well, though iron jewellery has been made and it is rare and fetches high prices. Iron has been used extensively for kitchen implements and for fire grates and andirons. Firebacks, large metal plates which stood behind the fire basket in large open grates, were usually in decorated cast iron. Early specimens, some of which include a date in the decoration, can still be found.

Lead

This was a popular metal during the eighteenth century for garden ornaments, figures, fountains and suchlike. Water tanks and flower boxes were also made of lead. All these are very much sought after and are collectors' pieces; though, once again, nineteenth century and present day copyists have tended to detract from their value. Smaller items, such as tobacco boxes, can be bought quite reasonably. Many of these were made from ammunition melted down after the Crimean War.

Pewter

Pewter is usually an alloy of tin and lead—and was used for centuries as the poor man's silver, particularly for household utensils.

There were three standards which might be described as hard, medium and soft—technically known as hard, trifle and lay. When pewter articles were first made they were highly polished and looked rather like a dull silver, but as soon as the air got to them oxidization took place and they took on the familiar grey pewter colour. Except for the oldest and rarest pieces, pewter is still quite cheap to buy, since its rather drab appearance makes it unsuitable for elegant settings.

The age of pewter can be judged by its patina, that is to say the depth and hardness of the surface oxidization; by the shape and style of the manufacture; and by the touch marks which are rather similar to the hallmarks on silver. These touch marks were stamped into the article by the maker and each was registered with the Pewterers' Company on a touch plate. One of the commonest touch marks is that of the Tudor rose surmounted by a crown. This was a mark of standard quality. Pieces of superior quality carry an 'X' mark. There are often initials of the maker and there is sometimes a date. Many pieces of pewter were illegally stamped with silver hallmarks with intent to deceive.

In 1824, it became obligatory to stamp all drinking vessels with their capacity, together with the initials of the reigning monarch. Tankards made since 1824 should, therefore, bear the initials G.R., W.R., or V.R., depending on whether they were made during the reign of George IV, William IV, or Queen Victoria. From 1877, a crown was added to the V.R. and this is an easy way to recognize a late piece.

Pewter made during the seventeenth century is rare because, as pieces became worn or were damaged, they were melted down and re-made.

Pewter is a very malleable metal. Treat it carefully: once dented it becomes stretched, making it difficult, if not impossible, to knock out the dent without leaving a mark. Great care should be used when cleaning all types of pewter. The touchmark (see Plate 13) corresponds to the hallmark on silver, and if this is worn away both the interest and value of the piece are reduced. Whether or not pewter should be cleaned is largely a matter of taste: some people like to see it dull, others like it highly polished to look almost like silver. But pewter does not polish easily and to burnish it with any sort of abrasive will destroy its value. There are several proprietory cleaners on the market which can be used safely: but in general it is true to say that old pewter should not be cleaned.

Tinware

Tableware made of tin was fairly common from the sixteenth century until the middle of the nineteenth century, but its metallic finish gives it little attraction. However, japanning, widely used in the eighteenth and early nineteenth century in imitation of Oriental lacquer work, was used on some tinware. Colour var-

nishes were applied to the metal, which was then baked to produce a hard glossy finish. All kinds of utensils were treated in this
way—coffee pots, water cans, tea canisters and buckets. The
bargees on English canals always favoured painted tinware. The
background is usually dark—black, brown, olive-green or deep
crimson—and the decoration usually consists of sprays of flowers,
festoons of leaves or birds with gay plumage. In the 1830s, painted
tin trays were common. One of the most famous factories producing this ware was at Pontypool.

Britannia Metal

'White metal', as it was called at the end of the eighteenth
century, or 'Britannia metal' to give it the later and more familiar
name, is an alloy consisting largely of tin with some antimony
and a small addition of copper. The metal was cheap and between about 1805 and 1830 captured the pewter market. It was
harder, brighter and less liable to crack than pewter, but was
nevertheless malleable and fairly easily worked. The chief pro-
ducer at this time was the Sheffield firm of Dixon and his work
is usually marked. At a later date Britannia metal was often
electro-plated with silver.

Britannia metal is regarded as the curse of the antique dealer's
life. In the words of John Bright: 'Silence is golden; speech is
silvern. But to say one thing and mean another is Britannia
metal.' Thousands of items were made from it—tea pots with
sugar basins and cream jugs, coffee pots, boxes etc—and so far
it has been of little value, though there are now rumours of a
developing American market. Unfortunately, many tea sets and
gilded clocks made from this base metal are sold for quite large
sums to unsuspecting buyers who, if they ever try to sell, will find
extreme difficulty in getting any offers at all. Remember that
when in good condition an item made from Britannia metal can
look magnificent. So, never buy without testing. If filed, the file
will bite deeply into the metal under very little pressure. Britannia
metal and other similar alloys are often referred to in the trade
as 'spelter'.

18. *Sheffield plate tray showing burred-over silver edge*

19. *Sheffield plate taper box showing 'bleeding'*

20. *Transfer printing on a Dr Wall Worcester mug*

21. *The base of a Worcester mug showing glaze shrinkage where rim joins base*

PORCELAIN

PORCELAIN is one of the most rewarding fields for the collector of antiques; so many of the pieces have great beauty. Many experts say that the making of high-quality porcelain began and ended in China. It was certainly being made there when William the Conqueror invaded Britain and by the middle of the seventeenth century Chinese porcelain was being imported in fair quantity when the East India Trading Company was bringing in tea. But we did not make any porcelain in this country until the middle of the eighteenth century. It is generally agreed that the first factories to produce English porcelain were at Bow and Chelsea in London, at Longton Hall in Staffordshire, and Lund's Factory in Bristol. They all started commercial manufacture between 1745 and 1750, using a soft-paste body. In 1768 William Cookworthy, a Plymouth chemist who had been experimenting for some years with local materials, founded the first English factory to make a type of hard-paste porcelain, although several Continental makers had already discovered the secret—the Meissen factory near Dresden, for one. Hard paste was an improvement on the soft paste of the early factories since it made it possible to reproduce on a hard-textured surface the high glazes which were so much admired in the imported Chinese porcelain. William Cookworthy's secret was later taken to Bristol and eventually to a factory at New Hall in Staffordshire.

Great emphasis is laid by many experts on the ability to distinguish between hard-paste and soft-paste porcelain and it is certainly useful to be able to do so because to identify a piece as made of soft paste places it as an early piece—as eighteenth century. However, this ability comes only with experience and the amateur need not worry overmuch if it does not come easily.

Much of the porcelain produced by the early factories was decorated in the blue designs derived from those that had become familiar on the imported Chinese ware. This decoration is often referred to as 'in the Chinese taste'. Although this early blue and white porcelain is widely collected, it can still be bought for comparatively small sums compared with later items decorated with coloured enamels.

Of all types of porcelain the figures, particularly if they can be found in pairs or sets, are probably the most desirable. Many of these figures were copied from Continental designs, though personalities of the day such as actors and actresses were also popular.

It will probably be useful here to make brief reference to the history of the best-known English factories making porcelain.

Chelsea

We know that this factory was making porcelain in 1745 as marked specimens exist with 'Chelsea 1745' under the glaze. George II interested himself in its output and encouraged German and other foreign workmen to come to work there. Indeed, the first name associated with the factory came from Belgium— Nicholas Sprimont—and most of the best work at Chelsea was done under his direction in the early years. But by then it had already been decided that the factory must be sold and Sprimont's influence declined. In 1770, it was bought by William Duesbury of the Derby factory, who carried on the Chelsea production for fourteen years. This is known as the Chelsea-Derby period and the work shows considerable French influence. It is thought that for much of the time the Chelsea factory was used as a centre for the decoration of porcelain made in Derby.

Bow

This factory was run by an Irishman, Thomas Frye, who took out patents for his methods of making porcelain 'not inferior in beauty and fineness' to the porcelain of China and Japan. He managed it from 1745 until 1759 but relatively few pieces are known which were made before 1750. Many figures were made, some of them in imitation of Meissen figures, others original. Some of these have a hole at the back into which a candle-holder could be placed. The factory closed between 1775 and 1778 (the actual date is uncertain) and it is probable that Duesbury of Derby took over the stock and equipment.

Derby

Porcelain was probably made at Derby as early as 1745 but early Derby porcelain, as we know it, is associated with the name of William Duesbury. Before he operated his Derby factory in 1756 he had controlled a workshop in London, decorating white porcelain mainly from Bow and Chelsea. Much of the early Derby work shows the influence of Chelsea but after the acquisition of the Chelsea factory in 1770 the style changed.

Duesbury employed first-class artists as modellers and decorators, as did his son who took over the factory after his death in 1786. Among them were John Bacon, William Coffee and Pierre Stephen. The painting in the years between 1770 and 1795 is often superbly done. The decorators specialized : landscapes were done by Boreman (who had learned his craft at Chelsea) and Hill; birds and fruit by Complin; flowers by Pegg and Billingsley; while Bamford specialized in the classical styles.

After 1795, there were many changes and other artists began to take over—John and Robert Brewer (landscapes), Dodson (birds) and Steele (fruit) were among them. But quality was beginning to decline a little, a decline which accelerated when Robert Bloor rented the factory from 1815. Even so, standards were still high when compared with the work of nineteenth-century porcelain makers. Bloor died in 1845 and the factory closed down in 1848. The present Royal Crown Derby Porcelain Company started in 1876.

Longton Hall

This factory was producing soft-paste porcelain in Staffordshire for some ten years from about 1750 to 1760. It is noted for moulded porcelain in the form of leaves on dinner ware, and for its figures. Longton Hall is thought to have pioneered the use of cobalt blue as a colouring.

Lund's (Bristol) and Worcester

A factory in Bristol known as Lund's was certainly making soft-paste porcelain in 1750, probably earlier, but by 1752 it had moved with a number of its workers to Worcester. The name usually associated with this move is that of Dr John Wall, though he was only one partner and did not assume the major direction of the factory until four years before he died in 1776.

Nevertheless, this early period from 1752 until the factory was sold to Thomas Flight in 1783 (seven years after Wall's death) is usually known as the 'Dr Wall period.' One of the chief decorators was Robert Hancock, who came from the Battersea factory in 1756 and worked in Worcester until 1774. In 1793, Martin Barr became a partner and the names of Flight and Barr were linked with the factory until 1840.

When Flight took over after the 'Dr Wall period', one of the decorators in the factory, Robert Chamberlain, established with his brother a second factory in Worcester which continued for many years and was so successful that it took over the Flight and Barr Company and the two continued as a single enterprise.

Meanwhile, in 1812, another porcelain factory was established in Worcester by Thomas Grainger, who was related to Chamberlain, but its work was not of particularly high quality. This factory was also taken over at a later date by the firm founded by Chamberlain which, in 1862, became the Worcester Royal Porcelain Factory.

Plymouth, Bristol and New Hall

When William Cookworthy of Plymouth was experimenting with hard-paste porcelain he had links with Richard Champion in Bristol, who fired some of his experimental pieces for him. It was not until 1768 that Cookworthy set up a factory of his own. Despite the fact that some excellent work was produced, it was not a commercial success—perhaps because there was too high a proportion of imperfect pieces. He moved his factory to Bristol when he was already a man of sixty-five. Within two years he had retired and Champion took over the manufacture of the new hard-paste porcelain, improving the technical quality. A number of well-known artists worked in Bristol, including Henry Bone who later became a Royal Academician.

Legal expenses involved in the protection of the hard-paste patent rights against attacks by Staffordshire interests led by Josiah Wedgwood were too much for Champion's resources. He was forced to sell to a company which started a factory at New Hall in Staffordshire. He also agreed to give advice and help. It specialized in ware decorated 'in the Chinese taste', much of it for export to the Continent.

Lowestoft

This factory, which was founded in 1757, produced porcelain similar in many ways to the Bow products and it seems more than probable that it had secured the services of someone who had acquired his 'know-how' from Bow. Much tableware was produced, decorated in blue 'in the Chinese taste' or, sometimes in later pieces, in a characteristic shade of pink.

Caughley

This Shropshire factory, which had been making earthenware for some twenty years previously, was acquired in 1772 by Thomas Turner (who had previously been at the Worcester factory) and started making porcelain. Caughley, like Worcester, used transfer-printing as a means of decoration and Robert Hancock was responsible for many of the engravings. The factory was the first to use the 'willow pattern' design which appeared in 1780, later to become so popular on both porcelain and pottery. In 1799, John Rose, who had worked at Caughley and had later established a pottery of his own, bought the Caughley factory. Its porcelain is very similar to that of Worcester. When unmarked, identification is usually based on decoration, the subject and the colouring.

Coalport

This was a second factory, often known as Coalbrookdale, set up by John Rose, in which much Caughley porcelain was decorated. In 1814, the Caughley factory was closed and the equipment and workers moved to Coalport. Later, Rose acquired the moulds from the South Wales factories at Nantgarw and Swansea. Today the Coalport China Company operates at Stoke-on-Trent.

Nantgarw and Swansea

The name of William Billingsley is closely linked with Nantgarw, a small village north of Cardiff. Billingsley was a rolling-stone. He had started as an apprentice in the Derby factory and worked there as a flower painter. He then spent five years at a small factory he had started near Mansfield (at Pinxton) where he made porcelain. (Specimens are now rare and expensive.) Billingsley then became a free-lance decorator, went to Worcester for several years and then started making porcelain again at Nantgarw. Here, and at the Swansea works of Lewis Dillwyn between 1813 and 1819, some superb porcelain was made. Much of it was decorated in London and connoisseurs value it as highly as some of the finest French porcelain. But Billingsley had his financial troubles. He moved on again to work for John Rose at Coalport and by 1823 the manufacture of porcelain at Nantgarw and Swansea had ceased.

Later English Factories

Early in the nineteenth century, four English factories were also making porcelain—Davenport, Spode and Minton in Staffordshire and Rockingham in Yorkshire. It was sometimes rather ornate and overdecorated but was extremely well made. At the Davenport factory, much Derby work was copied and decorators from the Derby factory were employed there.

The Spode factory specialized in tableware, adding to the prosperity of a thriving earthenware business, and is usually credited with having evolved bone china. It later became the Copeland factory.

Much of Minton's earlier output was decorated with Japanese designs and, later, Derby-style motifs with fruit and flowers were used.

At Rockingham, which only started to make porcelain about

1820, tablewares, especially in blue and green, were produced in quantity. Most of the output was gilded. Rockingham porcelain is now sought keenly by collectors, especially pieces with the celebrated 'griffin' mark.

The porcelain made at the Belleek factory in County Fermanagh, Ireland, gained a considerable reputation in the second half of the nineteenth century. Using a French process, the hard porcelain was glazed so that it gained a nacreous lustre (like mother of pearl). It could be worked into the thinnest of layers without losing its strength and this made it possible to model the most delicate baskets decorated mainly with small leaves of shamrock and tiny flowers such as lily of the valley. These usually had a handle like woven cane and sometimes a cover. The work was done by hand and it is sometimes possible to see faintly the finger prints of the modellers on the petals of the flowers. These baskets often carry the name of the factory in a ribbon of porcelain fixed to the base. Most of this work was done between about 1860 and 1880 when the owner was a wealthy man who could pay first-class artists and craftsmen without being overconcerned about his profit. The Belleek factory also produced Parian statuary, plant pot holders, and ordinary table ware.

BUYING PORCELAIN

Although much porcelain is marked, the only true safeguard when buying fine pieces is to be able to recognize the characteristics of products from the more important factories. Given this skill, the reader may at some time be fortunate enough to recognize a rare piece where he least expects to find it, perhaps in a shop where the owner may have dismissed it as unimportant. It is discoveries of this kind that make the whole business of antique collecting so exciting.

Chelsea

Much early Chelsea ware shows small, crescent-shaped bubbles in the paste when held against a strong light. These are known as 'Chelsea moons' and are distinctive of this factory. The glaze has a soft, 'cheesey' appearance.

Bow

This factory produced a ware that was extremely heavy for its size and the glaze on the so-called 'white ware' looks like a thick coating of condensed milk. Many of the figures have quite large firing cracks (Plate 22).

Chelsea-Derby

Many eighteenth-century Derby and Chelsea figures have three distinct 'patch' marks under the base rather resembling thumb prints (see Plate 23). These were made by the pads on which the figures stood when they were fired in the kiln.

Worcester

Early Worcester porcelain when held to a strong light shows a distinct greenish tinge in the paste. A pencil drawn around the inside ring of a foot rim will usually mark the porcelain in places where the glaze has shrunk, exposing the biscuit surface (Plate 21).

Caughley

Although superficially rather similar in appearance to early Worcester, Caughley porcelain shows a yellow or brownish tinge when held against a strong light.

Plymouth

Porcelain from the Plymouth factory is heavy for its size and often has small, black imperfections on its surface. It is particularly noted for its salt cellars and sweetmeat or pickle stands, which were made in the form of scallop shells.

For most people, early porcelain from the famous factories will be too expensive, but much attractive porcelain was made in the nineteenth century when mass production first came in and decoration was applied by transfer. The potters took advantage of new techniques and, because of this, there was less opportunity for expressing artistic flair. Colours, although much improved in their technical application, lost much of their vigour and figures particularly lost charm and spontaneity. This does not mean, however, that nineteenth-century porcelain is not worth collect-

22. *Bow figure showing typical firing cracks on the base. In the top left-hand corner are the impressed initials 'T.O.' said to be those of the famous modeller Tebo*

23. *Characteristic 'patch' marks on the base of a Chelsea-Derby figure made by the stands on which it stood in the kiln*

24. *Bloor Derby figure of about 1820, six inches high*

25. *The edge of a Delft plate showing characteristic chipping*

26. *Agate ware: note that the marbling goes right through the body*

27. *Stem of a drinking glass with spiral twist*

ing, for much of it, though not as beautiful as that produced by the craftsmen of the earlier famous factories, has a charm characteristic of the period, and often looks well in modern settings. It is still possible to buy quite important pieces from the Coalport, Davenport, Minton, Rockingham and Spode factories for less than £20 and they are nearly always clearly marked and are, as yet, not important enough for the forger to copy. Variations in style and decoration are limitless and nearly everything that could possibly be required—from vases to dinner services—are still plentiful. Beware, however, of vulgar decoration, brash, brightly applied gilding, garish colour combinations, and thoughtless design. Nineteenth-century porcelain is superior to earlier work in one respect. Technical advances greatly improved glazes and their application : they became clearer and smoother and were rarely damaged in the firing process.

It is worth noting that French biscuit porcelain is still very plentiful. This is usually seen in the form of figures produced by firing in an unglazed state so that the surface is left rough to the touch. They were coloured with rather anaemic shades, often highlighted with gilding, and are seldom marked, apart from a number of scratches made in the base before firing, though the telltale crossed ' $\mathcal{J}$ ' sometimes confirms their Continental origin.

Marks can be of great value in the identification of porcelain and pottery, and are discussed fully in the next chapter.

THE CARE OF PORCELAIN

Water used for washing decorated porcelain should never contain strong detergents as these might damage the enamels. Delicately-made pieces of porcelain should never be dried with a cloth, as it is difficult to judge how much pressure can safely be applied to the fragile parts—the fingers on a figure, for example. Instead, allow the piece to drain and dry at room temperature after rinsing it in clean water. The best way to clean intricate decorated work, such as Belleek baskets of flowers, is to keep the piece constantly on the move in the washing water, removing it occasionally to blow into crevices where dust may have collected. It is always dangerous to use a small brush as even a single bristle may stick and be enough to break some of the finer and thinner parts.

Fine hair-cracks in plain undecorated porcelain can be made less obvious by careful application of a diluted bleaching liquid.

It is still all too common to find antique plates which have been used in an oven. This results in a network of small cracks in the glaze known as 'crazing'. It is very pleasant to use antique china when possible, but always avoid overheating of this kind.

For many years damaged porcelain was regarded as worthless and was difficult to sell. In recent years the position has changed. There are now signs that some collectors are prepared to accept slight damage if the piece is rare enough or until they find a perfect piece to replace it. If the damage completely ruins the appearance of a piece, there are some very good porcelain restorers who will repair it so well that few people will spot the repair without the aid of ultra-violet radiation. Such repairs, however, cost a good deal of money and estimates should always be asked for before the work is commissioned. The names and addresses of porcelain restorers can be found in the *International Antiques Year Book*.

POTTERY

IN dealing with porcelain, we have described briefly the various factories where it was made. Earthenware or pottery has been made without a break since prehistoric times and many more factories have been involved since it began to be made on a commercial scale. We shall, therefore, approach the subject from a technical point of view, dealing with the various types of pottery and the development of techniques in the use of raw materials and decorative media.

Pottery is distinguished from porcelain by holding the object against a strong light. Porcelain will normally allow a certain amount of light to pass through it; pottery is always opaque. There are, however, certain articles made of heavy, thick porcelain which are also opaque. Pottery is literally the poor man's porcelain. Popular porcelain items of a period were often copied in pottery: they were cheaper to make because the raw materials consisted of simple clays which can be found in abundance in Britain, whereas porcelain required the careful mixing of many ingredients. The clays for porcelain were more difficult to obtain and the firing at higher temperatures was more hazardous.

Most pottery can be bought quite cheaply, except for some very early specimens and the very fine Wedgwood ware. Some of the best-known types are here described.

Slipware

Potters in the seventeenth and eighteenth centuries often worked in a small town or village producing articles for the home—dishes, pots, mugs etc. These were made from local clays and were decorated with slip—a white or coloured clay in a thick creamy condition which was 'slipped' across the surface of the article like decorative icing on a cake. Sometimes several different coloured slips were used, and these were trailed across the article from a spouted vessel or quill, or dropped or dotted on with a brush. Powdered lead ore was then dusted over the article before firing.

The earliest dated slipware was made at Wrotham and in London in the seventeenth century and signed dishes with pictorial designs were made in Staffordshire by Thomas Toft in the reign of Charles II. Fine slipware was also made in Derbyshire in the eighteenth century.

The making of slipware has continued until the present day and it is not easy to date a piece. Only the real expert can decide on the age and origin of certain pieces. Early slipware is much sought after by collectors but is often overlooked by antique dealers who regard the crude brown, yellow and red decoration as undistinguished. Yet a yellow-glazed and brown-decorated posset cup only five inches high made by Robert Stalbridge in 1623 recently fetched £44 at auction.

English Delft

The pottery known as 'Delft' is made by a process which has been used in many parts of the world for centuries; it was certainly perfected by the Italian potters as early as the fifteenth century for making majolica. Clay is used to make a plate or vessel and is then fired. The resulting article, which is porous like a modern flowerpot, is then dipped in an opaque white glaze containing an oxide of tin. On this white surface the decorators painted their designs, usually in cobalt blue. Over this, a transparent glaze was usually applied and the article was then fired a second time. Delft as we know it was first made in Holland from the sixteenth century and took its name from the town of Delft. By the middle of the seventeenth century it was being made in England; Lambeth, Bristol and Liverpool were the main centres, though there was also a Delft pottery at Wincanton in Somerset.

Portraits of royalty were a popular form of decoration and so were flowers, legendary scenes and landscapes showing Chinese influence. Perhaps the commonest examples of Delft are found in tiles which were made for use in fireplaces and kitchens. These often portrayed biblical scenes and some were decorated in such a way that it took several tiles to complete a picture.

The largest output of Delft was probably from Lambeth, where there are said to have been as many as twenty potteries. The white glaze was thin and some Lambeth Delft has a slight reddish tinge where the body shows through. The blue used in decoration has a grey tone.

Bristol Delft is noted for its polychrome decoration (i.e. using more than one colour), particularly for delicate shades of purple and green. Some pieces have a type of decoration known as *bianco sopra bianco*, in which white is painted over the enamel (often purple) to give a lace-like finish. It is seen particularly on the borders of plates. Most Bristol Delft has a greenish tinge in the glaze.

Liverpool Delft has a bluish tinge in the glaze. The punch bowls made in Liverpool are famous and the factory of Sadler & Green started transfer-printing on Delftware, a process which was to revolutionize the methods of pottery decoration in later years.

Salt-glazed Stonewares

Stoneware was made from a good plastic clay mixed with sand or some other form of silica. The shaped articles were placed in perforated boxes or saggers made from waste scraps. This was to protect the ware when it was fired at a high temperature in the kiln. With most clays the resulting colour was brown, ranging from a light buff colour to a dark sepia. The stoneware was glazed by throwing salt into the kiln when the heat was intense.

A grey salt-glazed stoneware was extensively made in Germany and Holland more than 300 years ago. By the end of the seventeenth century several potters were producing stoneware in England—John Dwight in Fulham, James Morley in Nottingham and John and David Elers, who started in London and later moved to Staffordshire. 'There were, about the year 1700, twenty-two glazing ovens in Burslem, each with eight mouths; and around each of them was a scaffold, on which men stood to throw salt into the ovens. The salt was decomposed by the heat of the oven; and holes in the saggers allowed the fumes to enter and act upon the wares within the saggers.' Shortly after this, new stoneware factories started in Derbyshire, notably at Chesterfield, using local clays.

Developments in Staffordshire

John and David Elers were Dutch and had had some experience as silversmiths. Much of their work had great artistic merit. They discovered a fine-grained, iron-stained clay at Bradwell Wood in Staffordshire which produced a red stoneware and their unglazed teapots of this material were beautifully made with decoration moulded in relief. It is said that the brothers were very jealous of their manufacturing secrets and looked to strategy rather than to the law for protection, keeping a careful guard against strangers and employing labour with little intelligence. However, their methods became known to Twyford and Astbury, according to some earlier writers, by stealth.

> Twyford applied for employment at the works, and proceeded to manifest entire carelessness and indifference to all the operations going on. Astbury was more of a hero; he suffered bodily in the cause. He assumed the garb and appearance of an idiot, got into employ, and submitted to the cuffs, kicks and unkind treatment of masters and men with meekness. He ate his food and went through the easy drudgery of his employment and comported himself in all outward matters with the same apparent imbecility. But his eyes and his mind were wide awake all the time. He watched every process by stealth; and on returning home in the evenings, he constructed models of all the different apparatus he had seen during the day, and made memoranda of the processes. This course he continued for two years; at the expiration of which period his employers began to think that he was not quite the fool they had imagined and he was discharged.

That is the story and there is no doubt that Twyford and Astbury had started to make ware similar to the Elers' products by about 1710, and other factories followed. Astbury later developed a white, salt-glazed ware by adding calcined flint to the clay. There is also a colourful story to account for this discovery.

> Mr Astbury, being on a journey to London, had arrived at Dunstable, when he was compelled to seek a remedy for the eyes of his horse, which seemed to be rapidly going blind. The

hostler of the tavern at which he stayed burned a flint-stone till quite red; then he pulverized it very fine, and by blowing a little of the dust into each eye, occasioned both to discharge much matter, and be quite benefited. Mr Astbury having noticed the white colour of the calcined flint, the ease with which it was then reduced to powder, and its clayey nature when discharged in the moisture from the horse's eye, immediately conjectured that it might be usefully employed to render of a different colour the pottery he made.

Whatever the source of his inspiration, and it seems more likely that it came from earlier potters such as John Dwight or from the glass makers who were already using calcined flint, the white-glazed stoneware (though it was, in fact, cream in colour) was certainly being made commercially by about 1720, and was widely used later by Aaron Woods and the two Ralph Woods, by Enoch Booth and by the Thomas Whieldon-Josiah Wedgwood partnership (Wedgwood was then in his twenties).

It is worth mentioning here that Wedgwood later made large quantities of a black, unglazed stoneware by adding manganese oxide to the mixture to be fired. It had a hard fine texture and was known as 'black basaltes' (after the hard, dark, volcanic, basalt rock). For this he established a factory at Shelton, which developed later into his main Etruria Works. All kinds of tableware were made in black basalt, together with decorative statues and vases which depended for their appeal entirely on form and character. The clay was pressed into moulds giving a decoration in bas relief, usually with classical motifs. By the early nineteenth century many Staffordshire firms were making black basalt.

A development which followed the manufacture of white, salt-glazed ware and involved greater concentration on decoration and colouring is associated with the name of Thomas Whieldon. Moulded flowers and leaves were placed as relief decoration on the main body and were joined by thin rolls of clay to provide the stems. He also perfected new colouring techniques, using a liquid lead glaze which could be dabbed with metallic oxides of various colours before firing, producing marbling, mottling, and tortoiseshell effects. Whieldon also produced agate ware, which was made by mixing layers of various shades of coloured clay together into a single mass before working. This gave the ware a streaked or variegated appearance. Whieldon agate ware is usually rather thin and light.

Josiah Wedgwood had fifteen years experience in the pottery industry, first as an apprentice and later as a partner with Whieldon, before starting a business of his own. He set himself to improve the stoneware on which he had worked with Whieldon in an attempt to produce an earthenware body which would have some of the properties of porcelain. He first succeeded in producing a cream-ware which was hard, attractive in appearance, and had a soft rich glaze. It is also extremely light in the hand. Wedgwood made a cream-ware tea-set as a gift for Queen Charlotte who allowed him to call this new earthenware 'Queen's ware'. This was in 1765; he had to wait another ten years before he could make a further improvement, though he had already solved the technical problems. Litigation was involved, since William Cookworthy had patented the use of Cornish clay and stone. However, by 1775, Wedgwood was able to add these ingredients to his raw materials. By 1779, he was producing 'pearl ware' which was whiter than his cream ware and lent itself to transfer decoration (see p. 81). This was to lead to a great expansion in the pottery industry and a considerable export trade. Other potteries were soon producing similar wares, notably a Yorkshire pottery at Leeds.

Among Wedgwood's best-known achievements was the manufacture of his jasper ware, a white stoneware in which the body consisted largely of sulphate of barytes with only about forty per cent of clay. It has fine texture and a smooth, almost wax-like surface. When it was introduced in 1775 it was coloured throughout, since the colour had been mixed with the body. Slowly, the solid jasper was replaced by what is known as jasper dip, in which the colour was applied to the white body. Blue is the commonest colour of jasper ware, but it was also made in black and shades of green, pink and lilac.

Apart from tableware and decorative vases, it was made into snuff boxes, scent bottles, plaques for interior decoration and even into earrings, cameos and buttons, the designs standing out in relief—white figures, medallions and classical motifs against a smooth, coloured groundwork.

28 *Base of an eighteenth-century drinking glass showing typical wear*

29. *Face of a Victorian automaton doll*

The Wedgwood firm employed many famous modellers and designers at Etruria, including artists from Italy. This was due to the influence of Wedgwood's partner, Thomas Bentley, a wealthy Liverpool merchant who was a student of the fine arts.

We have referred several times in previous pages to transfer printing which, in the first half of the nineteenth century, was used by almost every English pottery. Here is a contemporary account of the process.

> In that very useful production, the *blue-printed* ware, the pattern is engraved upon a copper plate; the ink or blue paint is a viscid mixture of cobalt, flint, oil, tar and other substances; and a print is taken from the plate with this ink on a piece of very thin but tough paper. The paper is handed to a girl called the *cutter*, who cuts away from it as much of the unprinted part as is not wanted; and a woman, called the *transferrer*, places the paper with the inked side downwards, on the biscuit ware which is to receive the pattern. She rubs the paper with a roll of flannel in such a way as to transfer the ink from the paper to the biscuit-ware; and by washing the ware immediately afterwards in water, all the paper is washed off in fragments, leaving the inked pattern on the ware. . . . The ink has a dirty brown appearance when laid on, but the heat of an oven and the subsequent glazing bring out its lively blue tint.

Vast quantities of this blue and white transfer ware were made, particularly large dinner services, and there was a considerable export to America.

The better-class transfer-printed ware was sold to middle-class people who could not afford to buy porcelain, the rougher pieces went to the homes of the workers. Certain patterns were widely used—the willow pattern 'in the Chinese taste', a design known as 'Asiatic pheasant' with flowers and birds, and the 'wild rose' pattern, which depicted a country scene with a river, a bridge, boatmen and some distant houses. The latter took its name from its floral border. Among famous makers of this type of decorated ware were W. Adams & Son, J. & R. Clews, A. Stevenson, and the Spode Factory, which produced work of very fine quality.

Most transfer-printed earthenware was produced in the first

F

half of the nineteenth century and, on the whole, the earlier work tends to be the better.

A summary of the main developments in the making and decoration of earthenware must include some reference to lustre ware. Its production involved coating the whole or part of the surface of glazed earthenware articles with a metallic oxide to produce a gold, silver or copper sheen. Its use was often combined with colour decoration. Lustre was certainly made before 1800 but the finer types came a little later, between 1810 and 1830. These are known as 'resist' lustres. Before coating with lustre, the desired design was painted on the article with fine china clay mixed with a sticky or resinous medium—glycerine, for example. This resisted the coating of metallic oxide which could be removed, so that the design was left against a lustred background.

Nearly every earthenware factory made lustre of some kind. Some specialized in a particular type, though few bear the maker's mark. At Sunderland, lustre was combined with transfer printing.

BUYING POTTERY

When an expert handles a piece of porcelain or pottery he almost invariably looks first at the base or the back to see whether it is marked in any way. The mark or marks give him some guidance about the maker and the date though, especially in the case of porcelain, he will treat marks with caution, since many have been copied or faked. Marks may have been impressed into the soft clay body before firing, much as a footprint is made in soft damp sand, or printed or painted in colour on the biscuit before glazing. These are 'under glaze' marks. Other marks have been painted on top of the glaze and these are obviously easier to fake at a later date. Factory marks can provide much useful information. The amateur will find it useful to remember the following facts when examining the marks on porcelain or pottery: they help to narrow the field for further investigation.

1. If the words 'England' or 'Made in England' are found, the article is not an antique. The former was used after 1891 (though a few firms used it from about 1880); the latter appears from about 1900 and is still used today. It became necessary to use

the 'England' mark on ceramics because the Americans insisted that all imported pottery and porcelain should carry the name of the country in which it was made.

2. The mark 'Bone China' was used after 1900. No antiques carry this description.

3. Some ceramics carry a registered number, sometimes printed, sometimes impressed, on a raised rectangular ribbon—e.g. 'Rd.No.265832'. Such numbers were only used after 1884.

4. Trade marks of limited liability companies which carry the mark 'Ltd.' or 'Ld.' are only found on ceramics made after 1860.

5. The words 'Trade Mark' appeared with the Trade Marks Act, which came into force in 1862, but were seldom used before 1875.

6. Beware of date marks included in a maker's mark: they nearly always indicate the date when the firm was first established, or even when its predecessor was established. The firm of George Jones & Sons of Stoke, for example, which operated from 1861-1952, shows the date 1790 on its 'Abbey' design mark which also includes the word 'England', indicating manufacture after 1891. Nineteenth-century porcelain from the Coalport factory often includes the date 1750 in its mark.

The above facts have now enabled the amateur to eliminate most marked porcelain and pottery made during the last hundred years. Much of it has charm and interest but it is not antique.

There are one or two other marks which help one to date nineteenth-century pieces. The word 'Royal' does not appear until after about 1850. The Worcester factory, for example, did not become the Worcester Royal Porcelain Works until 1862. The Royal Crown Derby Porcelain Company was formed in 1876.

Many Victorian pieces show a diamond-shaped pattern on the base (Fig 9) which was used from 1842 when the Copyright Act came into force. This mark makes it possible to determine the actual year when a design was registered but does *not* indicate the date of manufacture, since designs were only copyright for three years after registration. But it does suggest an approximate date. Fig 9 shows an actual mark. The 'IV' at the apex of the diamond indicates the class of goods—in this case china and glass. The figure '4' on the right indicates the day of the month, the 'D' on the left the month, the 'F' at the top, the year, and the '10' at the bottom was a parcel number at the Patent Office. A code is needed to determine the month and year of registration since the letters of the alphabet were not used consecutively.

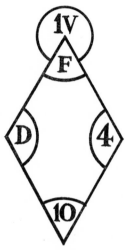

Figure 9   REGISTRATION MARK

The month letters were as follows :

C = Jan; G = Feb; W = Mar; H = April; E = May; M = June; I = July; R = August; D = Sept; B = Oct; K = Nov; A = Dec.

The year letters were:

X	1842	P	1851	Z	1860
H	1843	D	1852	R	1861
C	1844	Y	1853	O	1862
A	1845	J	1854	G	1863
I	1846	E	1855	N	1864
F	1847	L	1856	W	1865
U	1848	K	1857	Q	1866
S	1849	B	1858	T	1867
V	1850	M	1859		

Figure 9 therefore indicates a pattern or design registered on 4 September 1847.

From 1867 to 1883 a new mark was used with the information differently distributed on the diamond, but it need not concern us here: details with the code are available in all good dictionaries of marks. The most comprehensive and up-to-date is the *Encyclopaedia of British Pottery and Porcelain Marks* by G. A. Godden (Herbert Jenkins). A useful book to carry around is a *Pocket Book of English Ceramic Marks*, compiled by J. P. Cushion (Faber and Faber).

Although marks can be a useful guide, do not rely too much on them, particularly if they are on fine porcelain. They can easily be copied or added to, and often were. The Derby factory, for example, produced many porcelain figures which bore the Meissen factory mark of blue crossed swords. On less expensive ware, and certainly on pottery, more reliance can be placed on the mark since it would seldom be worthwhile to fake such a piece.

The range of items available to the collector of earthenware or pottery is enormous. We can deal briefly only with one or two types and have chosen transfer ware, pot lids, earthenware figures and what has come to be known as 'art pottery'.

Transfer Ware

Thomas Turner's introduction of transfer printing (p. 69) saw the beginning of mass production in the pottery industry, which resulted in a flood of printed earthenware. Almost every pottery in the country produced this ware and much of it was of rather poor quality. The interest to the collector lies in its availability and in the attractive designs and colours of some of the finer pieces. Many of the early designs were direct copies of those on imported Chinese ware or were 'in the Chinese taste'. Of these, the willow pattern, still in use today, has probably been the most popular. It is thought to have been first engraved by Thomas Minton at the Caughley factory in 1780. Subsequently, he worked as a freelance copperplate engraver and produced variations on the Caughley design for use in other potteries, notably those of Spode and Adams. Many other engravers copied this design but they all differ considerably from the 'three men on the bridge' pattern now in use, which appears to have become the standard pattern by the middle of the nineteenth century.

Romantic designs with classical ruins became popular early in the nineteenth century. The best known is perhaps Spode's 'Italian' design, introduced in 1816 and still being used today. Some makers produced series with English or American views, though the latter were for export and are rarely seen in Britain and even specimens of the English series are hard to come by. Their makers included Adams, J. & R. Clews, R. Hall, Charles Meigh, Pountney & Allies, John & James Rogers, Andrew & Ralph Stevenson, and Enoch Wood & Sons.

Some of the most interesting designs were those based on engravings taken from books which were popular at the time. Sydney B. Williams carried out some valuable research on the origin of the Spode designs and the results were published in his *Antique Blue and White Spode*. He reveals that some of these designs were adapted from *Oriental Field Sports* (1805) a book dealing with the story of the hunt in India—a country which aroused much interest in the early nineteenth century; others proved to be from Mayer's *Views in Asia Minor* (1803) and Merigot's *Views and Ruins in Rome* (1798). Later, William Ridgway, Son & Co. based designs for a dinner service on Hablot Browne's illustrations for *The Old Curiosity Shop*. This book was first serialized in a magazine called *Master Humphrey's Clock* and Ridgway used the words 'Humphrey's Clock' in his maker's mark. There were apparently insufficient suitable engravings in Dickens' book and so further engravings were made in a similar style. The partnership of Thomas and John Carey produced some superb quality blue and white ware with scenes illustrating Scott's *Lady of the Lake*, though we have not been able to trace that they were actually adapted from book engravings.

When buying these wares look at the quality of the transfer work. The skill acquired by the best transferrers was of a high standard and on the better quality ware the joins in the pattern are hard to find. Except when ironstone was used, most early transfer pottery is light in weight compared with modern earthenware. The glaze of the early pieces has a characteristic ripple, rather like the surface of the sand on the seashore when the tide has gone out. Look also for the marks left by the spurs or stilts which supported each piece in the kiln and kept it from contact with its neighbour. These are usually three marks spaced round the back of each plate or dish, though occasionally they are found on the front, masked by the pattern. Many early plates have no base rim and show signs of constant wear.

Until 1842, when copyright protection became possible, designs were freely copied. It is therefore unwise to assume that a particular design was used only by the originator. Some people assert that each pottery had its own border pattern for its transfer ware and that these borders were not copied. Do not assume that this was always so, for there is much evidence to the contrary. Pountney & Allies of Bristol used border patterns which were also used by Spode and Rogers, and the border of the 'wild rose' pattern was used by at least three potteries—Bourne, Baker & Bourne of Fenton, Samuel Barker & Son of the Don Pottery, and by the Middlesbrough Pottery.

Pot Lids

At the beginning of the nineteenth century men had started to use oil and grease on their hair. Macassar oil from the East Indies was widely used (hence antimacassars which the Victorians used to protect their upholstered furniture from the oil), and bear grease was also popular. The latter was sold in round, white pomade pots and many of these were made by F. & R. Pratt & Co., of Fenton, a firm run by two brothers who employed a particularly good decorator, Jesse Austin. Austin was not only a good artist but he had an inventive mind. By the time of the Great Exhibition in 1851, the firm had perfected a process by which colour printing could be done by transfers, each colour being produced from a separate engraving. Decorated pot lids made by the Pratt factory have long been favourites with collectors. The firm of T. J. & J. Mayer is also known to have made pomade pots.

Hundreds of different pictures appear on early pot lids—rural scenes, animals, historic events, famous buildings, sports, and some are based on well-known oil paintings. These pots were certainly used for the sale of pomade, as well as fish and meat pastes, until about 1880. By then, they had become so popular with collectors that they were specially produced for this new market.

Many of them were reproductions but a few were made using the original copper plates.

Collectors should bear the following points in mind.

1. The quality of the picture on a Pratt lid depended on very accurate placing of the coloured transfers which had to be applied in sequence, one for each colour. Small marks (usually dots or circles) were printed on the edge of the designs to help accurate superimposition. Always look for these marks near the edge of the lid.

2. Some of the earliest lids, since the pots were intended for bear grease, bore scenes with bears, which covered the entire lid. These are now rather rare.

3. Many of the popular early pot lids have been reproduced in recent years. Sometimes these modern lids carry a mark stating that they are reproductions—but not always. The amateur will need to assess the character of the earthenware and glaze before deciding on the age of the lid.

4. Try to compare a known original with a reproduction pot lid. The colours on the early lids are stronger and the detail is finer.

5. Finally, carry out a 'ring' test. If the lid produces a ringing sound when struck lightly with a metal object it is probably a reproduction. If it produces a dull sound it is likely to be a genuine early specimen.

Earthenware Figures

Various names have been given to earthenware figures at different times. In the middle of the eighteenth century they were called image toys, by 1800 they were merely toys. Twenty years later they were being advertised as chimney ornaments and today they are usually referred to as Staffordshire figures, though they were undoubtedly also made in other parts of Britain.

Some of the earliest figures are associated with the Wood family. Ralph Wood (1717-72) was a particularly fine modeller who coloured his figures before glazing. Well-known examples of his work are 'The Vicar and Moses', 'Old Age', 'Diogenes looking for an Honest Man', 'Charity', and the 'Toby Philpot' jug. They were sometimes signed 'R. Wood' and were later widely copied.

His son, also a Ralph Wood (1748-95), continued the tradition and made many figures similar to those made by his father, as well as some of his own design including busts of Handel and Milton. Ralph Wood Jr did some of his work in enamel: the colour was made to fuse with the glaze by adding a glassy flux before firing. His work is signed 'Ra. Wood'.

Enoch Wood, cousin of Ralph Jr, and more than ten years younger, not only modelled figures but was a keen collector of earthenware. John Wesley, when visiting the Potteries, gave sittings to the young Enoch Wood, and the bust he made has been much copied by other potters. By the time he died in 1840 at the age of 81, the modelling of well-known figures had become very popular. In the early part of the nineteenth century, toys or chimney ornaments and fairground pieces were turned out from the potteries in their thousands. Among the makers was John Walton whose figures are often backed by a spreading tree with foliage, a convention known as 'bocage' which was popular on the early porcelain figures made at the Bow and Chelsea factories. Another modeller of the period was Obadiah Sherratt, who became known for his bull-baiting group—a man with a staff, arms upraised, with dogs attacking a bull. He also made figures of famous people such as Napoleon, Wellington and Nelson, and milk jugs in the shape of a cow. It was jokingly said in the Potteries that Sherratt used the same mould for a cow's teat and Wellington's nose!

Other known figure-makers were J. Dale of Burslem, Ralph Hall of Tunstall, Ralph Salt of Hanley and Felix and R. Pratt of Fenton.

The manufacture of chimney ornaments continued throughout the nineteenth century. Figures included royalty, wartime leaders, politicians, evangelists (Moody and Sankey) and even criminals. Innumerable dogs were modelled, some sporting dogs, some lap dogs. Few can fail to have seen the flat-faced hearth dogs, like a King Charles Spaniel, which were made in large numbers and have been copied until quite recent times.

It is useful to know that the early figures were made by hand. The clay was pressed into the moulds with the fingers and the base was closed and recessed, though a small hole was left somewhere in the figure to release expanding air during firing. The colouring was often crude, but vigorous, usually under the glaze. Later figures were made by pouring a liquid slip into porous plaster moulds. These acted as blotting paper, soaking up the moisture from the slip, which then slowly hardened. These figures tend to be smoother, and they have an open base and often a flat, undecorated back. Colours were applied sparingly (since the cream-glazed surface was attractive in itself), usually over the glaze. Gilding was common.

Art Pottery

In the second half of the nineteenth century, when mass production was the rule, individual London artists were making and decorating various types of salt-glazed stoneware which has come to be known as art pottery. A great deal was made at the Doulton factory at Lambeth and some by the four Martin brothers at a small pottery at Southall. Many collectors now show a great interest in this ware. It is now nearly one hundred years since the Doulton factory, always well-known for its brown, salt-glazed ware decorated with hunting scenes in relief, started to employ individual artists, mainly young women who had been trained at the Lambeth School of Art, as decorators. The artist was able to select the stoneware piece she wished to work on and was free to use her own individual style of decoration. This was usually incised on the body and was hand coloured before firing. The vases, jugs, cups and candlesticks so produced found a ready market and within ten years of the beginning of this experiment Doulton's were employing over 200 artists, many of whom gained a considerable reputation. These decorators included Hannah, Florence and Arthur Barlow, Frank Butler, Mark Marshall, Eliza Simmance and George Tinworth. It is a field to be recommended for the amateur collector. This Doulton ware is inexpensive and all the pieces carry the name of the factory, the artist's mark and a date mark. The artists' marks are listed in several books of marks.

While these developments were taking place in the Doulton factory, four brothers by the name of Martin set up a factory at Southall in 1877 and, by dint of steady application and much

laborious experiment, succeeded in producing a salt-glazed
stoneware of fine quality, despite being handicapped by lack of
both experience and capital. They loved their work and made
themselves familiar with every process of their art which, as a
result, was highly individual. It was more expensive than mass-
produced ware and was bought privately, mainly by collectors.
There was no business organization in the ordinary sense of the
word. The organizer was Charles Martin who, after twenty years

Figure 10   MARTIN-WARE GROTESQUES
(From *The Ludgate*)

work with his brothers and despite a dislike of publicity, was per-
suaded in 1897 to give an interview to a journalist working for
The Ludgate magazine. He explained their policy thus:

> So as to separate ourselves as far as possible from the manu-
> facturers who turn out similar pieces by the hundred, we make
> it a matter of pride never to repeat a single specimen of our
> work. Even in the case of a pair of vases, you will find that
> the design, though of similar character, differs materially on
> each specimen . . . each of our designs is original and never
> repeated. They have to be engraved or etched, when the clay
> is sufficiently set, with some hard point, generally steel. The

clay is then so hard that a line once made cannot be obliterated, but must be included in the design.

The output of the Martin brothers consisted largely of shaped bowls, jugs and vases, and of grotesque figures of animals, fish and birds (particularly owls). Much of the work has unusual colouring for this kind of stoneware. Most of their pieces are signed and dated. The brothers were so engrossed in their work that money meant little to them and they kept many of their finer specimens for their own collection—most of these, fortunately, have since found their way into museums. The Martin-ware pottery collection is housed in the public library in Osterley Park Road, Southall, Middlesex.

Mocha Ware

Throughout the nineteenth century, mugs, jugs and other useful containers were produced cheaply in potteries all over Britain in a cream or white earthenware with a striking, tree-like decoration. This Mocha ware, as it is called, was used in public houses, markets and poorer homes, though there was also an export trade. The basic decoration is in coloured bands running around the body, usually of brown, blue or grey, with narrow black bands between them. The widest band is in the middle of the article and black, feathery shapes spread upwards on this band. The coloured bands were applied as slip while the dried pot was spinning on a lathe. The pot was then placed upside down while the slip was still wet and blobs of dark-coloured 'tea,' said to have been made from hops and tobacco juice, were dabbed on near the upper edge of the widest band. This 'tea' then spread outward through the coloured slip to form tree-like fronds.

Mocha jugs can still be seen in the bars of old inns and many of them carry a raised crown mark in white with the word 'IMPERIAL' on a ribbon beneath, showing that they have been approved as measures by the Weights and Measures authority. Sometimes the marks are printed on the body of the vessel and sometimes on a metal button fitted into a hole.

The amateur earthenware collector may wish to specialize in one type of pottery, or even in the products of a single factory, or he may like to cover a wide range of wares, collecting a specimen of each. In either case, it is wise to consider at an early stage the problems of display and storage. Plates look well on a Welsh dresser, on a high ledge around a room, or even resting on top of a wooden pelmet. Mugs or jugs need a shelf or windowsill, and a collection of these can look most attractive.

GLASS

GLASS vessels of various kinds have been made for centuries and much Roman glass still exists. In England, although glass was certainly made in Tudor times, the industry only became firmly established in the second half of the seventeenth century. This resulted from experiments carried out by George Ravenscroft, who discovered that lead oxide added in fairly large quantities to the molten glass greatly improved its quality and made it possible to produce an excellent glass that also showed more sparkle.

The variety of objects made from glass is enormous. Not only are there hundreds of types of drinking glasses and of bottles, jugs and decanters to hold the liquor, but all manner of tableware has been and is still being made—sugar basins, salt cellars, sweet dishes, cups for custard and dessert, cream jugs, finger bowls, cake-stands, fruit bowls, candlesticks, epergnes . . . the list is endless. In this chapter, we shall deal with transparent or crystal-glass drinking glasses and decanters made in the eighteenth and nineteenth centuries, and with a few of the many types of coloured glass.

Drinking Glasses

When trying to date a drinking glass it is necessary to study the bowl, the stem and the foot. Even then it is seldom possible to place it within narrow time limits because many shapes and styles persisted over long periods. It is possible, however, to state when a particular style was most popular.

Until well into the eighteenth century, English drinking glasses were usually fairly large and heavy in contrast to the

Figure 11   DRINKING GLASSES : BOWLS

Venetian glass which had previously been popular. They nearly always had a greenish grey colour, as it was not until the middle of the eighteenth century that ways were found of bleaching glass.

Let us first consider the bowls of drinking glasses. At the end of the seventeenth century these were mainly *funnel-shaped* (Fig 11a), or *fluted* (Fig 11d) but other shapes were evolving which gained great popularity in the eighteenth century. First came the *bell-shaped* (Fig 11b) and *waisted* (Fig 11c) bowls and a little later the *trumpet* (Fig 11e) bowl—an early shape which had been out of favour for a long time. Between 1715 and 1720, new shapes emerged, the *thistle-shaped* bowl (Fig 11f) and the *straight-sided* glass (Fig 11g) of which large numbers were made, probably for serving gin in inns. Just before 1750, new bowl shapes were introduced known as the *ogee* bowl (Fig 11h) and the *double ogee* bowl (Fig 11i). Then came the *bucket* bowl (Fig 11j) and its variant the *waisted-bucket*, which remained popular until about 1775. The seventeenth-century *round funnel* bowl produced its variant, thinned down and extended (Fig 11k). Throughout the eighteenth century glasses had become thinner and finer but the vogue for etched engraving and cut ornamentation towards the end of the period made it necessary to produce a slightly thicker glass again. The *ovoid* bowl (Fig 11l) appeared. In the nineteenth century, there were no startling new bowl shapes: existing types were modified to suit prevailing fashions.

When dating a glass, the stem is often more significant than the bowl it supports, and so are shaped enlargements in the stem which are known as knops. The shapes of stems and knops varied enormously and the periods when each style was being made overlapped. We give the main types below with the period during which they were in fashion.

1. The *Baluster* (Fig 12a) was popular from about 1685 to the 1720s though it was still made up to about 1760. It is usually found in the inverted form (Fig 12b) and, after 1720, often with knops above or below the baluster. The drawn stems often include a bubble or tear.

2. The *Drawn Plain* stems often include a bubble or tear (Fig 12c). They were turned out in their thousands because they were

30. *Faked bruising on reproduction furniture, probably done with a bicycle chain*

31. *An inkstain purposely made on the inside of a drawer of a piece of faked furniture*

32. *A Chelsea Red Anchor mark*

33. *A Worcester Crescent mark*

Figure 12   DRINKING GLASSES: STEMS AND KNOPS

easy to make. Though first seen in the seventeenth century, they appear to have been out of favour until about 1715. By 1740, they were well established and were widely used for the next thirty years or more.

3. The *Moulded Pedestal* (Fig 12d) was first made about 1715 and lasted until well past the middle of the century. Four, six and eight-sided varieties are known. It is sometimes known as the Silesian stem.

4. *Air Twist* stems (Fig 12e) were probably a direct challenge to the plain stem and many consider them an entirely English creation. They appeared in various forms between 1730 and 1770.

5. The *Opaque Twist* is similar in appearance to the Air Twist but the columns were of enamel instead of air. The twist was often white but colours were used after 1765. Their popularity waned after 1780.

6. The *Incised Twist* (Fig 12f) was only made for a short period round about 1750 : these stems are rare.

7. *Faceted* stems (Fig 12g) involved cut decoration. Various types of facet were cut into the glass in a regular pattern. They were made from about 1760 until the early nineteenth century.

After 1800, stems began to disappear and short stemless glasses gained favour.

The knops which appear in the stems of glasses usually take their name from their shape. They include the *Plain* knop (Fig 12h), *Flattened* knop (Fig 12i), *Ball* knop (Fig 12j), *Bladed* knop (Fig 12k), *Acorn* knop (Fig 12l), *Wide Angular* knop (Fig 12m), *Dumb Bell* knop (Fig 12n), *Drop* knop (Fig 12o), *Mushroom* knop (Fig 12p) and *Shoulder* knop (Fig 12q).

The foot of a glass does not lend itself to so many variations as the bowl and the stem. There are, however, several well defined types :

1. The *Conical* foot (Fig 13a) found in both plain and solid form.

2. The *Folded* foot (Fig 13b), so called because the outer rim is doubled back under itself, a form which gave the foot tremendous strength. It is more likely to break completely than to chip

Figure 13   DRINKING GLASS FEET AND DECANTER STOPPERS

but a good deal of force is needed to shatter it. The domed or bracket folded foot (Fig 13c) is a variant.

3. The *Firing* foot (Fig 13d) is a heavy, strong foot about a quarter of an inch thick, so called because it produced a loud sound like gunfire when banged on a table as a toasting glass.

In the early nineteenth century, the *Rummer* (Fig 13e) was probably the most popular type of glass. It gets its name from the German *Roemer* (meaning Roman), although it was often used to serve rum drinks.

When buying old glasses, examine the base carefully. When a glass is blown a sharp and jagged surface is left where it is snapped from the pipe. This is known as the pontil mark and will be found on the base of most glasses made before about 1750. After this date the makers began to grind the mark away. Few nineteenth-century glasses retain their pontil mark.

The bases of old glasses usually show scratches due to wear over long periods (see Plate 28). Scratching can be faked by rubbing the base of a glass with emery paper or a rough stone. Examine the scratching very carefully : faked scratches are often curved where the forger used a circular action with the abrasive.

Glasses which have been chipped are sometimes ground down and repolished. This destroys the proportions of the glass : the ground parts look too small for the rest. If the top rim has been ground it may have a flattened surface (Fig 13g) instead of the normal rounded one (Fig 13f).

Decanters

Many families have an old decanter among their inherited possessions, and these are much easier to date than drinking glasses. The shape of the body, neck and stopper of the decanter evolved in an orderly sequence, though many decanters have unfortunately lost their original or period stoppers. Many dealers and collectors hoard old stoppers in the hope of matching them to decanters which are incomplete.

During the first quarter of the eighteenth century, heavy-based decanters were popular. They are known as *Mallet* decanters (Fig 14a) and were usually six- or eight-sided, though they were sometimes cruciform with the body lobed in the shape of a cross

Figure 14   DECANTER SHAPES

(Fig 14b). The necks of these decanters were usually at least as tall as the body. A ring of glass was moulded around the top of the neck, so that string could be tied round the neck without slipping. Such rings certainly prevent a decanter from slipping through the fingers. In some cases there is more than one ring of glass. The *shaft* and *globe* decanter (Fig 14c) was also produced in this period. This was simply blown and looked rather like a bulbous bottle. The same shape became popular again in the Regency period. Early eighteenth-century decanter stoppers were usually ball-shaped and are not ground where they fit into the neck.

Decanters with broad (Fig 14e) or narrow (Fig 14d) shoulders had appeared by about 1740. They quickly gained in popularity and persisted into the nineteenth century. These were the first decanters to be decorated by cutting and gilding. Taper decanters with lozenge-shaped stoppers were popular during the 1760s and were also made well into the nineteenth century (Fig 14f). Decanters engraved or gilded with imitation wine labels and chains (Fig 14e) appeared at about the same time and were popular again in Regency times. They were also made in coloured glass (see page 104). Decanters shaped like a barrel (Fig 14g) were used during the last quarter of the eighteenth century.

Early nineteenth-century decanters include the Prussian and cylindrical types. In the *Prussian* decanter (Fig 14h) the bulbous body slopes in gently to the base. These usually have several rings set around the neck, and a mushroom-shaped stopper. The *Cylindrical* decanter (Fig 14j) has a straight-sided body decorated with vertical flutes and a ringed neck.

A special kind of decanter appeared in the 1780s which was designed for use on board ship. They were made with wide, heavy bases which made it almost impossible to turn them over. These ships' decanters (Fig 14i) which are sometimes called 'Rodneys' are much sought after.

It may be helpful to list and date some of the commoner types of decanter stopper. They include :

The *Ball Finial* (Fig 13h), early eighteenth century.

The *Vertical Lozenge* (Fig 13i), mid to late eighteenth century.

The *Pear-Shaped* (Fig 13j), late eighteenth century.

The *Mushrom* (Fig 13k) and the *Target* (Fig 13l), late eighteenth and early nineteenth century.

The *Cut Globe* (Fig 13m), early nineteenth century.

The Ball Finial was decorated with air bubbles after about 1710 and with tear-shaped bubbles from about 1720. Stoppers and the inner surfaces of decanter necks were ground about 1745 to ensure a good air-tight fit, and the bottoms of stoppers were ground flat and polished.

COLOURED GLASS

Coloured glass was first made in quantity in the second half of the eighteenth century, partly because the duty on clear crystal glass had been increased, partly in an attempt to compete with something 'new' against the large quantities of Chinese porcelain then entering the country. It is not surprising, therefore, that the glassmakers should attempt to produce an opaque white glass as a direct rival to imported porcelain. This was achieved at Bristol and much of it was decorated 'in the Chinese taste', as was early English porcelain, though some appears to have been sent to Liverpool to be transfer-printed. The only artist to have been identified as a decorator of this early white glass was Michael Edkins. Although this type of glass tends to be described as 'Bristol' glass, it is now certain that it was also made elsewhere in England during this period. Fine specimens cost a great deal of money : it is not a field for the collector of moderate means.

The name 'Bristol' is even more frequently associated with a deep blue, transparent glass, though similar glass was also made in the Midlands and the north-east of England. Many people think of 'Bristol Blue' as a type of glass. It is not. 'Bristol Blue' is a colour. The name probably derives from the fact that the finest smalt, the raw material which contained the cobalt colouring, was imported into Bristol for distribution to glass works all over the country. The blue glass actually made in Bristol seems to have been of such high quality that other manufacturers were anxious to imitate it, but it is doubtful whether even a glass expert could identify with certainty the place of manufacture of a piece of eighteenth-century blue glass. The amateur will find more interest in the style and decoration of the articles than in quibbling about the origin of the glass itself.

Decanters are the commonest 'Bristol' glass to be seen today. They were made long and tapering with a lozenge-shaped stopper; others were shouldered and were made in sets, each bottle bearing the name of the liquid it was to hold gilded on the glass, sometimes with a gilded chain added as though a wine label had been hung from the neck. Although the quality of the glass was good, the gilding was often poor and is frequently badly worn. A very few pieces of old Bristol glass are actually signed: 'I. Jacob, Bristol.' These, at least, are known to be authentic but beware of the single word 'Bristol' on blue glass. Modern glass made in central Europe is sometimes marked in this way.

The Nailsea glass-works established near Bristol in 1788 also gave its name to a type of coloured glassware that was made in other parts of the country. Its major output seems to have been after the tax on glass was lifted in 1845. It specialized in what have come to be known as 'friggers'—curiosities made in glass, like image toys in earthenware, probably for sale at country fairs. They include handbells, walking sticks, pipes, pocket flasks and hollow rolling pins which, legend has it, were given to sailors to use for smuggling tea into the country. The flasks and the bowls of the pipes often show festooning in white and coloured threads running through the clear glass. A special type of filigree work was said to have been done by French craftsmen working at Nailsea, and sometimes tiny glass top hats turn up which are thought to have been apprentice pieces. The Nailsea factory ceased to operate in 1873.

In Victorian times, new techniques were used to make glass articles, and in this connection it is useful to be able to distinguish between moulded glass and mechanically-pressed glass. Moulded glass is blown into the mould and any fluting or corrugation on the outside of the moulded glass has a corresponding fluting or corrugation inside. Except in the case of articles which would slip out of a mould without the need to open it, one can usually trace on the surface of the glass the faint thin mark where the sections of the mould met. Very often, the rim of the object was ground flat. On this type of moulded glass there is no pontil mark unless, of course, a glassblower worked on the piece after mould-ing.

Pressed glass was made by forcing the molten glass into a metal mould by pressing it down with a shaped plunger. In this case, only the outside of the glass object received the pattern from the mould, the inside taking the smooth surface of the plunger or whatever pattern the plunger itself may have imposed.

Although pressed glass was made as early as the 1820s, the output was relatively small until about 1870, when three glass factories in the north-east of England produced large quantities. These were Sowerby & Company of Gateshead, Greener & Company of Sunderland and George Davidson & Company of Gateshead. The latter made a most attractive type of glass known as 'Pearline', in which a clear coloured glass dies away into a pearly white glass. Some pressed glass is known as 'lace glass' because of its delicate patterns. Lace glass was sometimes used for commemorative pieces. An excellent account of late Victorian pressed glass is given in Mr G. A. Godden's *Antique China and Glass under £5* (Barker, 1966).

A number of other types of Victorian glass deserve mention.

Burmese glass, despite its name, has no connection with Burma. It is a translucent unpolished glass which shades from semi-opaque flesh-pink into a pale yellow colour. It was first patented by the Mt Washington Glass Company of America in 1885, and manufactured under licence by Thomas Webb & Sons of Stour-bridge in the following year. Queen Victoria became very interested in this glass which was later known as *Queen's Burmese*. It is highly valued.

Cameo glass was produced in the 1880s by a process developed by John Northwood nearly twenty years earlier. A rich-coloured glass was coated with white enamel on which a design was etched, cut or carved. By dissolving unwanted enamel with hydrofluoric acid, the design was made to stand out boldly against a coloured background. Cameo glass is greatly prized by collectors and fetches high prices.

Cased glass involved fusing one or more layers of coloured glass over clear flint glass. By cutting the outer layer or layers, the clear class was revealed. This cutting was sometimes done to create panels of clear glass which could be decorated with applied enamels. Cameo glass is often known as overlay glass.

Cranberry glass is a name given by Americans to what is often called 'ruby glass', though it varies a good deal in depth of colour. This red glassware was popular in early Victorian times and was made until about 1900. The earlier pieces are of blown glass: later pieces were often pressed. It was widely used for tableware and for every possible kind of decorative article—glasses, decanters, jugs, finger bowls, custard cups, sugar sifters, rose bowls, vases, epergnes, and powder bowls. Vases and glasses may have a clear glass base, jugs and decanters clear glass handles, and most decorative pieces carry pinched clear-glass ornamentation. Seen against plain walls, preferably with the lighting behind them, cranberry glass pieces add a warm richness to any room but, except for a few particularly fine or unusual specimens, they will not provide much excitement for the collector. Cranberry glass is, at the moment, too plentiful.

Opal glass, or *Opaline*, was a milky-white glass made by the addition of arsenic. It is recognized by the fiery glow seen when viewed against a strong light. In the 1870s, coloured opaline appeared in delicate shades of yellow, green and blue. The coloured vases were often painted with sprays of flowers or other ornamentation.

Spatter glass was made by gathering up small blobs of coloured glass on a larger mass of opaque white or cream-coloured glass before blowing into a mould. The resulting article has a surface spattered or streaked with several bright colours, but the inside is pure white or cream.

Vaseline glass is, as it's name implies, a pale, golden-green colour which, especially in later examples, may show a pearly cloudiness in places.

THE CARE OF GLASS

Glass should be washed in clean soapy water, rinsed in warm water and dried on a linen cloth. Never immerse glass in very hot water.

One of the most difficult problems is the decanter. When they have not been used for some time a white chalky deposit may often be seen over the inside surface and there may be a ring of thicker deposit where the liquid it contained evaporated from the surface. This white deposit is not easily removed and can seldom be washed away. There are, however, some time-honoured tips which are useful : this 'hint to servants' in *The Young Housewife's Daily Assistant* of 1864 is still valid. 'Decanters should be cleaned with tea leaves and a bottle brush, and well rinsed with cold water, then turned upside down to drain. Be careful never to use soda, or any acid, it makes them look thick, cloudy and white, instead of clear and brilliant.'

Another method is to put several dozen dried peas into the decanter and to swill them round and round with water, but to date the most satisfactory method we have found is to obtain fine lead shot and to swill this around in the same way.

The removal of decanter stoppers which are stuck is always a problem. Try filling a deep bowl or bucket with hot water into which you can put your hand with comfort. Place the body of the decanter, including the neck, upright in the water, making sure that no part of the stopper is in contact with the hot water. Keep up a steady twisting action on the stopper as though you were continually turning a tap on and off. At the moment when the heat has expanded the glass of the neck but has not yet reached the stopper, the latter should be released. If this does not happen the first time, allow the decanter to cool down completely before trying again.

Valuable glass occasionally gets chipped. If this unfortunately happens, a small chip can be removed by careful grinding and polishing—a job which must be done by an expert glazier. This does, of course, seriously diminish its value but it does mean that it can be kept for display as an example of its period, or because of its beauty.

Photographers should be warned when recording rare pieces that considerable heat is radiated by a photographic lamp and it should not be allowed near a glass object for more than a few seconds at a time. Many fine glasses have been shattered before the camera.

Some Victorian glass bottles and decanters have a metal mount around the rim, secured to the glass with a mixture of plaster and size : never immerse such articles in water.

Coloured Victorian glass is often decorated with clear glass ornamentation. This can sometimes act as a lens in sunlight, concentrating the rays on the main body and causing it to crack. In hot weather, such articles should be kept away from the direct rays of the sun.

CHAPTER NINE

ORIENTAL ANTIQUES

ORIENTAL antiques are usually regarded as those which
have come from the Far East—from China and Japan.
Chinese porcelain is world-famous, and rightly so. It
was probably being made at least a century before the birth of
Christ, and by the thirteenth century the Chinese were making
fine quality wares in considerable quantity. Their porcelain was
of a hard-paste type not made in England until Cookworthy discovered the secret of manufacturing a similar paste at Plymouth
in 1768.

The word 'Ming' is often lightly and wrongly used by amateurs
to describe Oriental ware. In fact, the name signifies a dynasty
covering nearly three hundred years, from 1368 to 1643. The
oldest examples of Chinese porcelain one may now hope to find
come from this period, though the chances of doing so are very
slight: even though a piece may look 'right' and be correctly
marked, it is very unlikely to be genuine. Chinese potters have
always copied the great patterns and marks of the past and continue to do so today. Most Chinese porcelain to be found in shops
was made in the nineteenth century, but the most fruitful period
to which hopeful collectors may look is the Chien Lung period
from 1736 to 1795. This porcelain, if held in a certain light, often
reveals a surface pitted like the skin of an orange.

The symbols used by the Chinese when decorating their porcelain are of great interest. The *Bat* (which often looks like a pair
of elephant's heads complete with trunks) was their symbol of
happiness. The *Dragon* with five claws was the Imperial emblem :
with four claws it indicated royal blood, and with three claws,
nobility. *Two Fish* signified married bliss. A plant looking rather

like a vase with two leaves projecting from the neck, called the *Che plant*, was the sign of longevity, as was the *Hare*. The *Rabbit* was the sign of fertility, and the *Leaf* an emblem of goodness. These were often incorporated in the decorative designs on porcelain and were sometimes used as marks.

Chinese porcelain is also famous for its *Famille Verte* and *Famille Rose* wares. These names refer to a predominance of a single colour—green or a delicate rose pink. *Famille Noire* (black) and *Famille Jaune* (yellow) are also found, but rarely.

During the eighteenth century, which covers the Chien Lung period, the trade routes between Europe and China were numerous and tea was one of the main commodities. The Chinese took this opportunity to produce great quantities of porcelain for the European markets and one type, known as armorial, bears the coats-of-arms of families in England. Services were specially ordered and drawings of the crests or coats-of-arms were sent with the order for the Chinese artists to copy. Chinese armorial porcelain fetches very high prices. Another type of eighteenth-century Oriental decoration is known as 'Jesuit'. The designs— often with a religious motif—were usually executed in black and gold. Some of this porcelain was commissioned by Jesuit priests in China. Only study, experience and constant handling will enable a new collector to learn to distinguish between old and new Chinese porcelain.

Many people either own or come across old Chinese bronze vessels. Most of these were made in the nineteenth century to sell to unsuspecting tourists. A genuine old Chinese bronze is usually covered with an emerald green patina. This is so hard that a finger nail scraped across it has no effect. Many of the later copies have had this green layer artificially added, but it is soft and can be scraped away with the nail.

The Chinese were not noted for outstanding work with precious metals and silver and gold are seldom seen in their artistic work. They did, however, make magnificent objects in jade, a natural translucent mineral varying in colour from almost white to many shades of green. It was too hard to carve and had to be worn into shape by constant rubbing with an abrasive. True jade is so hard that if a knife edge is run across it, the knife will be blunted without making any impression on the jade. True jade is also ice-cold to the touch no matter what the temperature of the surrounding air. This is why an expert will test a jade object by touching it with the tip of his tongue, or holding it against his forehead.

Cloisonné enamel work was made famous by the Chinese. Thin wires were soldered to the body of a metal vessel to form the design. The decoration was then split up with more wires to form little cells which were then filled with different coloured enamels. An old piece of *cloisonné* may often be distinguished from later specimens by the small blobs of solder seen where the wires meet each other, though this is not an infallible criterion. Old *cloisonné* also tends to be heavier than the more modern pieces.

Carved red lacquer was used by the Chinese to decorate boxes and small cabinets, though it has also been used on large pieces of furniture. The surface of the article to be decorated was covered with a thin layer of bright red lacquer. This was allowed to dry until completely hard and then another coat and another was added, until perhaps one hundred or more layers had been built up. The thick rubbery surface was then delicately carved. When looked at under a magnifying glass, the layers which have been cut through can be distinctly seen looking like the edges of a closed book. Sometimes several colours of enamel were used, beginning with layers of one colour and continuing with layers of another. This gave the carving a relief effect. Black and red were a common combination. The many nineteenth-century copies of this lacquer can easily be detected : the article to be decorated was coated with a thick layer of clay which was carved and then covered with a single coating of red lacquer. The general appearance is much softer because of the rounded outlines and no tell-tale layers can be seen under a magnifying glass. A pin carefully stuck into the object will reveal the clay when pulled out.

Japan

Porcelain made in Japan has never seemed to appeal as widely as Chinese porcelain. It is certainly regarded by many as being some way behind in quality. Perhaps the most famous of all Japanese ware is *Imari*, named after the port from which it was exported. The decoration is in dark reds and blues with some gilding. The early *Imari* porcelain was of good quality but much *Imari* ware exported to Europe late in the nineteenth century was not so good : smaller pieces of this can still be bought for a matter of shillings. The larger vases, however, are now fetching higher prices.

The porcelain of Japan may have lacked artistic merit but the skill of the Japanese carvers in ivory has never been surpassed. Japanese clothing had no pockets : people usually carried a small box with drawstrings to keep it closed and to suspend it from the wearer's belt. The toggle which secured the strings to the belt was known as a *netsuke*. *Netsuke* were usually made of ivory, bone or wood, and were nearly always delicately carved. Among the finest are those in the form of a mushroom with deeply carved gills. Great skill and craftsmanship was required for this work and artists became famous for the originality and execution of their carvings. Most of the finer *netsuke* were made in the eighteenth and early nineteenth century and were often signed by the craftsmen who carved them. Towards the end of the nineteenth century, however, European clothing increased in popularity and fewer *netsuke* were made. It was not long, however, before they were being sought by collectors as minor works of art and this new demand eventually became so great that they were actually made again purely to sell to collectors. Today, beautifully carved and signed early *netsuke* fetch high prices at auction.

Japanese prints or, strictly speaking, woodcuts, have a grace, charm and simplicity of line unequalled in the history of art. (Copper plate printing did not come to Japan until the nineteenth century.) In the seventeenth and eighteenth centuries many coloured woodcuts were produced which have been eagerly purchased whenever offered for sale. The recognition of these early woodcuts is a job for the specialist. Realizing the demand for them, Japanese artists have recut the original blocks many times and have cut many exact copies in order to meet it. Often, only careful comparison with a known early version makes it possible to date one of these prints. To the trained eye, the later versions are stiffer and lack the flow of the originals. This is not surprising. If you take a pencil and draw a waving line on a piece of paper it comes naturally and quickly. Now copy this line exactly. This will need some care and, because of the lack of flow, it will look stiff and harsh in comparison with the original, however well-executed.

The Japanese were also noted for their skill in making arms, particularly swords and armour, but this is a very specialized field.

CHAPTER TEN

ANTIQUES FOR THE WALL

ALL kinds of antiques can be used to decorate interior walls —oil paintings, water-colour drawings, prints of all kinds, maps, miniatures, silhouettes, needlework pictures, samplers, decorative plates and weapons. Each one could provide study for a lifetime: we can do no more here than give a few notes on each which may help the prospective buyer to explore the field in more detail.

In the nineteenth century, painting in oils and water-colours was a common accomplishment or pastime. Thousands of people fancied their skill. Today, the pictures they painted are scattered throughout the antique and *bric-à-brac* shops of Britain and there are few auction rooms where paintings are not offered for sale. Most of them are by unknown, unrecognized and second-rate or amateur artists and as such do not command high prices, though some are attractive enough to hang on the wall. As John Ruskin said: 'They are good furniture pictures, unworthy of praise, and undeserving of blame.' This is a field in which personal taste is all important. If you like a picture well enough to live with it, it can be a good buy. It may even appreciate in value, for many pictures by Victorian artists which would have attracted little attention a few years ago are now being bought for quite high prices.

Always be a little suspicious when buying a signed picture. Many artists whose work now commands a good price were copied and most of the copies bear a faked signature. Some auctioneers have a catalogue convention to deal with this situation. If they are quite certain that a picture is genuine they will print the artist's name in full—e.g. 'Edwin Landseer'. If the catalogue simply states that the picture is by 'E. Landseer', it may only mean that the picture is attributed to Landseer. The name 'Landseer' alone, without christian name or initial, means that the picture is possibly not genuine: it has probably been painted by some unknown artist 'in the manner of Landseer.' The amateur would be very unwise to buy an expensive picture without the prior opinion of an art expert.

Many old paintings are too large for the wall of a modern home and the smaller ones tend to fetch relatively higher prices. For this reason, old prints provide an attractive alternative. They are seldom very large and those that have originated as book plates, even when framed with a mount, will seldom be more than a foot in width. Many people like prints in colour and for this reason black and white engravings are often tinted or coloured before they are offered for sale. However, it is still possible to obtain early colour prints relatively cheaply, especially if they are bought unframed. We have recently seen prints by famous caricaturists of the late eighteenth and early nineteenth centuries offered in antique shops for less than £1 each and it is sometimes possible to pick up an old and worn book with prints which can be used, though we do not recommend the 'breaking' of well-bound complete volumes for the sake of the prints. It is often done, but it is sacrilege to the booklover.

Look out for coloured prints by Rowlandson (1756-1827), who was a great traveller in the hey-day of the stage-coach and loved the English inn. He had a fertile imagination and a light touch: his illustrations for the *Tours of Dr Syntax* are delightful and can still be found. James Gillray (1737-1815), a friend of Rowlandson, is known for his broad satirical humour aimed mainly at Napoleon, George III and the main political figures of his day. A useful book has recently been published under the title, *Fashionable Contrasts*, which tells us a good deal about him.

Coloured sporting and equestrian prints, especially those by well-known artists such as H. Alken and J. F. Herring Sr, are much sought after, especially by horse-riding and hunting enthusiasts. They were usually produced in sets of four or six and these can fetch up to £50 or more for a set, though single prints cost relatively less.

Black and white prints are more easily come by : they are to be found in many old topographical books and in the 1830s it was fashionable to bind up the illustrations engraved for the books of famous authors in separate volumes; Finden's *Illustrations to Lord Byron's Life and Works* (1834) and *Illustrations of the Waverley Novels* (1833) are examples. It is sometimes possible to find old volumes of this kind with the prints still in good condition. They contain landscapes and portraits of well-known contemporary writers or fictional characters, which look most attractive when mounted in black and gold frames.

Prints and water colours often suffer from what is known as 'foxing', the name given to the brown spots or patches which often develop when they have at some time suffered from damp. These marks are not easily removed without damage to the picture. Expert treatment can be expensive and is probably merited only if a print is rare or has special value for the owner. When hanging prints and water-colours see that the frame does not rest against the wall if there is the slightest possibility that it may at any time suffer from dampness. This can be done by sticking small pads of rubber behind the lower corners of the frame.

Prints normally carry a good deal of interesting and useful information. On no account cut this away, or any other portion of a print, and do not buy prints which have been framed down to the edges of the picture, because this almost certainly means that the border with the title of the picture and the names of the artist and engraver have been removed. In fact, the cut-away portion can sometimes be seen pasted on the back-board. Prints that have been cut have little value.

The name of the artist is usually seen at the bottom left-hand corner of the print. If an engraving has been based on a painting, the name will be followed by 'pinxit' (or some variant); if based on a drawing, by 'delin' or 'del'. The name of the engraver is usually on the right-hand side and his name will be followed by 'fecit' or 'sculp' (sometimes 'sculpsit). Thus :

D. Teniers, pinxit.   T. Major, sculp.

beneath an engraving would mean that Thomas Major had made the engraving from a painting by David Teniers. A good deal of other information is often included on a print—usually a title, the name and address of the publisher and often the date when it was printed.

Old maps, framed and hung on the wall, are full of interest, particularly if they show a county or district you know well. It is fascinating to compare the settlements, roads and by-roads with those of the landscape you know today. Celebrated map-makers were Christopher Saxton (sixteenth century), John Speed and John Ogilby (seventeenth century) and Hermann Moll (eighteenth century). Their original maps with contemporary colour are of considerable value, but there are many fakes and even more reproductions. The latter are easy to identify but hand-coloured fakes which have been washed over with a colouring agent to make them look old are not so easy to recognize. The key to authenticity is the water mark. Hold the map up to the light. Very early specimens will often show a watermark of vertical lines a little less than two inches apart. In seventeenth century maps the lines were closer and are crossed by many other lines to form a close grid. There is often a coat-of-arms, monogram or maker's name. Those who wish to delve into the subject are advised to consult Raymond Lister's book on *How to Identify Old Maps and Globes* (G. Bell & Sons).

The little portraits known as miniatures were originally made to be worn on the person but in Victorian times they were already being used for wall decoration. Miniatures were made from the sixteenth century onwards and the earliest examples were painted on parchment or specially treated paper. By the first decade of the eighteenth century ivory was being used, a material which proved to be very suitable as a base for water-colours. Sometimes oil paint or enamel was used on a copper base. Many colour reproductions have been framed to look like miniatures but they are not difficult to recognize once removed from behind the glass.

Prices of miniatures vary enormously. Those which bear the signatures or monograms of the famous seventeenth and eighteenth century miniaturists may be worth several hundred pounds, par-ticularly if the subject is named. A miniature of the Duke of Wellington by Henry P. Bone was recently sold at a London auction for £320. On the other hand, an unsigned miniature of a 'lady' or a 'gentleman' may sell for between £10 and £20.

Many people could not afford to have miniatures painted and contented themselves with simpler and cheaper silhouettes, profiles cut with a knife from black paper and mounted on a white or coloured background of card, vellum or ivory. Early examples were mounted in oval brass frames usually with a border of ribbon work, clearly in imitation of the more expensive miniatures, but later examples were framed in wood or *papier mâché* for wall decoration. The best silhouettes were made in the reign of George III.

Samplers are often used for wall decoration. They were originally specimen stitches or patterns embroidered on linen in coloured thread, but in the eighteenth century children were given samplers to make as a needlework exercise. They often embroidered the letters of the alphabet, a motto or a proverb, usually adding their name and often the date. Proud mothers framed them for all to see, and the more colourful ones still have a certain charm. More elaborate pictures embroidered by expert needlewomen, often in silk, were sometimes framed in gilt. These are more expensive than samplers which can often be bought very cheaply.

Porcelain or pottery plates are sometimes used for wall decoration, though some people frown on this practice. However, good quality, transfer-printed ware or hand-painted porcelain can look most attractive and is certainly preferable to poor-quality paintings.

THE CARE OF PICTURES

Oil paintings may need to be cleaned but never try to do so yourself : it is a job for an expert. Surface dirt accumulated over the years can, however, be carefully removed at home. A soft face cloth dipped in tepid, soapy water and wrung out can be used to wipe a varnished picture very gently. This will remove a great deal of the ingrained dirt without damage, though no water should be allowed to seep through to the canvas as damp may cause the oil paint to rise.

It is often said that gilt picture frames can be cleaned by careful application of a solution of bicarbonate of soda (one teaspoonful to a pint of water), but we have never succeeded in using this method without some slight damage to the gilt, which tends to rub off its plaster ground if any pressure is applied during the process.

The method recommended in *The Young Housewife's Daily Assistant* is gentler.

> A gill of good vinegar in a pint of cold water, a *large* camel's hair brush (a shaving brush will do), and clean soft cloths. The frame must be perfectly free from dust. Dip the brush into the liquid, and squeeze it slightly, that it may not be too wet; brush the gilding (a small piece at a time) lightly, up and down, till it is quite restored. The brush must be constantly washed; and in finishing it should be squeezed dry, and the gilding brushed till dry.

One thing is certain, 'gold paint' should never be used on gilt frames.

SMALL ORNAMENTAL ANTIQUES

T HERE are many small decorative objects which look well on a side table or on the shelves of an alcove, and antique jewellery can be most attractive to wear. In this chapter, we mention a few items which may be bought reasonably today.

Dolls

Today, our fashion houses display their creations at special shows using live models. During the eighteenth and nineteenth centuries, before the days of modern transport, the model was a doll used as a traveller's sample and when their primary purpose had been fulfilled these dolls became playthings for children. In early Victorian times, of course, dolls were also specifically manufactured as toys and often took the form of babies or small children. Many of these were made so that the eyes would open and shut by pulling a wire. It was much later, in the 1870s, that a lead weight was used which caused the eyes to shut automatically when the doll was laid down.

A dressed doll usually wore little shoes and stockings, and often gloves, so that the only part of the body visible would be the face and much care and attention was given to making this realistic. Although all kinds of materials were used for doll-making, wax and china provided the greatest opportunities for artistry (see Plate 29). The name of Montain is particularly associated with the modelling of beautiful wax dolls, and Jumeau with the use of unglazed or 'bisque' porcelain dolls.

The costumes, when original, usually help to determine the date when a doll was made but there are one or two useful pointers in their construction. Early dolls of the eighteenth and early nineteenth centuries usually had brown eyes. In Victorian times, the colour changed to blue in honour of the Queen. Parian ware was used for doll-making in the middle of the nineteenth century and the white material evidently suggested a Nordic type, for it is usually associated with fair hair. Dolls made of *papier mâché* date from the early nineteenth century.

Painted Enamels

The small enamel objects made at the Battersea and South Staffordshire factories in the eighteenth and early nineteenth centuries often show superb artistry. Little boxes to be carried in the pocket or *étui*, in which ladies kept small articles such as scissors, bodkins and snuff spoons, were produced in large numbers. They were made of copper to which was fused a thin layer of opaque coloured glass. The surface was then usually decorated with painted panels or with transfer work. The edges of most of the early examples were finished with a small strip of gilded metal. So precise was the workmanship that the lids of the boxes closed snugly, obviating the need for a catch.

Factories in South Staffordshire at Bilston and Wednesbury probably started production in the early 1750s and were still operating in the early nineteenth century. The Battersea factory, however, was a financial failure. It started in 1753 and was forced to close down three years later.

It is difficult even for the expert to distinguish between the Battersea enamels and those from South Staffordshire : there is no sure method of deciding which was made where. Colours are said to differ slightly, though even this is a matter of opinion. However, since there is little difference between the quality or current value of the work produced at any of the factories this is relatively unimportant.

When buying enamel work it is as well to remember that the surface, though hard, chips and cracks very easily. Many pieces have been damaged and repaired with paint. When this has just been done it is difficult to detect, but as time passes the paint discolours, making the repair work more obvious.

Small enamel boxes inscribed with mottoes or the name of a

resort are quite common. Many have a mirror inside the lid. These boxes were produced in their thousands for the tourist trade during the nineteenth century. They are now being collected and, for their size and often indifferent quality, are commanding quite high prices, often between £15 and £20.

Both the Battersea and South Staffordshire factories produced limited numbers of larger pieces such as kettles, candlesticks, knife boxes, etc. These are comparatively rare and therefore valuable.

The Samson factory in Paris, which has copied old porcelain of many kinds, also copied enamel work, and many fakes were imported from Europe during the nineteenth century.

It is worth mentioning one or two other types of enamel which can be seen in some of our larger museums. *Cloisonné* enamel has already been described.

Champlevé enamel is the reverse of *cloisonné*. Instead of building up cells to hold the enamel on the surface, the metal body was carved to provide the design and the incised depressions were filled with coloured enamels. The surface was then polished. *Champlevé* enamels date from as early as the ninth and tenth centuries and the early work is very rare.

Limoges enamel is named after the French town where it was made over a very long period of time, especially during the sixteenth and seventeenth centuries. As with the Battersea and South Staffordshire work, the enamels were painted on a copper base. The early work is superb. It was copied profusely during the nineteenth century.

Jewellery

This is a wide and very specialized field which the amateur should study carefully before buying, unless an experienced friend is at hand to give advice.

Early jewellery, made before the eighteenth century, is rare but it does occasionally turn up in small shops and is often unrecognized. Quite recently, a seventeenth-century Spanish pendant with large rose-cut diamonds set in filigree gold was sold for £12 by a dealer who thought that the crude workmanship and irregularities of the stones meant that it was a piece of little value. In fact, it was worth well over £100. As with many such pieces, the diamonds were greyish-brown in colour and the setting was fashioned by hand in a carefree way. This mistake was simply due to lack of knowledge and experience : early Spanish jewellery has a distinctive style which, once seen, is never forgotten.

We can do no more, however, than give a little basic information about jewellery. First, remember that there are three common qualities or standards of gold—9 carat, 18 carat and 22 carat (pure gold is 24 carat). The value of any piece which has gold in its make-up depends very much on the carat standard. Gold is measured in pennyweights of which there are twenty to the ounce. The value of gold varies daily with world markets but it is usually about £4 13s 0d for a 9-carat ounce, £9 6s for an 18-carat ounce and £11 10s for a 22-carat ounce. Although colour can give some idea of the quality of gold—9-carat gold is often yellower than the reddish, 22-carat gold—it must be remembered that gold can be found in colours and tones ranging from green to white. These colours are sometimes used by goldsmiths to decorate pieces with flowers or geometrical designs.

Most gold jewellery is stamped with the carat value, together with a hallmark, but if this is missing a jeweller can rub the gold on a porous black stone known as a touchstone, dab the mark on the stone with acid, and determine the purity of the gold by the effect the acid has on the mark. But let us issue a warning here : we have come across several brass pieces, notably watch-chains, stamped with a 9-carat mark. All objects thought to be gold should be tested with nitric acid, which has no action whatsoever on gold. The object to be tested should be filed in an inconspicuous place in order to remove a surface layer of gold should the object be plated. If the acid turns green then the gold plate is on copper or brass : if it turns grey it is on silver.

When buying Alberts (nineteenth-century gold watch-chains) which have been made into charm bracelets, remember to check the links for wear where they rub together. At the same time, check the rings and padlock at the ends for hallmarks; unscrupulous dealers sometimes put cheap, plated ones on hallmarked chains. Among the most sought-after charms for bracelets are the gold-mounted seals which were often attached to old watch-chains.

Victorian jewellery was, on the whole, bold, imaginative and very well made. There was also a great deal of it, which is all to the good since it is at present very fashionable. Though gold seems to have been used without stint, the cost was kept down by the skilful use of semi-precious stones and seed pearls. However, before buying, it is as well to remember that 'all is not gold that glitters' for the Victorian jeweller was very fond of using an alloy of copper and zinc called 'Pinchbeck' (invented by a London watchmaker of that name) which looks remarkably like gold. Most jewellery in which gold or silver was used can be dated from the hallmarks.

In many old rings the amateur may jump to the conclusion that the clear sparkling stones are diamonds : it is probably wise to assume that this is not the case. They will often turn out to be zircons, or white sapphires or paste—another name for ordinary glass. Remember that diamonds can only be positively valued in daylight because the value depends largely on the colour (i.e. whether it is tinged in any way) and this cannot be determined under artificial light. Many of the cheaper precious stones have flaws—cracks or marks within the actual stone. Contrary to popular belief, diamonds are not the only stones which will scratch the surface of glass. In fact, many hard substances will scratch glass if sharp enough and applied with enough pressure.

Diamonds are valued in carats but this is a measurement of volume and not weight as in the case of gold : they increase rapidly in value as the volume increases. Large stones are rare and value is related to this rarity. Precious stones should be taken to a reputable jeweller or gemologist for accurate identification.

Glass Paperweights

Decorative glass paperweights are all of nineteenth-century date. They were first made in England between 1820 and 1840 and consisted of a clear glass bun into the base of which was set a bust or profile cast in relief in china clay. These profiles were usually of the king, but famous personalities of the day were also used. They are said to have been the work of apprentices in the glass factories, who made them in their spare time and sold them as curios to boost their poor pay. They were made at Bristol and Nailsea, in London and Stourbridge and Birmingham. Nailsea produced domes of green glass in which air bubbles were made to form flower-like shapes.

Until 1845, there was an excise tax on coloured glass. Its removal encouraged an expansion in the trade. Weights were made by covering clear glass with several layers of coloured glass and then grinding parts of it away to end with a panel of clear class surrounded by a border of coloured stripes.

At this time (1845), the St Louis glass works in Paris started to make the superb *millefiori* (thousand flowers) paperweights. These were buns of clear glass into the base of which were inserted canes of coloured glass. Each cane was made in a different shape and colour and contained pictures of animals or designs or letters. The design ran right through the canes like the lettering in a stick of rock. The most famous of these paperweights were made at the Clichy and Baccarat factories. Some have the initial of the factory and the date running through the canes. A few rarer weights contain glass insects, reptiles or flowers. Some weights produced at Stourbridge are very similar in style to the French types.

In most weights, the pontil mark has been ground out deep enough to reveal the lower end of the canes: on others the bottom has been ground flat and then cut with a multi-pointed star.

Good quality paperweights are now quite rare and command high prices. King Farouk, who was a great collector, was probably partly responsible for their rapid appreciation.

Buyers should beware of the many imitations. Thousands are at present being imported from Japan. Beware also of weights which have been chipped and subsequently ground and repolished. These usually appear to be rather small for the size of the decoration they contain.

Tea Caddies and Work Boxes

'Britain is a nation of tea-drinkers'. How true this is and has been for a very long time. During the eighteenth century, tea-drinking was a social ritual and a great deal of money was spent on silver kettles and teapots. 'Taking tea' provided an opportunity for assessing the social standing of one's hosts. It is easy to see, therefore, why so much trouble was taken over the appearance of a tea caddy. They were made in a great variety of materials, including silver. Most were made of veneered or inlaid wood or of *papier mâché* : some were covered or inlaid with ivory or tortoiseshell. Most early caddies were fitted with locks to prevent pilfering by members of the household staff. After all, tea was expensive : in 1714 the cheapest tea, 'Bohea', cost from 9s to 25s a pound : 'Pekoe' was 45s a pound and green tea 16s a pound. Prices dropped a little during the 1720s and 1730s but by 1750 they were up again. During the Regency period mahogany, rosewood and walnut were used to make caddies in the shape of a sarcophagus. The majority of these later caddies had at least two compartments, one for green tea and one for black, and many had a mixing bowl for blending the teas to suit a personal taste.

Tea caddies supported on a pillar and taking on the role of a piece of furniture were an early nineteenth-century development and are known as 'teapoys', a name often used to describe the small mid-eighteenth century three-legged table from which tea was served.

Tea caddies cover a vast range of shapes and sizes and are decorative and useful things to have in the home.

Workboxes tended to be larger and more cumbersome than tea caddies. During the eighteenth and early nineteenth centuries, when needlework was a common pastime for ladies of leisure, they were used for keeping the silks, wools, needles and thimbles needed for tapesty and embroidery work. Most were made of wood and were lined inside with coloured paper or cloth. A padded pincushion usually occupied a prominent place and the rest of the box was divided into trays and receptacles for scissors, buttons, hooks and ribbons. Many of the accessories were made of ivory or boxwood and rather conspicuous 'secret' drawers were often included. These were sometimes padded and may have been intended for jewellery. As with tea caddies, workboxes were sometimes built as pieces of furniture supported on various types of pillar or leg, often with a cloth bag slung underneath to take wools. These were known as work tables.

Snuff Boxes and Vinaigrettes

During the eighteenth and early nineteenth centuries, snuff-taking was a popular habit indulged in by both sexes, though the ladies were more secretive about it. Craftsmen recognized the need to produce small, decorative boxes with tight-fitting lids in which the snuff could be carried. The decoration of these boxes allowed the artist great freedom and the range is vast. Many people collect snuff boxes and they are commonly used for carrying pills. Gold and silver examples are most sought after and are very expensive when the actual weight of precious metal is considered (see p. 217).

Similar in many ways to the snuff box was the vinaigrette. These were small boxes of various shapes, sizes and decoration. They were usually of gold or silver and can be distinguished from the snuff box by the secondary pierced and hinged lid fitted inside. Beneath this grill was placed a small sponge soaked in aromatic vinegar. When the smells from candles, inadequate sewage disposal or unwashed clothing heavy with body odours became too much to stand, the box was opened and a 'whiff' was taken of the sweet-smelling vinegar. The grills of these boxes were often beautiful, chased with scrolls and flowers etc. The silver vinaigrettes were always gilded inside to prevent the acid vinegar reacting with the silver. Vinaigrettes are as popular with collectors as snuff boxes.

Silver Buckles

These are usually Continental, most frequently Dutch. They have intricate moulded designs and there is always a ready market for them as there is a tradition among nurses always to wear a silver buckle on their uniform belts when they are qualified.

CHAPTER TWELVE

SUGGESTIONS FOR THE NEW COLLECTOR

ONE of the most frequent questions asked of any person with an interest in antiques is: 'I would like to begin collecting. How do I start?' The answer depends very much on the amount of money the enthusiast has available and the reasons behind this urge to collect. Some want to invest capital; others want to collect and furnish at the same time; and there are those who want to do it for the fun they hope to get out of it. The would-be-investor should consult a reputable dealer. Those who want to furnish should decide on a style and a maximum expenditure and then keep looking until they find the things they want at a price they can pay. (The auction sale records on pages 161 to 218 should be of assistance in estimating costs.) This chapter is addressed to those who want to start collecting as a hobby and who have little money to spare.

The first and obvious fact is that anything that is generally regarded as beautiful or rare will be too expensive: the sights must be set lower. Here are a few suggestions.

Porcelain

Collections of porcelain made by well-known factories can be acquired quite cheaply if you are prepared to accept slightly damaged pieces. The accumulation of representative specimens from the different factories makes it possible to handle the pieces, to distinguish between them and between the genuine and the fake. A collection of odd cups and saucers from the famous eighteenth-century factories can be made without spending a great deal of money. They look attractive when displayed in a cabinet and can occasionally be married.

Drinking Glasses

Odd eighteenth-century glasses constantly crop up in junk shops and in job lots at salerooms. They can usually be bought quite cheaply. There is a vast range of shapes and sizes but, nevertheless, they can look very attractive when set out on a tray and, once again, there is always the chance of making up a set. The great thing about collecting glasses is that they can be used, but don't be tempted to buy damaged glasses : these can be both dangerous and unhygienic.

Silver Spoons

Attractive representative collections can be made of odd silver spoons. Aim at finding one of each style and period from George I onwards. The size of the spoons will depend on the size of your wallet.

Oriental Blue and White

Porcelain decorated with underglaze blue and made for export from China during the nineteenth century, often referred to as Nankin ware after the port from which it was shipped, can be seen in most antique shops. It has so far been rather frowned on by collectors because it does not reach the high quality of eighteenth-century work. However, it is slowly gaining in favour, is still within the range of the average collector, and is very decorative.

Commemorative Medals and Small Plaques

These seem to hang around antique shops for ever and we know of no serious collectors of these medals. They can be bought for a few shillings each, since they are usually made of bronze or brass. Silver ones, of course, are more expensive because of their scrap value. This is a wide new field for collectors because any occasion of note in the late eighteenth century and during the nineteenth century, both here and overseas, seems to have had a plaque or medal struck to commemorate the event.

Silk Pictures

The city of Coventry has always been noted for the weaving of silk ribbon : in the first half of the nineteenth century it was the

I

chief occupation of its people. Then, about 1860, came a serious slump in the ribbon trade and unemployment became so acute that several thousand people left the city to look for work elsewhere. At this time a certain young man, Thomas Stevens, who by hard work and inventiveness had already acquired his own business, had been experimenting on his looms, trying to produce pictures in silk. The slump gave him his opportunity. He successfully turned out all manner of small decorative ribbon articles which could carry his pictures—birthday and Christmas 'cards', Valentines, bookmarks, scent sachets, badges and hat ribbons; by 1880, his woven silk pictures were being mounted and framed as pictures. During the phenomenal expansion of his business a new factory had been built, the Stevengraph Works, and the term Stevengraph is now the name given to these Coventry silk pictures.

Great interest has recently been shown in the articles made by Thomas Stevens and a Stevengraph Collectors' Association has been formed in America. We mention them briefly here so that if you come across a Stevengraph between the pages of an old book, among old letters, or when clearing out a drawer, you will recognise it for what it is and know that it has value.

Art Nouveau

Although it is not antique, *art nouveau* decoration has been accepted in the fashionable world and has recently come into the limelight. It followed the work of people such as William Morris and Burne Jones and continued from the 1890s into the early years of the present century.

In Britain, the best known names are those of Aubrey Beardsley, the artist, and Rennie Mackintosh, the Scottish designer. A well-known firm of London auctioneers has recently held *art nouveau* sales, where it became obvious that the things to collect are signed pieces by artists of the *art nouveau* movement. These are more plentiful than one might imagine. Look out for names such as Gallé and Daum, the famous French glass-makers of the period, and for the name of Tiffany, the big American store that sponsored so many artists of the movement and commissioned work from them.

Collectors' Societies

For the benefit of those who may wish to get in touch with other people interested in the same field, we give below a list of collectors' societies with the addresses of the secretaries:

Arms and Armour Society, 40 Great James Street, London, W.C.1

Society of Caddy Spoon Collectors, 43 Pine Avenue, Gravesend, Kent.

English Ceramic Circle, 8 Church Row, London, N.W.3.

Oriental Ceramic Society, 31b Torrington Square, London, W.C.1.

Glass Circle, 50a Fulham Road, London, S.W.3.

Map Collectors' Circle, Durant House, Chiswell Street, London, E.C.1.

Society of Pewter Collectors, Pelham House, 80 Denton Road, Newhaven, Sussex.

The Pot Lid Circle (The Colour-Printed Pottery Collectors' Association), The Vines, Hildenborough, Kent.

Society of Silver Collectors, 168 Lupus Street, London, S.W.1.

Stevengraph Collectors' Association, Irvington-on-Hudson, New York, U.S.A.

Wine Label Society, Hook Norton Rectory, Banbury, Oxfordshire.

One of the great thrills of collecting is the purchase of an article which intrigues you for reasons which you cannot really understand. The detective work and research involved slowly lead to an understanding of the article and, having solved your problem, you will hardly be able to wait before you get involved again. Many dealers who have given up the antique business because of its stresses and strains, continue to collect because they cannot live without the excitement of the chase. As they say in the trade; 'The big buy is just around the corner.' It could be yours tomorrow.

CHAPTER THIRTEEN

SOME MUSEUM COLLECTIONS

EVERY lover of antiques will enjoy seeing the many fine examples of early craftsmanship in our art galleries, museums and historic houses, even though he will seldom have the opportunity actually to handle them. Most large museums cover many fields, others specialize, and provincial museums usually pay particular attention to exhibits of local products or of special local interest. Many of the finest collections of porcelain, pottery, silver and glass can be seen in the districts where these products were made. We have selected for mention in this chapter some of the museums where the classes of antiques we have dealt with in this book can be profitably studied. All our large cities have fine museums and art galleries: we have concentrated in the following list on some museums and collections which have special interest for the keen amateur.

(Places marked * may normally only be visited by appointment.)

Periods and Styles

Many museums show furniture, porcelain, needlework and other household objects in rooms or settings characteristic of certain periods or styles. These give a much better insight into the social life of the times and the use made of particular items than any study of individual pieces can possibly do. Such museums include:

London

The Victoria and Albert Museum, South Kensington, which has a unique collection of artistic masterpieces. The furniture is displayed in period rooms and the galleries contain antiques of every age and many countries. The booklets on specialized subjects issued from time to time by the Museum are particularly useful.

Chiswick House in Burlington Lane, Chiswick, has rooms which were decorated by William Kent (see p. 25).

Geffrye Museum in Shoreditch has rooms representing every period from early Stuart times.

Osterley Park House, Isleworth, and Syon House, between Isleworth and Brentford, give a fine impression of the work of Robert Adam—the style of architecture, furniture and decoration.

Barnsley

The Cannon Hall Art Gallery and Museum. Period rooms in an eighteenth-century country house.

Brighton

The Royal Pavilion. A museum of Regency furniture 'in the Chinese taste' and 'in the classical taste.'

Bristol

The Georgian House, in Great George Street. Entirely furnished as a period piece.

Colchester

The Minories Art Gallery, High Street. Period rooms with Georgian furniture.

Hove

The Hove Museum of Art, New Church Road. Rooms furnished in Georgian, Regency and Victorian styles.

Hull

Wilberforce House, High Street. An Elizabethan building with period rooms.

Huntingdon

Cromwell Museum, Market Square. Deals with the Cromwellian period.

Leeds

Abbey House, Kirkstall. A folk museum with nineteenth-century houses, shops and workshops laid out in streets.

Northampton

Abingdon Museum, Abingdon Park. Period rooms, especially nineteenth century.

Plymouth

Elizabethan House, New Street. Furnished in period style.

Salford

Museum and Art Gallery, Peel Park. Contains a nineteenth-century street.

Scunthorpe
Normanby Hall, Century Street. Regency-style furnishings in Regency mansion.

Southport
Botanic Gardens Museum. Room of the Victorian period.

Wakefield
City Museum, Wood Street. Rooms and shops furnished in period styles.

West Bromwich
Oak House Museum, Oak Road. A fifteenth-century house furnished in the style of the period.

York
York Castle Museum. A cobbled street, and period rooms in folk museum.

FURNITURE

Brighton
Art Gallery and Museum, Church Street. French and English furniture with some fine satinwood pieces.

Chorley
Astley Hall, Art Gallery and Museum. Old furniture of various periods.

Edinburgh
Lauriston Castle, Cramond Road South. Furniture of various periods.

Great Yarmouth
Elizabethan Museum, South Quay. Old furniture.

High Wycombe
Art Gallery and Museum, Castle Hill. A good range of chairs with emphasis on the Windsor type.

Port Sunlight
Lady Lever Art Gallery. English furniture of various periods.

Richmond
Ham House, Petersham. Fine Restoration furniture.

Shugborough
Staffordshire County Museum, near Stafford. Eighteenth-century French furniture.

South Queensferry
Hopetoun House Museum. Chippendale furniture.

CLOCKS

Basingstoke
The Willis Museum, New Street. Clocks, watches and watchmakers' tools.

Colchester
The Minories Art Gallery, High Street. Colchester clocks.

London
Guildhall Museum, Royal Exchange. Houses the museum of the Clockmakers' Company.

SILVER AND SHEFFIELD PLATE

Abingdon
Guildhall Art Gallery. Corporation silver and plate dating from the sixteenth century.

Bath
The Holbourne of Menstrie Museum of Art, Great Pulteney Street.

Belfast
Ulster Museum, Stranmillis. Fine collection of Irish silver.

Birmingham
The Assay Office, Newhall Street. Good collection of early silverware.

London
Goldsmiths' Hall, Cheapside. A fine collection of old and modern silver.

Newcastle
Laing Art Gallery and Museum, Higham Place.

Oxford
The Ashmoleum Museum, Beaumont Street.

Sheffield
City Museum, Weston Park. Particularly fine collection of cutlery and old Sheffield plate.

York
The Yorkshire Museum, Museum Street.

NON-PRECIOUS METALS

Abingdon
Borough Museum Collections, The County Hall. Pewter plate.

Battle
> Battle Museum, Old Church House. Exhibits of local iron-industry products.

Berwick-on-Tweed
> Museum and Art Gallery, Maygate. Brasswork, useful and decorative.

Coalbrookdale
> Museum of ironfounding.

Great Yarmouth
> Old Merchant's House. Collection of domestic ironwork.

Lewes
> Anne of Cleves House, High Street, Southover. Collection of iron firebacks.

Newcastle-upon-Tyne
> Laing Art Gallery and Museum, Higham Place. Ironwork.

Swansea
> Industrial Museum of Wales, Victoria Road. Local industrial history with copper, iron and steel relics.

York
> The Yorkshire Museum, Museum Street. Pewter.

PORCELAIN AND POTTERY

Alton
> The Curtis Museum, High Street. Porcelain and pottery, especially Leeds creamware.

Bath
> Victoria Art Gallery, Bridge Street. The Bristol and West of England Delft collection.

Birkenhead
> Williamson Art Gallery and Museum, Slatey Road. Good collection of Liverpool pottery and porcelain.

Bootle
> Museum and Art Gallery, Oriel Road. Collections of earthenware figures and Liverpool pottery.

Bournemouth
> Rothesay Museum, Bath Road. English porcelain.

Brighton
> Art Gallery and Museum, Church Street. Stevens Collection of

Worcester porcelain and Willett Collection of pottery, which includes good Staffordshire figures.

Bristol

City Art Gallery, Queen's Road. Fine collection of porcelain and pottery (including Bristol Delft).

Cambridge

Fitzwilliam Museum, Trumpington Street. General collection of ceramics.

Cardiff

National Museum of Wales, Cathays Park. Ceramics include Swansea porcelain.

Cheltenham

Art Gallery and Museum, Clarence Street. Good collection of pottery and porcelain.

Chorley

Astley Hall, Art Gallery and Museum. Leeds pottery.

Derby

Museum and Art Gallery, Strand. Porcelain collection, including local products.

Glasgow

Art Gallery and Museum, Kelvingrove. Porcelain in the Burrell Collection.

Leeds

City Art Gallery. Local and Staffordshire pottery.

Manchester

The Athenaeum Annexe to the City Art Gallery is a museum of ceramics.

Newcastle-upon-Tyne

Laing Art Gallery and Museum, Higher Place. Collection of porcelain and pottery.

Nottingham

City Museum, The Castle. Fine collection of ceramics, especially Wedgwood and local stonewares.

Paisley

Paisley Museum and Art Galleries, High Street. Large collection of porcelain and pottery.

Plymouth

City Museum and Art Gallery, Tavistock Road. Good collection of porcelain, including Plymouth and Bristol.

Port Sunlight

The Lady Lever Art Gallery. Collection of Wedgwood.

Reading
  Museum and Art Gallery, Blagrave Street. Collection of Delft ware.

Stoke-on-Trent
  City Museum and Art Gallery, Hanley. A large and superb collection of pottery and porcelain.

  * Spode-Copeland Museum and Art Gallery, Church Street. Early blue transfer-ware and porcelain made by the firm.

  * Wedgwood Museum, Barlaston. A collection of Wedgwood ware.

Sunderland
  Museum and Art Gallery, Borough Road. Local pottery.

Swansea
  Glynn Vivian Art Gallery, Alexandra Road. Welsh ceramics, including Swansea and Nantgarw porcelain.

Warrington
  Municipal Museum and Art Gallery, Bold Street. The Edelstein Collection (ceramics).

Wolverhampton
  Municipal Art Gallery and Museum, Lichfield Street. Collection of Staffordshire pottery.

Worcester
  Dyson Perrins Museum of Worcester Porcelain, the Royal Porcelain Works, Severn Street. The finest collection of Worcester porcelain in existence.

GLASS

Accrington
  Haworth Art Gallery, Haworth Park. Collection of Tiffany glass (see p. 130).

Bath
  Victoria Art Gallery, Bridge Street. The Carr collection of English glass and the Huth Collection of Bohemian glass.

Belfast
  Ulster Museum, Stranmillis. Collection of Irish glass.

Bristol
  City Art Gallery, Queen's Road. Bristol and Nailsea glass.

Newcastle-upon-Tyne
  Laing Art Gallery and Museum, Higher Place.

Nottingham
City Museum and Art Gallery, The Castle.

Preston
Harris Museum and Art Gallery, Market Square.

South Shields
South Shields Library and Museum, Ocean Road. Locally-made glass.

Stourbridge
* Council House. Fine collection of coloured glass.

Swansea
Glynn Vivian Art Gallery, Alexandra Road.

Warrington
Municipal Museum and Art Gallery, Bold Street. Locally-made glass.

ORIENTAL ANTIQUES

Bristol
City Art Gallery, Queen's Road. Oriental ceramics.

Durham
Gulbenkian Museum of Oriental Art, Elvet Hill. Chinese pottery, porcelain, jade and ivory. Japanese bronzes and swords.

Guernsey
Lukis and Island Museum, Cornet Street, St. Peter Port. Chinese porcelain.

Leeds
Temple Newsam, near Leeds. Chinese porcelain.

London
Percival David Foundation of Chinese Art, Gordon Square. Ceramics.

Manchester
Whitworth Art Gallery, Oxford Road. Japanese coloured woodcut prints.

Northampton
Abington Museum, Abington Park. Chinese ceramics.

Oxford
Ashmoleum Museum, Beaumont Street. Chinese and Japanese porcelain.

Port Sunlight
Lady Lever Art Gallery. Chinese ceramics.

Sheffield
Graves Art Gallery, Surrey Street. Chinese ivories.

DECORATIVE ANTIQUES

Dolls

Bangor
  Penrhyn Castle, near Bangor, has a unique collection.

Miniatures

Lincoln
  The Usher Gallery, Lindun Road.

London
  The Wallace Collection, Manchester Square.

Oxford
  Ashmoleum Museum, Beaumont Street.

Scent Bottles

Preston
  Harris Museum and Art Gallery, Market Square.

GLOSSARY OF TERMS USED IN THE ANTIQUE TRADE

Acanthus: A type of leaf decoration popular since the classical period and widely used on items made from wood or metal (see Plate 14).

Andirons: Firedogs used to support lengths of burning wood on the hearth.

Apron: The box frame above the legs and beneath the top of a table or the seat of a chair.

Argyle: A spouted vessel, usually of silver or silver plate, in which gravy was kept hot by means of a liner filled with hot water. The name is said to be after a Duke of Argyll who was irritated when his gravy arrived at the dining-table, which was some distance from the kitchen, with a skin of cool fat on the surface.

Armorial: The crest or coat-of-arms of a family or families was often engraved on silver, carved on wood, or painted on china belonging to that household. This is armorial ware. Armorial porcelain is particularly sought after by collectors.

Astragal: A convex moulding : a term used in furniture to describe the bars between the panes of a glazed bookcase or cabinet.

Bail Handle: A form consisting of a half-loop of metal secured by bolts; it was popular between 1720 and 1780.

Ball and Claw: A type of decoration usually used for feet or supports representing a lion's paw (or sometimes a bird's foot) with the claws extended over a ball. It is used on furniture, silver and occasionally on porcelain. It was much used during the eighteenth century and was favoured by Chippendale though it was not his original design.

Balloon Back: The shape of a chair back which resembles a partly-inflated balloon. It developed during the Victorian period.

Baluster: The bulbous, almost pear-shaped part of the stem of a drinking glass; the leg of a piece of furniture or any supporting column.

Banding: A decoration of the edges of a piece of furniture with a thin strip of veneer of a different colour and texture from the main body.

Baroque: A seventeenth-century style of decoration with extravagant curves and much foliage. It is often fussy, but full of life.

141

Bas Relief: Modelling on the surface of an article in low relief—i.e. the modelling has very little depth.

Bentwood: Wood for making furniture which has been bent into shape in one piece by steam heating. Commonly found in Victorian rocking chairs.

Bergère: A French term used for a padded and upholstered armchair. It is now used for English chairs made in the same French style and also for chairs with caned panels.

Bijouterie: A term for jewellery or trinkets, but sometimes used to describe a small display table on which the objects on view are protected by a glass-topped case.

'Billies and Charlies': Billy and Charlie were the names of two London workmen who made small leaden objects, mainly figures, with early dates impressed on them. They buried these objects in the ground on the site where they were digging and later dug them up again and sold them as genuine finds to eager unsuspecting spectators who were watching their excavations. They are now much sought after by collectors.

Birdcage Table: A single-pillared table which has a small box at the top of the column the sides of which are formed of four vertical columns. The table top rests upon this and it enables the table to be both revolved and tipped.

Biscuit: The name given to pottery and porcelain when it has been fired in an unglazed state.

Bocage: A background of flowers or trees to porcelain or pottery figures.

Bombé: The shape of a piece of furniture which is bulbous, the lower part being the widest. French in origin.

Bonbonnière: A box or container for bonbons or sweets.

Bone China: A hard-paste porcelain containing bone ash which can be modelled thinly and still retain its strength. It is very translucent and has superceded most other types of porcelain in Britain.

Bonheur du jour: A ladies' writing table of delicate proportions.

Boulle or *Buhl:* A term used to describe a piece of furniture made in the style introduced by a seventeenth-century French furniture-maker of that name. He specialized in brass and tortoiseshell inlay work.

Bracket Foot: Feet formed from two shaped or square pieces of material—usually wood—mounted at right angles to form a bracket. This style of foot is used in place of a leg to raise the object above the surface on which it stands.

Breaker: A book which is to be broken up for the prints or maps it contains.

Breakfront: A term used to describe a piece of furniture in which the central portion either projects slightly forward or is recessed, breaking the main horizontal line set by the two ends. It is usually found in bookcases or in sideboards or dressers.

Britannia Metal: An alloy of antimony, copper and tin which was often silver-plated. It was first used in the eighteenth century and was popular during the Victorian period. It is cheap, very malleable, and has a dull ring when tapped.

Bunfoot: A bun-shaped foot commonly used during the William and Mary period and in much early oak furniture, particularly on chests.

Cadogan Teapot: These teapots are usually made of brown-glazed earthenware with Chinese influence decoration in relief. They are lidless and have to be filled through a hole in the base and with tea that has already been strained.

Candle Box: A small wooden box with a base extended lengthwise in one direction. A hole is cut in this extension to make it possible to hang the box on a wall. It is usually made of oak with a sliding top, and was used for storing candles.

Canapé: A sofa (French).

Canted: A term used to describe a bevelled corner.

Canterbury: A small piece of furniture, rather similar in design to a modern magazine rack, made for storing sheet music. They usually stand on short legs with castors and often have a carrying handle in the centre. Larger versions were made to store artists' portfolios of drawings. They were first made in the Georgian period and are much in demand today.

Canton: A port of southern China noted for the export of delicately coloured enamel or copper objects of all types. They were sent to Europe during the eighteenth and nineteenth centuries. Much English porcelain was sent to Canton to be decorated.

Carcase: The basic structure of a piece of furniture before the finishing veneers and inlays are applied : it is usually made of oak, deal or pine.

Card-cut: A term usually applied to a method of decorating silver and occasionally furniture. A flat piece of silver with the edges cut in a decorative fashion is laid on the surface of the main body, much as a decorative hinge may be laid upon a door. It is commonly found in early silver.

Carlton-House Table: A rather elegant D-shaped desk or writing table with long rounded tapering legs and with banks of drawers in a semi-circle on the top at the back. Carlton-House tables look severe and functional with their undecorated clean lines. The design for these tables was made for the Prince of Wales when he lived at Carlton House.

Cartouche: Now a generally accepted term in the antique trade for a decorated frame within which a coat-of-arms, crest, or the initials or trade mark of a firm, are carved, drawn or etched.

Carver: The name generally given to an open-armed dining chair. There are usually two carvers to every six ordinary dining chairs and they were used by the heads of a household, who were usually responsible for carving the meat at dinner. It is sometimes said that the name was derived from a chair used by Admiral Carver.

Cassolette: A vessel or box for burning perfume.

Caster: A vessel originally used for shaking or dredging brown sugar over sweets. It resembles a large pepper pot and was made of silver or pewter.

Castor: The small wheel mounted on the legs of furniture to facilitate movement. Initially made of wood or leather, later of brass or porcelain.

Cat: A form of three-legged trivet or tripod usually made of wood but sometimes of brass or silver. Used for warming dishes in front of a fire.

Caudle Cup: A cup used for a mixture of spiced gruel and ale or wine.

Celadon: Chinese porcelain decorated with a pale jade-green translucent glaze.

Chafing Dish: Portable metal dish, often of silver, in which food could be kept warm.

Chaise-longue: A long couch usually with one end and a partial back normally used as an individual day bed.

Chalice: A cup or goblet usually associated with religious service.

Chamfered: A term describing the result of cutting away the wood which forms the edge between two flat surfaces to form a bevelled edge.

Champlevé: A method of decorating a metal object with enamels in which small cells are scooped out of the main body and filled with molten coloured enamels. This work is often found on French ecclesiastical items. It reached its peak of popularity at Champlevé in the fifteenth century.

Chapter Ring: A circular piece of metal on which the hours are marked on a clock or sundial. On older clocks they were usually of brass which had been silvered.

Charger: A large dish.

Chatelaine: An attachment which could be clipped on a lady's belt. From it, a number of useful articles were suspended by a chain— scissors, an ivory notepad, pencil, case containing needles, button-hook, etc. Chatelaines were often made of silver.

Chiffonier: A small narrow sideboard, often with a shelf or shelves at the back and a cupboard beneath. The cupboard doors were often fitted with grille fronts backed with pleated, coloured silk. They were popular during the Regency and Victorian periods.

Chinoiserie: A term used to describe decoration which has been influenced by the popularity of Chinese art. It reached its height in England during the eighteenth century and is found in all materials.

Chocolate Pot: A large pot similar in shape to a coffee pot for serving hot chocolate, a popular drink during the early eighteenth century. Spouts on chocolate pots are usually placed high up on the body to try and avoid the risk of pouring out any thick residue which may have settled on the bottom. The knob of the pot can often be removed to allow a long thin spoon to be inserted for stirring.

Clapper or *Knocker:* A dealer who normally works without a shop, travelling around the country knocking on people's doors in the hope of buying any antiques they may be willing to part with. He normally sells these or he might even work for another dealer.

Clean Piece: Unrepaired and undamaged.

Cloisonné: A type of decoration made popular by the Chinese, in which wires were soldered to the body of a metal vessel (usually copper) to form a design. The decoration was then split up with more wires to form little cells which were filled with different coloured enamels. It was then fired and polished.

Coaster: A small, round dish, often of silver or Sheffield plate, with a turned wooden base on which decanters or bottles were stood. The base was covered with baize so that it would slide or 'coast' over a polished surface. These coasters were usually made in sets of four. More elaborate types were fitted with wheels so that they resembled small waggons.

Cock-beading: The thin strips of wood which fit around the front edge of a drawer.

Coffer: A chest.

Commode: A chest of drawers in the French style : or a chair, a small cupboard, or a small flight of steps for use in a bedroom, concealing a chamber pot.

Comport: A dish for fruit or sweets on a stand which raises it above table level.

Console Table: A small table with a single front leg which stands against and is given support by a wall. Console tables are often gilded.

Corner Chair: A chair with its legs so arranged and the back so shaped that it will stand in a corner.

Court Cupboard: An open-shelved oak cupboard of the Tudor period. These continued to be fashionable until the Commonwealth.

K

Crazing: A network of fine cracks in the glaze of porcelain or pottery.

Credence or *Credenza:* An Italian sideboard or serving table.

Crossbanding: A strip of decorative veneer chosen so that the grain of the wood runs in a different direction from the grain of the ground into which it is mounted.

Dolphin Foot: A decorative foot in which a dolphin's head becomes the base and the upturned tail the support. William Kent used this design between 1730 and 1740.

Dovetail: The fan-shaped joint most commonly seen where the front of a drawer is attached to the sides.

Dowel: A wooden pin used on most old oak furniture to secure joints. Dowels were used in preference to nails : their roughly circular heads can usually be clearly seen.

Drop Handles: Brass handles resembling elongated drops of moisture. They were popular during the reign of William and Mary.

Drops: Pear-shaped pieces of cut glass hanging from a chandelier or glass ornament.

Duchesse: Two facing *bergère* chairs with a stool between them.

Dumb Waiter: A tall column or pillar supporting wooden trays of various sizes and levels. Dumb waiters were usually made of best-quality mahogany. They were used to hold food and drink so that servants could be dispensed with during meals and also for more informal occasions to provide what we should now call a 'buffet' meal.

Engine-turned: A term used to describe pottery that has been decorated, before firing, on a lathe specially designed to produce the pattern. Small metal articles such as snuff boxes, were sometimes engine-turned.

Epergne: A multi-branched stand, usually of glass or silver, or a combination of the two, though sometimes of porcelain. Each branch terminated in a vase or dish for flowers or sweetmeats. On some epergnes, there was a large dish at the top of the stand for fruit. An epergne usually stood in the centre of a dining-table and is typically nineteenth century.

Escritoire: A writing cabinet on a stand or chest of drawers. They were popular in the late seventeenth century.

Escutcheon: A brass or ormolu plate which surrounds a keyhole. The name derives from the shield-shaped ground on which coats-of-arms are found.

Étui: A small decorative container, often of silver or enamel, in which ladies kept items such as needles, bodkins, toothpicks and snuffspoons.

Faience: A Continental tin-glazed earthenware, especially important in France during the eighteenth century. It was sometimes enamelled over the glaze and this type of faience can sometimes be mistaken for porcelain.

Farthingale Chair: An armless chair with a tall, thin, tapered back used by ladies wearing hooped petticoats or farthingales.

Fauteuil: A French chair with unpadded arms, similar in design to the padded *bergère*. It may, however, have padded elbows.

Fine: A term used by the trade to describe high quality.

Finial: An ornamental projection such as the knob on a cover or the decorated apex of a pediment or canopy.

Fluting: A series of grooves cut or pressed into an article.

Foxing: The discolouration produced by the brown spots or patches which appear on paper that has been affected by damp.

Frieze: The horizontal band of wood beneath a cornice on furniture. Originally an architectural term.

Friggers: Articles made of glass more for diversion than for use. They were often designed to test the skill of the glass blower and included glass hats, pipes, walking sticks, rolling pins, etc.

Frit: A type of glass used by potters when glazing their wares.

Gadrooning: A form of decoration on the edges of furniture, silver and ceramics made up of convex curving lobes, or sometimes straight lobes.

Gesso: A relief decoration modelled with a mixture of size and plaster or whiting over which gold leaf has been applied. It is found on furniture, mirrors and picture frames.

Gilding: Gold leaf applied to smooth surfaces—often to softwood coated with plaster of Paris—to enrich the decoration.

Gimmel: Two glass bottles fused together.

Glaze: A translucent vitreous coating applied to porcelain and pottery which gives the finished articles a sheen. Different mineral substances in the glaze produce various colours in glazing.

Girandole: A carved and gilded candleholder for the wall, often with a mirror back plate.

Grisaille: Paintings which give a three-dimensional effect using only tones of one colour, usually grey.

Handcooler: A small egg-shaped object of glass or stone. It was held in a lady's hand to prevent perspiration on the palm.

Herringbone: A type of veneered decoration using a dark and light wood alternatively in a series of small arrowheads.

Hood: The top portion of a long case or grandfather clock which contains the glass. It will slide forward and off to make the working parts accessible.

Hoof-foot: A foot in the shape of an animal's hoof.

Horsehair: The hair from a horse's mane and tail used for covering or padding upholstered furniture because of its long-lasting resilience. It was sometimes woven to form a covering and was first used in the seventeenth century.

Incised: Decoration cut into the surface of the body.

Inlay: Pictures and decorative motifs, made up of woods of various colours, set into the actual body of a piece of furniture. Bone, ivory, tortoiseshell, mother-of-pearl and brass were also sometimes used in inlay work.

Intaglio: An incised engraving in a hard surface.

Ironstone: A form of pottery with a very hard glassy body, obtained by adding furnace slag to the clay of which it was made.

Japanning: A lacquer finish which is very hard, usually applied to softwood and to *papier mâché,* iron and tin articles. It is most often seen in red or black. The process originated in Japan.

Jardinière: A classical vase-shaped container or stand used for plants or flowers. *Jardinières* vary greatly in size.

Joynt: Catalogues sometimes refer to a joynt stool. This means a jointed piece in which mortice and tenon joints are secured with a dowel pin.

Kaolin: The name given to the white hard-paste china clay dug in Devon and Cornwall and first used in England by William Cookworthy.

Key Pattern: A design of straight lines joining at right angles (Plate 15) used to decorate borders, especially of furniture and silver.

Knee: The outward curving part of a leg which marks the change of direction from the near horizontal towards the near vertical.

Knocker: See *Clapper.*

Knife Box: A container in which knives were kept, usually on a sideboard. Knife boxes were sometimes incorporated in designs of sideboards, particularly those of the Adam style.

Knocked Down: Sold at auction.

Knock-out: A term used for a private auction which may take place among dealers after they have completed their transactions in an ordinary saleroom.

Knop: A decorative knob or finial to a lid, or a shaped enlargement included in the stem of a glass which may take many forms, e.g. an acorn, a ball, a cushion.

Knurled: Scrolled. A term applied to the foot of a chair or table.

Lacquer: A coating of the sap of the lac tree. Applied by dissolving shellac in alcohol which evaporates, leaving a thin layer on the lacquered article. See *Japanning.*

Ladder Back: The back of a chair with several bracing struts which run horizontally like the rungs of a ladder.

Library Chair: A chair popular during the eighteenth century which could be sat on or astride. It had a bookrest which could be raised on a ratchet at the back. The arms often contained hinged compartments for ink, pens, etc. The chair was bestridden for reading or writing.

Library Steps: Elegant flights of steps which enabled the user to reach books from high shelves. The tread of the steps could often be raised revealing useful storage space. Much ingenuity was used by cabinet-makers to design library steps which would fold to form a chair or a table.

Limoges Enamel Ware: Copper articles decorated with coloured enamels, usually black, white or terra-cotta, and depicting classical legends. The finest Limoges enamel was produced in the sixteenth century : it was much copied in the nineteenth century.

Lion's Mask: The lion's head was ideal as a design for decorative handles often with a ring hanging from the nose. It was widely used on silver and furniture, especially during the eighteenth century and during the Regency period. It is also seen on porcelain.

Lithograph: A reproduction of a picture or drawing taken from a limestone block.

Lithophane: A small plaque of white or cream porcelain into which a picture is moulded in relief giving varying degrees of translucency. In Victorian times, they were placed in front of candles which gave the picture depth when seen from the front.

Loper: The vertical slide which is drawn out on either side of a fall-front bureau or desk to support the writing surface.

Lot: An article or group of articles to be sold at auction for a single sum of money.

Love Seat: An upholstered couch for two people.

Loving Cup: A two-handled mug or goblet.

Lustre: A vase from the top rim of which are suspended a number of cut-glass drops which catch the light. They were usually made in pairs.

Lustre Decoration: A thin film of metal on pottery or porcelain.

Lyre: A shape derived from the musical instrument of that name. It was popular during the French Empire and Regency periods for the backs of chairs, ends of tables, etc.

Majolica: Italian tin-glazed earthenware decorated with brightly coloured enamel and dating from the sixteenth century. Imitation majolica was also made by English factories in the second half of the nineteenth century.

Marbling: Decoration intended to produce a variegated pattern like marble.

Marquetry: Decorative motifs covering the surface of a piece of furniture made up of veneers of various colours and contrasting grains inlaid in the darker veneered background.

Marrow Spoon or *Marrow Scoop:* A silver or plated spoon with a long shallow bowl, often double-ended, used for scraping the marrow from bones.

Millefiori: A decoration normally found at the base of paperweights. The floral appearance is created by a series of coloured glass rods cut off to leave the exposed ends uppermost encased in a clear glass bun.

Mote-skimmer: A long thin teaspoon, often of silver, the bowl of which is pierced with holes, the end of the handle terminating in a barb. The bowl was used to remove leaves from a cup of tea; the barb was used to clean the strainer in the teapot.

Mother-of-pearl: The nacreous iridescent lining from a sea-shell.

Nailer: A term used by clappers or dealers for an object which first excites the curiosity or greed of a buyer or seller. For the buyer, it is often a quality antique displayed among poorer quality items in the shop window of an unscrupulous dealer. It is usually unpriced and not for sale. For the seller, it is usually a valueless item on which the unscrupulous dealer places a high value with no intention of buying in the hope that the seller will be so impressed that he will be willing to sell other and better items at low prices.

Nutmeg Grater: A metal plate similar to a modern kitchen grater usually contained in a decorative mount. The larger ones were in carved ivory, the portable ones in silver or gold boxes.

Ogee Foot: A bracket foot with a double curve (convex above and concave below) commonly used from the time of George II (see Figure 7).

Opaline: A white translucent glass that shows a fiery-red glow when seen against a strong light.

Ormolu: Decoration cast in brass or bronze and gilded.

'Over the Odds': Above current market value.

Oyster Veneer: A veneer selected for its grain, which resembles the concentric rings on an oyster shell.

Pap-boat: An oval-shaped vessel with a small lip or spout for feeding babies. In the early eighteenth century they were made of silver but they can also be found in porcelain or pottery.

Papier mâché: A term used for articles made from layers of pulped paper soaked in a mixture of chalk or flour and glue compressed into shape, and heated. Nearly all *papier mâché* articles are finished with black lacquer and decorated.

Parcel Gilt: This term, often used in the trade, is the old English way of saying partly gilt or partly gilded.

Parian Ware: A soapy white unglazed porcelain used for making figures and busts.

Parquetry: A mosiac of geometrical pieces of wood fitted together as a veneer on furniture. Today, we use the word 'parquet' to describe a wood-block floor.

Paste: The clay or mixture of which a piece of porcelain or pottery is made.

Paste Jewellery: Jewellery in which glass is used in imitation of precious stones.

Pastille Burners: Small decorative pottery and porcelain ornaments, often in the form of houses or cottages. They have an aperture in the back into which a small pastille was placed. When ignited, this gave off a perfumed vapour.

Pâte-sur-Pâte: A method of decorating porcelain using a thin white translucent slip on a coloured ground. It was introduced by Mark Louis Solon when he came over from France in 1870 to work at the Minton factory. It originated in the Sèvres factory.

Patera: A small decorative disc used on furniture especially during the Adam period.

Patina: The surface condition acquired by wood or metal through years of polishing and normal household use.

Pestle and Mortar: The mortar is a brass, bronze or stoneware bowl; the pestle is a short, heavy, round-ended rod usually of the same material used to powder or pulverize materials—usually drugs— in the mortar.

Pewter: An alloy of tin with lead, copper or antimony.

Pie-crust: A method of decorating the edge of an object with carved concave depressions so that it resembles a pie-crust after it has been thumbed.

Pinchbeck: This is often known as 'Poor man's gold'. It was an alloy of which the basic metal was brass invented by Christopher Pinchbeck, a clockmaker. The alloy looks very like gold and does not tarnish quickly : it was used a great deal in making Victorian jewellery.

Pontil Mark: The point at which a glass article is snapped from the pontil or punty—the iron rod on which it was worked. In most old glass this shows as a sharp and jagged surface. In later glass the pontil mark was ground off or sometimes covered with a blob of molten glass.

Porringer: A double-handled bowl used for porridge. Porringers were popular during the seventeenth and early eighteenth centuries.

Posset: This was a drink made from hot milk curdled with ale or wine, and was often spiced. It was taken as a remedy for colds and drunk from posset pots or posset cups which were often lidded.

Posy Holder: A cone-shaped vase, often of silver, into which a posy could be inserted without water. A pin which was attached to the holder by a chain could be pushed through a hole in the holder and out the other side to hold the posy in place. The posy holder itself was often attached in some way to the wearer.

Potato Ring: A circular, pierced silver ring, usually three to four inches high, which was used on a dining-table to support a dish of hot potatoes and so prevent damage to the polished surface beneath. Another school of thought believes that they were placed on wooden platters with the hot potatoes inside. They were commonly made and used in Ireland in the second half of the eighteenth century.

Pricket: The spike on the sconce of old candlesticks which was driven into the base of the wax candle to support it.

Printies: Concave cuts, round or oval in shape, used to decorate glass vessels, especially decanters.

Privates: A term used by dealers for private individuals with no trade connections who bid at sales.

Prunt: A small blob of molten glass, often decorated to resemble a raspberry, applied to the main body of a glass article, as decoration. They were occasionally used to hide the pontil mark.

Puffer: The trade term for a person at an auction sale, in league with an unscrupulous auctioneer, who bids against a genuine buyer in order to run the price up.

Punter: A purchaser who is prepared to take a chance.

Putto: A small boy. *Putti* in art are Cupid-like figures used for decoration. They frequently adorn paintings, sculpture, carved furniture, porcelain and silver, and occur in profusion in baroque decoration.

Queen's Ware: The trade name for the creamware made by Wedgwood.

Reeding: A decoration made up of a series of convex parallel mouldings in relief.

Refectory Table: A large long rectangular table, often of oak, used for dining large parties. They were originally used by monks in monastic establishments.

Rent Table: A round or octagonal table—also called a capstan or drum table because of its shape—around which fit a series of wedge-shaped drawers. The top is supported on a central column or stand and has a round lidded hole in the centre into which the money was heaped. Rent tables usually stood in the hall of a country home and rent books and monies of each tenant were kept in one of the lockable drawers.

Reserve: A price placed by the vendor upon an object to be offered at auction, below which he is not prepared to sell.

Resist: A lustre decoration combined with overglaze painting.

Repoussé: Embossed work on metals such as silver or copper.

Reproduction: A fair copy of an original.

Ribboned: A term used to describe decoration in the form of trailing ribbons and bows.

Right: Genuine.

Ring: A group of people, usually dealers, who elect one bidder in advance of a sale to avoid the price being raised as a result of competition between them. See also *Knock-out.*

Rococo: A style of decoration made up of flowing symmetrical curves, delicately balanced so as not to disturb the flow or line of the object.

Rummer: A large short-stemmed glass which came into fashion in the late eighteenth century. It derives its name from the traditional Rhenish wine glass. Many people wrongly associate the name with the drinking of rum toddy.

Salt glaze: The frosty glaze achieved on early pottery and porcelain by throwing salt into the kiln during the firing.

Salver: A tray, sometimes standing on feet, for handing round drinks, etc.

Sampler: An embroidered panel; most frequently a child's needlework exercise.

Sconce: The part of a candlestick on which, or into which, the candle is placed. The word is sometimes used to describe the complete candlestick fitment when attached to a wall.

Scrapper: The term applied to a gold or silver object which is either badly worn or of no re-sale value and which will be consigned to a box of similar metal to be sold for its scrap weight value.

Scroll Feet: Feet resembling rolled up scrolls of paper or vellum.

Serpentine: A term used to describe the front of a piece of furniture of which the two ends curve inwards and the centre curves outwards all in one flowing line.

Settle: A chest with lid which also has arms and a back so that it can be used both for storage and as a seat.

Shagreen: A skin covering often used for small boxes and wallets. It is usually green or black and is thought by many to be the skin of the shark. Although this is sometimes true, it is more often ordinary animal skin into which seeds have been pressed and the whole then coloured.

Ship's Decanter: A decanter with a very broad base and sloping sides, often known as a Rodney. It was less likely to tip over in rough seas than an ordinary decanter.

Skewer: A large, silver-plated, flat-bladed object with a ring handle which was pushed through barons of beef to secure them for carving. They are now popular for use as paper knives.

Skirt: The pieces of wood around a chair below the seat. The front skirt is normally referred to as the apron.

Slip: A creamy mixture of clay and water trailed over the surface of pottery as decoration.

Snuffers: A cone of metal used to extinguish a candle flame without damaging the wick, or a pair of tongs (rather like sugar tongs) with flat blades which pinched the wick. Later examples were rather like a pair of scissors with a box on one blade. The blades cut off the burning portion of the wick which was caught and extinguished in the box.

Soapstone: A soft stone which is easily carved. Most soapstone carvings come from the East.

Spandrels: Decoration which radiates from and is confined to the corners of a square or rectangle—e.g. the relief ormolu ornaments mounted in the corners of a clock face.

Spelter: A cheap alloy, mainly of zinc.

Splat: The panel of wood running down the centre of an open chair at the back.

Squab: A stuffed cushion.

Standish: An inkstand on four small feet and with a curved edge.

Stirrup Cup: A drinking vessel without a base to stand on, used by members of a hunt when in the saddle. They may be of glass, silver, porcelain or pottery and often take the form of an animal's head, particularly, of course, the fox.

Straw Work: A form of delicate marquetry where the design is built up from straw which has previously been dyed different colours.

Stretcher: The horizontal pieces of wood used to brace the legs of chairs, tables, etc.

Stringing: A thin band of inlay usually no more than one-eighth of an inch wide used to decorate the edges of furniture. Brass strips were also used for the same purpose, particularly during the Regency period.

Style: A term used in auction sale catalogues to convey their belief that the article is not of the period although the design and general appearance might lead one to believe it to be genuine— e.g. a *Sheraton-style* china cabinet could have been made by a Victorian or Edwardian cabinet-maker.

Swagged: Festooned with flowers, fruit, leaves or draping.

Syllabub Glass: A small glass used for serving syllabub, a dish made with cream, wine and sugar.

Taking bids off the ceiling: When an auctioneer takes an imaginary bid in an attempt to raise the genuine bids. Also referred to as 'off the wall'.

Tantalus: An open stand in which decanters were kept. It had a bar fitted with a lock which prevented anyone from removing the decanters and stealing the liquor, and was called a tantalus because it was tantalizing to see the liquor without being able to imbibe.

Taper Stick: A miniature candlestick for holding tapers.

Taper Jack: A box or stand which contained a rolled-up taper which could be pulled out as required. Sometimes called a wax-jack.

Tazza: A saucer-shaped bowl or cup, usually mounted on a foot. Originally an early wine-cup with a round shallow bowl.

Tea Poy: A pedestal table with a lifting top which forms a large tea caddy containing compartments for tea and a mixing bowl.

Terra Cotta: A hard earthenware fired once. It is usually a brownish-red colour.

Toddy Lifter: A hollow tube with a bulbous end and a hole at each end used (rather like a pipette in a laboratory) to lift hot toddy from bowl to glass. The bulbous end was immersed in the toddy, and a finger was then placed over the hole at the top to prevent air from entering. The finger was removed to release the toddy.

Torchère: A tall column surmounted with a small round platform on which a candlestick could be placed to illuminate part of a room. They were generally made in pairs.

Totter: A 'rag and bone' man. Totters now deal mainly in scrap metal but usually keep an eye open for antiques and generally appreciate their value.

Treen: A generic name for all small domestic articles made of wood.

Trivet: A stand, usually of iron or brass, which was kept in the hearth for hot saucepans and kettles.

Tunbridge Ware: Decorated woodwork which was made in Tunbridge Wells from about 1680 until the 1890s. The early work was marquetry but the best known is the wood mosaic made in the nineteenth century. The method was to build up a bundle of multi-coloured strips of wood to create a picture at the end, rather like the lettering in a stick of rock. The bundle was then secured and thin sections were sliced off and stuck to the object to be decorated. This bundle gave many identical mosaics as the result of a single design operation.

Tyg: An early drinking vessel with three or more handles.

Vellum: Cured skin used for early manuscripts.

Vinaigrette: A small box, often resembling a snuff box, usually in precious metal or enamel but always gilded on the inside. Inside the main lid was a secondary lid pierced to allow perfume to rise from a sponge soaked in scented vinegar which was held inside.

Vitrine: A display cabinet with glazed door and sides.

Volute: In the form of a scroll.

Waiter: A small silver salver.

Waxjack: See *Taper Jack.*

Weeder: A dealer who puts aside the best goods for his own use.

Wine Cooler: A vessel, often of silver or plate, but sometimes of wood lined with lead. Bottles were placed in the cooler and ice was packed around them.

Work Table: A small table, often supported by a single pillar. The top formed the lid of a shallow box for holding needles, cotton etc., and beneath the box hung a bag of material which would slide out. This was for keeping the wools and silks used for embroidery.

Wrong: An adjective used to describe an antique or any part of an antique which is not genuine.

BIBLIOGRAPHY

BOOKS FOR THE POCKET

A Pocket Guide to the Marks of Origin on British and Irish Silver Plate (1544-1960) and old Sheffield Plate Makers' Marks (1743-1860) Frederick Bradbury, (J. W. Northend, Sheffield).
Pocket Book of English Ceramic Marks: J. P. Cushion, (Faber).
'Country Life' Collectors' Pocket Book: G. Bernard Hughes.
'Country Life' Pocket Book of China: G. Bernard Hughes.
'Country Life' Pocket Book of Glass: Geoffrey Wills.

HISTORICAL AND DESCRIPTIVE

1. *General*
   Antiques and Their Periods (1600-1830) Hampden Jackson, (Murray).
   Antiques: The Amateur's Questions: Hampden Jackson, (Murray).

2. *Furniture*
   Short History of English Furniture (H.M. Stationery Office).
   English Furniture Styles: Ralph Fastnedge, (Herbert Jenkins).
   English Furniture: John Gloag, (A. & C. Black).
   A Social History of Furniture Design: John Gloag, (Cassell).
   Old English Furniture: A Simple Guide : Hampden Jackson, (Murray).
   'Country Life' Book of English Furniture: Edward T. Joy.
   Antique English Furniture: L. G. G. Ramsey (Editor), ('The Connoisseur').
   Victorian Furniture: R. W. Symonds & B. Whineray, (Country Life Ltd.).
   Papier mâché in Great Britain and America: Jane Toller, (Bell).
   Old Furniture: Edward Wenham, (Spring Books).
   English Looking-Glasses: Geoffrey Wills, (Country Life Ltd.).

3. *Clocks*
   Old Clocks: Edward Wenham, (Spring Books).

4. *Silver and Sheffield Plate*
   Introduction to Old English Silver: Judith Banister, (Evans).

English Domestic Silver: Charles Oman, (A. & C. Black).
Antique English Silver and Plate: L. G. G. Ramsay (Editor), ('The Connoisseur').
English Silver of the Eighteenth Century: J. Stone, (Cory, Adams & Mackay).
Victorian Silver and Silver Plate: Patricia Wardle, (Herbert Jenkins).
Old Sheffield Plate: Edward Wenham, (G. Bell & Sons).

5. *Non-Precious Metals*

    (a) Brass and Copper
    Horse Brasses: George Hartfield, (Abelard-Schuman).
    Horse Brasses: G. Bernard Hughes, (Country Life Ltd.).
    Collecting Copper and Brass: Geoffrey Wills, (Arco).

    (b) Iron
    Iron and Brass Implements of the English House: Seymour Lindsay, (Alec Tirani).

    (c) Pewter
    Pewter: John Bedford, (Cassell).
    Antique Pewter of the British Isles: R. F. Michaelis, (G. Bell & Sons).

6. *Porcelain and Pottery*

    Delftware: John Bedford, (Cassell).
    Old English Lustre Ware: John Bedford, (Cassell).
    Old Worcester China: John Bedford, (Cassell).
    Staffordshire Pottery Figures: John Bedford, (Cassell).
    Wedgwood, Jasper Ware: John Bedford, (Cassell).
    English Delftware: F. G. Garner, (Faber).
    Victorian Porcelain: Geoffrey A. Godden, (Herbert Jenkins).
    English Pottery and Porcelain: W. B. Honey, (A. & C. Black).
    English Pottery and Porcelain Figures: G. Bernard Hughes, (Lutterworth Press).
    Victorian Pottery and Porcelain: G. Bernard Hughes, (Country Life Ltd.).
    The Story of Wedgwood: Alison Kelly, (Faber).
    English Slipware: Dorothy Kemp, (Faber).
    Porcelain: G. Savage, (Pelican Books).
    Pottery Through the Ages: G. Savage, (Cassell).
    Victorian Pottery: Hugh Wakefield, (Herbert Jenkins).
    'Country Life' Book of English China: Geoffrey Wills.

7. *Glass*

    How to Identify English Drinking Glasses and Decanters (1680-1830): Douglas Ash, (Bell).

Bristol and other Coloured Glass: John Bedford, (Cassell).
English Crystal Glass: John Bedford, (Cassell).
'Country Life' Book of Glass: Frank Davis.
English and Irish Cut Glass: E. M. Elville, (Country Life Ltd.).
English Glass: W. A. Thorpe, (A. & C. Black).

8. *Antiques for the Wall*
   English Watercolours: Laurence Benyon, (A. & C. Black).
   How to Identify Old Maps and Globes: Raymond Lister, (Bell).
   English Portrait Miniatures: Graham Reynolds, (A. & C. Black).
   Art Collecting for Amateurs: Richard Seddon, (Muller).
   British Silhouettes: John Woodiwiss, (Country Life Ltd.).

9. *Oriental Antiques*
   (a) China
   Handbook of Chinese Art: Margaret Medley, (Bell).
   Chinese Jade: G. Savage, (Cory, Adams & Mackay).

   (b) Japan
   The Japanese Print: J. Hillier, (G. Bell & Sons).
   Japanese Porcelain: S. Jenyns, (Faber).
   The Prints of Japan: Frank A. Turk, (Arco).

10. *Collectors' Books*
    Art Nouveau: (Dutton Vista Picturebook).
    Small Boxes of all Kinds: John Bedford, (Cassell).
    Wine Labels: John Bedford, (Cassell).
    Talking about Teapots: John Bedford, (Cassell).
    Victorian Jewellery: E. Bradford, (Country Life Ltd.).
    Victorian China Fairings: W. S. Bristowe, (A. & C. Black).
    Scent Bottles: K. Foster, ('The Connoisseur').
    Antique China and Glass under £5: Geoffrey A. Godden, (Barker).
    Silver Collecting for Amateurs: James Henderson, (Muller).
    Collecting Antiques: G. Bernard Hughes, (Country Life Ltd.).
    More about Collecting Antiques: G. Bernard Hughes, (Country Life Ltd.).
    Jewelry: Graham Hughes, (Studio Vista).
    Small Antiques for the Collector: Therle Hughes, (Lutterworth Press).
    More Small Antiques for the Collector: Therle Hughes, (Lutterworth Press).
    How to Repair and Dress Old Dolls: Audrey Johnson, (Bell).
    Collecting Victoriana: Mary Peter, (Arco).
    Collecting Victorian Porcelain: Ernest Reynolds, (Arco).
    Victoriana: A Collector's Guide : Violet Wood, (Bell).

11. *Reference Books*

The Concise Encyclopaedia of Antiques: issued by 'The Connoisseur' in five volumes, 1955-1961.

The Shorter Dictionary of English Furniture: Ralph Edwards, (Country Life Ltd.).

A Short Dictionary of Furniture: John Gloag, (Unwin Books).

Encyclopaedia of British Pottery and Porcelain Marks: Geoffrey A. Godden, (Herbert Jenkins).

Illustrated Encyclopaedia of British Pottery and Porcelain: Geoffrey A. Godden, (Herbert Jenkins).

Handbook of Pottery and Porcelain Marks: W. B. Honey and J. P. Cushion, (Faber).

The Collector's Dictionary of Clocks: H. Alan Lloyd, (Country Life Ltd.).

Dictionary of Marks, Ceramic, Metalwork and Furniture: Margaret Macdonald-Taylor, ('The Connoisseur').

International Antiques Year Book: published annually by Studio Vista.

APPENDIX

ANTIQUES AND THEIR VALUES

Some Auction Room Prices

The prices in the following lists were paid at public auction sales in Great Britain and Northern Ireland since 1 July 1966. Many of the items listed occur fairly frequently in saleroom catalogues but a few rarer items have been included when they seem to be of special interest. No information is given, or can be given, about the condition of the articles listed, although we have done our utmost to ensure that they were sound and we have 'sampled' a number of salerooms for this purpose. Variations in the price paid for similar lots may nevertheless be due to the difference between the fine piece and the piece which shows signs of wear. Some auctioneers indicate in their catalogues when an item is in poor condition (*a.f.*), or is slightly damaged (*s.d.*).

Since prices for a particular type of article may vary from one part of the country to another, the area where each lot was sold has been indicated by a letter in the first column. These correspond with the areas on the map (Fig 15) overleaf.

We believe these lists to be representative of current values and we hope they may prove useful to owners, buyers and sellers alike.

FURNITURE

		£	s
Bookcases, Bureau-bookcases and Bookshelves			
Sheraton banded mahogany secretaire bookcase, the upper part enclosed by glazed astragal doors, the base with secretaire drawer opening to reveal concave drawers and recesses and green tooled leather writing panel over two panelled doors	M	480	0
Dutch Queen Anne walnut bureau-bookcase	SE	360	0
Regency figured-mahogany wing bookcase with centre secretaire compartment and two side drawers: four cupboard doors below: the upper cabinet enclosed by four glazed doors with astragal mouldings. Width 7 ft, height 7 ft 1 in	SE	290	0

Figure 15

MAP OF
SALE AREAS

L—London; M—Midlands and East Anglia; N—North of England;
NI—Northern Ireland; W—Wales; S—Scotland; SE—South and South
East England; WE—West of England

	£	s
Early nineteenth-century breakfront bookcase with three glazed doors and nine drawers below, on plain plinth, 7 ft 4 in wide	M 180	0
Nineteenth-century mahogany bureau-bookcase inlaid with foliate scrolls, the upper cabinet with two glazed drawers; lower part with slant fall-front enclosing a well-fitted writing compartment; two-door cupboard below; on ogee bracket feet, 3 ft wide	SE 160	0
Red and gold Chinese-lacquered bureau-bookcase, interior fitted drawers and pigeon holes, having fall front, four long drawers under the double dome top fitted two shelves enclosed by a pair of glazed doors, on bracket feet	L 132	0
Late Georgian bookcase of Chippendale style, the open top with two tiers, with carved frieze and fretwork sides, the base with secretaire drawer opening to reveal drawers and recesses and green tooled leather writing panel, over three long graduated drawers	M 125	0
Eighteenth-century mahogany open wall-bookshelf of three tiers, 30 in wide	SE 110	0
Set of Georgian mahogany graduated open bookshelves with drawer under	M 100	0
Georgian banded mahogany open bookshelf with cupboard below two open shelves; shaped top and bun feet. Width 2 ft 6 in	SE 75	0
Burr walnut cross-banded open breakfront dwarf bookcase fitted six shelves, divided by square fluted columns, 7 ft 6 in wide	L 64	0
Regency mahogany secretaire bookcase with ebony line-inlay above the secretaire drawer in a pair of barred glass doors and below a pair of panelled doors, 3 ft 6 in wide	L 56	0
Georgian-style mahogany bookcase having dentil and fret cornice enclosed pair of glazed bar panel doors, fitted drawer and cupboard, 2 ft 11 in wide	WE 46	0
Mahogany secretaire bookcase with two lattice glazed doors above secretaire and two doors below with lion ring handles, 2 ft 11 in wide	SE 38	0
Georgian mahogany four glazed astragal door breakfront bookcase on shaped supports	S 32	0
Mahogany library breakfront bookcase enclosed five bar panel doors, 7 ft 6 in wide, 5 ft 9 in high	WE 31	0
Victorian mahogany bookcase, the top part enclosed by two glazed doors, having drawer and two panel doors under, 3 ft 6 in	L 29	0
Victorian mahogany glazed bookcase/cupboard	WE 23	0
Regency rosewood open bookcase with adjustable shelves, 6 ft 6 in wide	WE 22	0
Victorian mahogany bookcase, enclosed pair of glazed and pair of panelled doors, two drawers to frieze, 3 ft 11 in	L 15	0
Victorian mahogany bookcase, enclosed pair of glazed doors, 39 in	L 8	0

Bureaux, Writing Cabinets, and Escritoires
Eighteenth-century marquetry inlaid and banded Dutch writing cabinet in two parts, fitted ten short drawers, cup-

		£	s
board and three long drawers below writing fall, and having moulded cornice with dome centre and raised on bun feet, 2 ft 8 in	SE	200	0
George I cross-banded walnut bureau, brass swan-neck handles, shaped back plates and escutcheons, shaped bracket feet, 3 ft 8 in by 3 ft	WE	190	0
Cross-banded and inlaid Queen Anne walnut bureau, five short and two long drawers, brass drop handles and escutcheons, on shaped bracket feet, 36 in wide	WE	170	0
George III mahogany bureau, 3 ft 3 in wide	L	100	0
Early eighteenth-century walnut bureau inlaid with chevron bands; with slant fall-front enclosing drawers, pigeon-holes and secret compartments; four graduated drawers below fitted brass drop handles; on bracket feet, width 3 ft	SE	98	0
Rosewood bureau with pigeon-holes enclosed by drop-flap inlaid with classical group in engraved copper, brass pewter, ivory and mother of pearl marquetry; the three-drawer front and top inlaid with similar floral motifs; the sides brass-banded; fitted brass-loop handles; on bracket feet, width 29½ in	SE	90	0
Walnut bureau with floral marquetry inlaid panels having a fall-front enclosing drawers, pigeon-holes, cupboard and well, two short and two long drawers below with brass escutcheons on bracket feet, 3 ft 2 in wide	L	60	0
Sheraton inlaid mahogany fall-front bureau with concave interior fittings, two short and three graduated long drawers under, on bracket feet, 3 ft 8 in	L	60	0
Georgian mahogany bureau with slant fall-front inlaid with a conch shell medallion; two short and three graduated long drawers below fitted chased ormolu drop-handles and escutcheons, on bracket feet, 3 ft 10 in wide	SE	60	0
Late eighteenth-century French cylinder-front bureau fitted three deep drawers, 3 ft 2 in wide	WE	56	0
Mahogany bureau, 3 ft 9 in, with line inlay, fitted two short and two long drawers with brass handles, on bracket feet	M	52	10
Early Georgian cross-band inlaid walnut bureau, brass swan-neck handles, ring backplates, shaped escutcheons, shaped bracket feet, 36 in wide	WE	45	0
Georgian inlaid mahogany bureau three long and two short drawers under, bracket feet, 3 ft 6 in	L	44	0
Early eighteenth-century oak bureau with fitted interior, writing slide, and seven drawers to base on bracket feet, 3 ft	SE	44	0
Georgian mahogany bureau with slant fall-front enclosing drawers, pigeon-holes and secret compartments; four graduated drawers below fitted plain brass-loop handles, on bracket feet, 3 ft 6 in wide	SE	44	0
Eighteenth-century oak fall-front bureau, fitted four graduated long drawers, on bracket feet, 2 ft 9 in	L	40	0
Georgian mahogany bureau, the sloping fall inlaid with coloured woods and opening to reveal maplewood drawers and recesses; a single frieze drawer and three drawers to the base	M	40	0

		£	s
Georgian mahogany bureau, four graduated drawers, brass swan-neck handles and bracket feet	WE	40	0
Inlaid mahogany bureau, the fall flap with broad cross-banding and fine oval to centre, three long drawers below, fitted brass plate handles, 2 ft 5 in	WE	28	0

Cabinets

Georgian olive-green lacquer display cabinet, decorated with chinoiseries in gilt and red, with a single glazed door; the domed top surmounted with Prince of Wales plumes and with a panelled door below	M	230	0
George III mahogany corner cabinet	WE	170	0
William and Mary walnut china cabinet	WE	130	0
Nineteenth-century burr-walnut dwarf display cabinet inlaid with amboynawood bands and boxwood and ebonized lines; embellished with ormolu mounts and beading; single glazed door enclosing two baize-lined shelves, width 31 in, height 44 in	SE	72	0
William and Mary oyster walnut cabinet of drawers enclosed two doors	S	70	0
Mid-nineteenth century ebonized cabinet with amboynawood bandings and gilt incised decoration mounted with six porcelain figure and portrait medallions: ormolu mounts and beading; panel door in centre and two quadrant glazed wing doors, width 5 ft 10 in, height 3 ft 8 in	SE	58	0
Victorian inlaid walnut and ormolu mounted china cabinet having bowed glazed doors with centre door, 4 ft 10 in wide	WE	50	0
Black lacquer and gilt decorated china cabinet enclosed pair glazed doors fitted two drawers and cupboard with undershelf, 3 ft 1 in wide	WE	38	0

Canterburys

Georgian mahogany boat-shaped Canterbury with drawer	M	62	0
Rosewood music Canterbury	SE	32	0
Nineteenth-century Canterbury with a drawer in base, 18 in	L	21	0
Victorian Canterbury whatnot	SE	18	0
Victorian walnut wood Canterbury with bow ends, 30 in	L	11	0

Chairs—Arm

Chippendale carved mahogany open-arm chair upholstered in tapestry	SE	70	0
Eighteenth-century oak frame armchair, on front baluster support and stretcher rails, and with padded seat and back, upholstered blue tapestry	SE	68	0
Small Jacobean open-arm chair, on baluster legs with plain under tails, the back carved with arch, fan and scroll decoration, and with blue squab seat	SE	62	0
Sixteenth-century oak open-arm chair with carved arch and fan decoration to back, and on baluster supports with plain stretchers	SE	56	0
Seventeenth-century open-arm chair with leather upholstered seat and back	SE	54	0
Eighteenth-century Windsor armchair, with pierced splat and crinoline rail	SE	50	0

		£	s
Jacobean open-arm chair in oak, raised on baluster legs, panel back and with inlay holly and diamond decoration. Brown velvet squab	SE	42	0
Lady's sixteenth-century oak plank-constructed armchair with chip carved roundel to back	SE	32	0
Chippendale carved mahogany open-arm chair, tapestry seat	WE	30	0
Chinese Chippendale mahogany armchair, seat in repp	S	27	0
Late eighteenth-century yew wood Windsor arm chair, with wheel and spindle back and crinoline rail	SE	26	0
Spindle-back Windsor armchair	SE	21	0
Painted carved frame open-arm single chair with upholstered seat and back in the French manner	SE	20	0
Sixteenth-century oak open-arm chair, carved scrolls and holly inlaid panel back	SE	19	0
Spoon-back armchair with buttoned back in peach velvet	SE	16	10

Chairs—Children's

Queen Anne-style child's walnut elbow chair having a shaped splat back on carved cabriole legs with shell motifs to the knees and ball and claw feet, loose seat in blue-ground floral needlework	L	36	0
Child's eighteenth-century Windsor elbow chair	WE	23	0
Child's Georgian cane-back high chair on table base	SE	17	0

Chairs—Countrymade

Six eighteenth-century Yorkshire oak chairs	SE	54	0
Three wheelback Windsor chairs	SE	50	0
Four rush-seat spindle-back chairs	S	46	0
Sixteenth-century oak chair, with spindle back and gouged frame	SE	28	0
Eighteenth-century yew wood Windsor chair, with pierced centre splat and crinoline rail	SE	22	0
Early Windsor comb-back corner chair	SE	18	0
Yolk-top Windsor chair with comb and shield back	SE	12	10
Windsor comb-back elbow chair	SE	8	0

Chairs—Dining—Eighteenth-century Sets

Eight Georgian mahogany dining chairs, two carvers and six standard	L	345	0
Six Chippendale mahogany dining chairs	SE	310	0
Six single and one carver Chippendale period mahogany chairs	M	240	0
Twelve mahogany dining chairs of Hepplewhite style	N	215	0
Eight Hepplewhite-design mahogany shield-back dining chairs	M	190	0
Eight (six and two arms) Chippendale mahogany spring-seat dining chairs	WE	160	0
Two carving and ten single Hepplewhite-design mahogany dining chairs, with pierced splats	M	135	0
Eight Chinese-Chippendale-design mahogany chairs	L	135	0
Six Sheraton mahogany dining chairs (two with arms), the low four-rail backs having label cresting rails; stuffed seats covered in green leatherette; on turned ringed legs	SE	130	0
Two carving and six single Hepplewhite mahogany shield-back dining chairs, the pierced vase splats with floral scrol-			

		£	s
ling and wheat ears, the tapestry seats supported on square and tapering legs	M	100	0
Five Sheraton mahogany dining chairs	WE	67	0
Four Dutch marquetry dining chairs with shaped cresting rails and splat backs, on cabriole legs with carved shell knees, slip-in serpentine seats covered machine tapesty	SE	64	0
Four Sheraton dining chairs	SE	56	0

Chairs—Dining—Regency Sets

		£	s
Eight Regency mahogany dining chairs (two with arms) with reeded frames and sabre legs; drop-in seats covered in leatherette	SE	340	0
Eight Regency beechwood dining chairs	L	340	0
Nine Regency chairs with simulated-rosewood frames, brass inlay, caned seats with drop-in seats and sabre legs	M	250	0
Seven Regency simulated-rosewood standard chairs, having brass mounts, cane panelled seats with squab cushions, and sabre legs	SE	160	0
Six Regency mahogany dining chairs	SE	120	0
Ten (two arm, eight single) late Regency mahogany dining chairs	WE	100	0
Eight early nineteenth-century mahogany dining chairs in the Hepplewhite manner, the dip seats upholstered in hide	SE	90	0
Six Regency mahogany rail-back chairs with seats covered in striped material, on sabre legs	SE	70	0
Six (two elbow, four single) Regency chairs with open rail and spindle backs and brass centre roses, rush seats on turned legs	M	70	0
Six George IV mahogany square-back dining chairs, the top rails inlaid with maplewood oval panels and horizontal splats carved with roundels, the over-stuffed seats covered in red-figured brocatelle, and supported on turned and tapering legs	M	40	0
Four Regency ebonised and gilt open-back chairs with stuffed seats, on fluted legs	SE	18	0

Chairs—Dining—Regency Pairs

		£	s
A pair of Regency mahogany sabre-leg dining chairs with carved rail backs, loose seats upholstered green leather	WE	26	0
Pair of Regency simulated-rosewood sabre-leg chairs having carved pierced backs and cane seats	WE	21	0
Pair of late Georgian mahogany dining chairs, carved rail backs, the seats in grey tapestry	L	16	0
Pair of Regency chairs with brass inlay, on sabre legs, loose seats covered floral wool tapestry	L	12	10

Chairs—Dining—Victorian Sets

		£	s
Eight Victorian rosewood dining chairs with rope rail, cane-seats and velvet cushions	SE	92	0
Six Victorian rosewood chairs, the upholstered seats covered old gold fabric	L	56	0
Six early Victorian mahogany dining chairs	N	52	0
Six Victorian Gothic dining chairs with cane seats and bobbin-turned backs and legs with loose green cushions	SE	35	0

		£	s
Five Victorian mahogany chairs with carved roll-backs on turned legs with loose seats	WE	22	0
Four Victorian walnut hoop-back chairs with serpentine seat-rail and well-shaped cabriole legs	WE	21	0
Three Victorian walnut open-back chairs with stuffed serpentine seats, on cabriole legs	SE	15	0
Four Victorian mahogany spoon back dining chairs with seats and backs in red velvet	WE	9	10

Chairs—Easy

Chippendale wing easy chair	S	56	0
Georgian mahogany frame high-back easy chair having square chamfered legs, upholstered blue	WE	41	0
French black and gilt shaped-back easy chair on cabriole legs	M	20	0
Victorian small buttoned chair	SE	18	0
Victorian carved walnut frame and button-back easy chair	SE	17	10
Small Victorian spoon-shaped easy chair on turned legs	M	16	10

Chairs—Elbow

Pair of Regency elbow chairs	WE	120	0
Pair of Adam-style elbow chairs	WE	90	0
James I elbow chair in oak on baluster legs and plain stretchers, and with carved arch and diamond motif to panel back	SE	72	0
Georgian mahogany upholstered open elbow chair with serpentine seat rail	WE	57	0
Hepplewhite painted mahogany-framed elbow chair	M	50	0
Pair of Regency mahogany elbow chairs with X-shaped backs, stuffed seats, on stretcher frames	SE	42	0
Hepplewhite gilt and ebonised elbow chair	SE	40	0
Victorian walnut elbow chair	SE	27	0
Late eighteenth-century ebonised and carved frame elbow chair with claw carving to elbows and spiral fluted legs	WE	19	0
Victorian mahogany elbow chair with back, seat and elbows in Genoese-style velvet	SE	12	0
Victorian button-back elbow chair in tapestry with carved walnut frame	WE	7	0
Eighteenth-century elm ladder-back elbow chair with wide back and well-shaped outswept arms, solid seat on square legs	W	9	0

Chests of Drawers

Sheraton crossbanded satinwood bowfront chest of four graduated long drawers with fitted top drawer, brass-ring handles and splay feet, 3 ft 3 in	M	590	0
William and Mary oyster and marquetry chest of drawers	SE	260	0
Eighteenth-century marquetry inlaid oyster walnut chest with satinwood banding, fitted two short and three graduated long drawers, on bun feet, 3 ft 1 in	SE	160	0
William and Mary oyster walnut chest inlaid and banded with satinwood, fitted four graduated long drawers, on bun feet, 3 ft 2 in	SE	120	0
Georgian mahogany bachelor chest of four graduated drawers, brushing slide, brass drop-handles, pierced back plates and escutcheons, shaped bracket feet	WE	110	0

		£	s
George II walnut-wood bachelor's chest, with conventional folding top, and fitted with two small and three long drawers, 2 ft 10 in wide	M	105	0
William and Mary oyster-wood straight-front chest of three long and two short drawers with brass drop-handles, on bun feet, 3 ft 3 in	L	86	0
Georgian mahogany square front chest with brushing slide and four graduated drawers, fitted brass-loop handles; on bracket feet; plate glass protector; 2 ft 9 in wide	SE	72	0
George III figured bow-front chest of drawers	SE	60	0
Sheraton banded mahogany chest of three long drawers, 3 ft	SE	60	0
Eighteenth-century walnut chest of three short and three long graduated drawers. Front richly figured and top cross-banded, on bracket feet, 3 ft 5 in by 1 ft 11 in	SE	56	0
Hepplewhite mahogany bow-front chest, four long drawers on splay feet with brushing slide, 3 ft 4 in	M	46	0
Georgian mahogany chest of drawers of four long graduated drawers, oak lined, and with brass drop-handles, splayed feet, 2 ft 9 in	L	44	0
Yew chest of two long and two short drawers with brass bail handles, 3 ft	SE	42	0
Georgian mahogany bow-front chest	WE	40	0
Georgian mahogany chest of four drawers, brass swan-neck handles, ring back plates, on bracket feet	WE	37	0
Georgian mahogany and inlaid bow-fronted chest of five drawers with brass handles, on splayed feet, 3 ft 6 in	SE	35	0
Georgian mahogany straight-front chest of four graduated drawers, brass drop-handles, shaped bracket feet, 33 in by 35 in	WE	34	0
Georgian fruitwood chest of two short and three long drawers, on bracket feet	SE	30	0
Stuart oak chest of four drawers	WE	26	0
Georgian mahogany bow-front chest of two long and two short drawers on splayed feet, 3 ft 5 in	L	24	0
Jacobean oak chest of two short and three long drawers with old drop brasses and on ball feet, 3 ft 1 in wide	SE	23	0
Georgian mahogany chest of two short and three long drawers, bracket feet, 3 ft 5 in	L	19	0
Eighteenth-century oak chest of five drawers on bracket feet, the drawer fronts veneered in figured walnut with contemporary brass drop-handles, fretted back plates and escutcheons, 3 ft	M	16	0
Early nineteenth-century mahogany bow-front chest on splay bracket feet having reeded top and ebony stringing, two short and four long drawers, 3 ft 6 in	WE	15	0
Georgian walnut wood chest of two short and three long drawers, on bracket feet, 3 ft 5 in	L	15	0
Nineteenth-century mahogany chest of three long and two short drawers, with a scrolled plinth, 3 ft 6 in	L	14	0

Chests—Military

		£	s
Teak military chest with secretaire drawer, 2 ft 4 in	SE	106	0
Teak military chest with secretaire drawer, two short and three long drawers; on bun feet, 3 ft 3 in	SE	88	0

		£	s
Oak military chest with secretaire drawer, 3 ft	SE	82	0
Military secretaire chest of drawers	S	75	0
Oak military chest of drawers	SE	66	0

Chiffoniers

		£	s
Regency rosewood chiffonier	M	240	0
Small Regency rosewood chiffonier	SE	72	0
Regency olive-green lacquer chiffonier, with two doors with oval panels decorated with figures in garden landscapes in gilt on vermillion lacquer, and with open superstructure	M	65	0
Rosewood chiffonier, fitted one long drawer and cupboard under, 3 ft 6 in wide	L	15	0

Coffers

		£	s
Carved coffer, *circa* 1590, 3 ft 8 in	SE	68	0
Carved seventeenth-century oak coffer, panel divided into a symbolic life of Christ, 5 ft	SE	50	0
Eighteenth-century domed-top oak coffer, 33 in	SE	42	0
Early sixteenth-century oak coffer with gouged and carved panel decoration, 3 ft 9 in	SE	40	0
Early sixteenth-century oak coffer with diamond decoration, on solid supports, 3 ft 10 in	SE	34	0
Carved and panelled oak dower chest with lift-up lid, 3 ft 7 in	SE	25	0
Jacobean carved and panelled oak coffer, 4 ft 2 in	M	22	0
Old oak coffer with carved three-arch front, 3 ft 3 in	L	16	0

Cupboards

		£	s
Early eighteenth-century oak bacon-cupboard with two doors enclosing original wood pegs, two short and four long drawers below with drop ring brasses	SE	78	0
Early seventeenth-century oak court-cupboard with two panelled doors to top, a long drawer and open base, the whole carved in the manner of the period, 3 ft 9 in	SE	58	0
Early seventeenth-century oak court-cupboard with carved and panelled front and sides enclosed by six doors, on bun feet, 4 ft 4 in	SE	44	0
Small seventeenth-century oak cupboard, panelled door with gouged decoration	SE	38	0
Oak cupboard, with carved panelled door and wide wrought-iron hinges, 32 in	SE	38	0
Early eighteenth-century oak food-cupboard, with panelled doors, enclosing shelves	SE	34	0
Georgian bleached pine linen-cupboard enclosed pair panel doors and fitted four drawers to base, 4 ft wide	WE	33	0
Elizabethan cupboard with open base, plain panels, styles, frieze and other borders of simple carved design, 3 ft 10 in wide, 4 ft 9 in high	WE	30	0
Oak court-cupboard with open compartment above and cupboard under enclosed by carved quartered panel door, wrought-iron hinges, 27 in wide	L	27	0

Cupboards—Corner

		£	s
Early eighteenth-century small Dutch pine hanging corner-cupboard, painted in floral design in reserved panels; the single door enclosing three shelves	WE	50	0

		£	s
George III mahogany bow-front corner-cupboard with two doors on brass 'H' hinges, enclosing three shelves and three small drawers, width 26 in, height 43 in	SE	46	0
Inlaid mahogany double corner-cupboard	S	44	0
Carved oak Dutch double corner-cupboard with domed glazed door, flap and two doors below, standing on ball feet, 3 ft 6 in wide overall, 7 ft high	SE	40	0
Mahogany and inlaid bow-front hanging corner-cupboard enclosed by two doors, 2 ft 2 in	SE	38	0
Welsh oak hanging-cupboard, with three drawers in base and with panel front and ends, 3 ft 10 in wide, 5 ft 4 in high	SE	32	0
Late eighteenth-century English black and gilt lacquer bow-front hanging corner-cupboard decorated in the Chinese style, 24 in wide	WE	31	0
Mahogany standing corner-cupboard with four shelves enclosed by four panelled doors, 3 ft 6 in	SE	25	0
Georgian mahogany hanging-cupboard with dentil and fluted cornice and one drawer in the base, on bracket feet, 4 ft 4 in	SE	20	0
Queen Anne lacquer corner-cupboard with shaped shelves	WE	19	10
Oak corner-cupboard, fitted shelves, enclosed by a pair of panel doors, bracket feet, 3 ft	L	19	0
Georgian inlaid oak bow-front hanging corner-cupboard	WE	18	0
Georgian cross-banded oak bow-front hanging corner-cupboard enclosed two doors, 2 ft 8 in wide	WE	16	0
Nineteenth-century hanging-cupboard enclosed by two panelled doors with scroll pediment and pillar sides, four drawers, 4 ft	SE	16	0
Eighteenth-century inlaid corner-cupboard containing two shaped shelves, 2 ft 6 in	M	13	0

Davenports

Regency rosewood Davenport with gallery	M	60	0
Victorian mahogany Davenport fitted lined writing slide enclosed by a piano front and fitted four drawers, 21 in wide	L	46	0
Victorian inlaid rosewood Davenport, the lid inset with a leather panel and the interior containing two small drawers, with four pedestal drawers and on circular feet, 1 ft 9 in	M	36	0
Victorian figured-walnut Davenport with rising superstructure, pull-out writing slide and fittings and four drawers below (in need of repair)	WE	25	0
Victorian rosewood Davenport, fitted four drawers, 21 in	L	21	0

Desks

Georgian mahogany kneehole writing-desk with two long and six short drawers and cupboard to recess with original handles, on bracket feet, 2 ft 6 in	SE	160	0
Nineteenth-century mahogany and satinwood writing-desk with tambour front and drawers above; two frieze drawers, painted with swags, and portrait medallions; on square tapering legs, 3 ft wide	SE	155	0

		£	s
Chippendale mahogany kneehole desk with sliding carved door and centre cupboard and brass handles, on bracket feet, 3 ft	SE	150	0
Mid-nineteenth century mahogany kneehole writing-desk with frieze drawer and eight drawers fitted chased brass knob handles; red leather top with gilt tooled border (stamped W. Priest, Blackfriars), width 3 ft 11 in	SE	70	0

Dressers

		£	s
Early eighteenth-century Welsh oak dresser	SE	88	0
Old English oak dresser with three drawers and carved front on turned club legs; fitted brass handles and key-plates, width 5 ft 6 in. No shelves	SE	65	0
Georgian oak dresser bordered in mahogany, arranged with three drawers and three panel doors, furnished in brass bow handles on cut plates, 6 ft	L	50	0
Eighteenth-century oak dresser, fitted three drawers, on turned legs and platform base, 5 ft 11 in	L	39	0
Oak dresser base with three drawers having drop-ring brasses, turned supports with bun feet, 6 ft 3 in in length	SE	37	0
Oak Welsh dresser with three drawers and three panelled doors to base, 5 ft 6 in	SE	30	0
Early eighteenth-century oak dresser containing four short and four long drawers, on bracket feet, metal fittings, 6 ft	M	26	0

Firescreens

		£	s
Georgian pole-screen with carved tripod and claw feet, the panel with Jacobite needlework figures in a formal garden	M	75	0
Pair of Victorian rosewood pedestal pole-screens with wool-work panels	M	32	0
Regency inlaid mahogany brass pole banner-screen with lacquer panel	WE	27	0
Mahogany pole-firescreen with needlework octagonal panel, on tripod base	M	12	0
Victorian rosewood pole-firescreen on carved scroll tripod base, the banner in wool and tapestry work with a parrot	SE	11	0
Mahogany pole-screen with *papier mâché* panel	WE	8	10
Nineteenth-century pole firescreen with shaped banner	SE	7	10

Jardinières

		£	s
Square carved Oriental hardwood *jardinière* stand with in-set marble top, 16 in	L	9	10
Victorian mahogany drum-shaped *jardinière* with metal liner and on cabriole legs	SE	7	0
Mahogany *jardinière* stand, pillar and tripod support	SE	5	10
Pair of Chinese hardwood *jardinières*	SE	2	10

Library Furniture

		£	s
Regency library table	SE	560	0
Georgian mahogany breakfront library bookcase	L	200	0
Regency mahogany-framed library chair-steps	WE	120	0
Small Regency oval satinwood library table	SE	72	0
Set of eighteenth-century mahogany library steps	SE	56	0

Mirrors—Cheval

		£	s
Domed-top mahogany cheval mirror	WE	12	10

		£	s
Georgian mahogany cheval mirror on shaped supports	SE	6	10

Mirrors—Mantel

Regency mantel mirror of three panels in giltwood frame	WE	5	5
Regency mantel mirror of three panels in giltwood frame	WE	5	0

Mirrors—Pier Glasses

Chippendale giltwood pier glass, 48 in by 25 in	L	280	0
Queen Anne gilt-framed pier glass	M	22	0
Pair of large gilt-framed pier glasses	M	20	0

Mirrors—Toilet or Dressing

Sheraton mahogany bow-front box toilet mirror with shield-shaped glass	M	32	0
Eighteenth-century inlaid mahogany oval toilet mirror on serpentine base containing three drawers, ogee feet, 14½ in	M	25	0
Nelson mahogany swing dressing mirror	NI	22	10
Georgian mahogany swing-frame toilet mirror with antique bevelled glass and three drawers	SE	20	0
Toilet wig-patch mirror with magnifying glass on turned pillar and frame	WE	11	0

Mirrors—Wall

Eighteenth-century Chippendale gilt mirror	SE	505	0
Eighteenth-century wall mirror in Chippendale carved gilt-wood	SE	200	0
Eighteenth-century gilt-framed wall mirror	SE	100	0
Carved giltwood and pierced frame wall mirror in the Chippendale-style having rococo floral and husk decoration, 5 ft 1 in by 3 ft	WE	88	0
Walnut frame wall mirror of Chippendale-design	M	74	0
Late eighteenth-century convex wall mirror in gilt frame with an eagle at the top and carved leafage decoration, two candle sconces with Irish glass sconces and drops 32 in by 39 in high	SE	62	0
Chippendale mahogany frame wall mirror with bevelled plate, 1 ft 7 in by 1 ft 1 in	SE	40	0
Queen Anne domed pinewood wall mirror with original hand-bevelled plate, 3 ft by 1 ft 8 in	SE	38	0
Gilt frame oval girandole with two pairs of candle brackets, 45 in by 35 in plate	L	36	0
Queen Anne upright wall mirror	WE	32	0
Carved gilt frame mirror with scrolled leaf decoration, 34 in by 20 in plate	L	28	0
Gilt frame mirror with carved surmount of horses and flowers, 25 in by 17 in plate	L	26	0
Gilt carved girandole mirror	M	24	0
Sheraton wall mirror with bevelled glass, set in carved and inlaid frame	SE	22	0
Early English gilt-framed wall mirror	M	12	0
Oval wall mirror with gilt frame, carved with ivy leaf design	SE	5	0
Mahogany-framed wall mirror	M	4	10
Rosewood-framed wall mirror	M	3	0

Settees, Couches, Chaise-longues, etc.
Winged-back *bergère* of Louis XV-design with finely carved

		£	s
giltwood frame; figured pink silk upholstery; on cabriole front legs with knurled feet	SE	135	0
Sheraton painted settee	SE	80	0
Chaise-longue in the Louis XVI-style with double canewood panels, carved ribbon cresting and turned fluted legs, comprising two fauteuils, each with a squab cushion and footrest	L	68	0
Victorian carved walnut frame and button-back settee upholstered crimson velour	WE	47	0
Louis XVI-style gilt frame salon settee, seat and back covered beige tapestry, floral and figures, 4 ft 5 in	L	30	0
Victorian carved walnut-wood couch, covered fawn moquette	L	30	0
Regency rosewood lyre-shaped settee with upholstered seat and back, and cushions, 7 ft long	M	25	0
French painted beechwood chaise-longue or duchesse, with seat back ends, frame painted pale green with slight floral decoration with *bergère* back panels and seat on turned legs, 6 ft 6 in	WE	25	0
Victorian double-ended open-back settee on spiral twist supports	M	19	0
Victorian settee of Regency-design carved mahogany horsehair covered seat and bolster cushion	L	12	0

Settles

		£	s
Early eighteenth-century Welsh oak settle	SE	50	0
Settle with a box seat, panel front and back, of the Stuart period, 4 ft 9 in	SE	42	0
Carved oak settle with lion arms and rising box seat, 3 ft 4 in wide	L	28	0
Nineteenth-century carved oak hall settle having lift seat, 3 ft wide	WE	15	0
Seventeenth-century oak settle carved and panelled, 3 ft 9 in	SE	14	0

Sideboards

		£	s
Hepplewhite mahogany serpentine-front sideboard, fitted centre drawer and two deep side drawers, on six taper supports with spade feet, 5 ft 1 in	SE	300	0
Sheraton bow-and-breakfront inlaid mahogany sideboard, 6 ft	M	275	0
Hepplewhite bow-fronted sideboard	SE	155	0
Sheraton mahogany and satinwood inlaid serpentine sideboard with drawers and cellarette, brass handles, on taper legs, 5 ft	SE	150	0
Georgian mahogany bow-fronted sideboard on square tapered legs, fitted three drawers, 4 ft 10 in wide	WE	142	0
Regency mahogany sideboard, 3 ft	SE	106	0
Georgian mahogany bow-front sideboard	L	102	0
Early nineteenth-century bow-front mahogany sideboard, cross-banded in coloured woods	M	78	0
Georgian mahogany serpentine sideboard, with two cupboards and a drawer, 6 ft 4 in wide	M	60	0
Inlaid mahogany bow-front sideboard, square tapering supports and box toes, 9 ft 4 in long	WE	42	0
Late Georgian mahogany bow-fronted sideboard with three drawers and two cellarette drawers, on six tapered supports, 5 ft 4 in wide	M	28	0

		£	s
Stools			
Queen Anne period stool in original condition	WE	90	0
Pair of Chippendale stools with upholstered tops	M	85	0
Regency ebonised and gilt scroll X-frame cane seat stool	WE	80	0
Early eighteenth-century oak stool	SE	70	0
Regency bamboo duet stool	M	48	0
Sixteenth-century oak coffin stool	M	42	0
Seventeenth-century oak joynt stool	SE	40	0
Eighteenth-century joynt stool on turned legs	SE	38	0
Seventeenth-century oak joynt stool	SE	30	0
Eighteenth-century oak joynt stool on baluster supports	SE	28	0
Early Victorian carved walnut serpentine shape stool on cabriole legs	WE	26	0
Early seventeenth-century stool on stretcher base, 14 in	SE	26	0
Square upholstered stool on cabriole legs with spade feet	WE	16	0
Georgian revolving piano stool	M	16	0
Victorian rosewood stool, the square top in floral needle-work on curving X-shaped supports	WE	12	0

Tables—Card			
Ormolu-mounted kingwood cross-banded folding shaped card table	SE	175	0
Ebonised and red buhl card table with serpentine folding top, ormolu beading and mouldings, etc; mask mounts on knees of the cabriole legs, width 3 ft	SE	160	0
Georgian mahogany card table of rectangular form with projecting corners, triple folding top, baize-lined and in-laid for chess and backgammon; on cabriole legs with club feet, width 24 in	SE	125	0
Sheraton inlaid and painted satinwood card table	M	120	0
Late nineteenth-century mahogany card table with brass mounts	M	90	0
Sheraton inlaid and cross-banded mahogany card table on tapered supports and original castors, 3 ft	SE	70	0
Sheraton mahogany half-round card table on taper legs	M	66	0
Victorian rosewood pedestal card table, with baize-lined top, on stem and four splayed feet, elaborately carved with foliage, width 3 ft	SE	60	0
Sheraton mahogany D-shaped card table on taper legs	M	50	0
Nineteenth-century inlaid rosewood envelope-topped card table with green baize interior, tapered supports on castors and with drawer, 21 in wide to 2 ft 6 in, 2 ft 3 in high	SE	46	0
Hepplewhite mahogany rectangular folding-top card table with polished interior, deep banded top, square tapered supports on spade feet, 32 in wide	SE	32	0
Victorian walnut card table	N	27	0
Victorian burr-walnut card table	M	20	0
Victorian mahogany card table, the folding-flap lined with green baize, on flat end supports and turned stretcher, 18 in wide	L	20	0
Victorian mahogany folding-top card table on carved pillar and quadruple support with brass nosings	L	17	0
Victorian rosewood card table on pillar and shaped base, 3 ft	L	12	10

	£	s
William IV mahogany card table with fold-over flap top, half-reeded column and circular base with scroll carved feet, 3 ft	L 12	0
Nineteenth-century mahogany folding card table with red baize interior and on pedestal and quadruped platform base, 36 in wide	SE 5	10

Tables—Centre

Rosewood centre table the top of oysterwood with floral and pictorial inlays	S 38	0
Georgian mahogany centre table on turned pedestal, tripod support having claw feet, pie-crust top and birdcage underframe, 2 ft 9 in diameter	WE 24	0
Victorian inlaid walnut oval centre table on carved pedestal, 4 ft 6 in by 3 ft	WE 22	0
Victorian rosewood centre table on carved pedestal supports, fitted two drawers either side, 4 ft 2 in	WE 18	0

Tables—Dining

George III three-pedestal dining table	L 560	0
Twin pedestal dining table of Georgian design	WE 240	0
Georgian mahogany twin-pillar dining table	L 190	0
Late Georgian mahogany circular tip-up dining table on pillar with quadruple legs, inlaid with boxwood stringing, 49 in	SE 125	0
Georgian mahogany dining table with double flaps and two 'D'-ends, supported on reeded and tapering legs, overall length 7 ft 5 in, width 3 ft 4 in	M 100	0
Late Georgian twin-pillar dining table	M 95	0
Regency mahogany twin-pedestal dining table	WE 92	0
Heavy Chippendale circular mahogany dining table	SE 90	0
Eighteenth-century yew wood cottage dining table on turned supports, 2 ft 10 in	SE 76	0
Mahogany 'D'-end dining table, a Georgian-style table with two semi-circular ends and a gate-leg centre section on square taper legs with inlaid stringing and chains of husks, 10 ft 1 in by 4 ft 3 in	WE 61	0
Georgian faded mahogany dining table having satinwood banding, comprising 'D'-shaped end sections with square tapering legs and centre leaf, 5 ft 9 in	L 36	0
Georgian mahogany tilt-top dining table on turned pedestal with four carved splay legs, brass-nosed feet, 5 ft by 4 ft	WE 33	0
Georgian mahogany cross banded 'D'-end dining table with centre leaf, 5 ft 9 in by 4 ft	WE 30	0
Mahogany dining table on fluted legs, two leaves	S 25	0
Victorian walnut-wood oval top table on turned pillar and quadruple claw, 4 ft 6 in	L 21	0
Victorian inlaid walnut-wood oval top table on carved pillar and tripod support, 4 ft 6 in wide	L 20	0
Mahogany drop-leaf dining table on club feet, top 3 ft 6 in by 1 ft 2 in, extending open to 3 ft 5 in	SE 18	0

Tables—Gatelegged

Early English fruitwood gateleg table	SE 180	0
Seventeenth-century oak gateleg table	WE 70	0

		£	s
Oak gateleg table with drawer	M	42	0
Oak gateleg table, 3 ft 3 in	M	28	0
Old English oak gateleg table having oval top, drawer and turned baluster legs, 3 ft 5 in	L	25	0

Tables—Occasional

		£	s
Pair of Sheraton-period oval mahogany occasional tables	SE	420	0
Sheraton satinwood occasional two-flap table with unusual quartering to the veneer	M	400	0
Pair of Victorian inlaid walnut occasional tables of French design with serpentine tops and cabriole legs; each with one drawer, width 28 in	SE	90	0
Fruit-wood occasional table, with drawer	S	32	10
Gilt-decorated mahogany circular occasional table, 38½ in diameter	N	28	0
Inlaid mahogany rectangular nineteenth-century occasional table with satinwood band, square tapered supports and cross stretchers, top 27 in by 15 in	SE	15	0
Georgian mahogany tripod table having 'birdcage' square top and turned column, 2 ft square	L	13	0
Victorian figured-walnut oval top occasional table, on carved quadruple support, 2 ft 9 in	L	10	10
Rectangular nineteenth-century mahogany tip-top occasional table on pedestal and tripod, top 26 in by 18 in	SE	6	10

Tables—Pembroke

		£	s
Sheraton mahogany Pembroke table	M	100	0
Mahogany Pembroke table on taper legs	M	42	0
Sheraton mahogany oval Pembroke table, the frieze drawer inlaid with boxwood stringings, 3 ft 9 in	M	40	0
Oval mahogany Pembroke table	SE	37	0
Regency mahogany Pembroke table, one drawer with wood knop handles, cylindrical pillar on four scroll supports	L	20	0
Georgian Pembroke mahogany table, fitted drawer, on square tapering legs, 30 in	L	10	0

Tables—Refectory

		£	s
Seventeenth-century oak refectory table of fine colour on turned legs and ground stretchers, 6 ft 10 in	SE	85	0
Early oak refectory table, fitted drawer, on turned supports and ground stretchers, 7 ft by 2 ft 8 in	L	60	0
Old Flemish oak refectory table in the seventeenth-century style having turned legs with square stretchers, 5 ft 2 in by 2 ft 4 in	L	45	0
Solid elm refectory table, the rectangular top 6 ft 2 in by 2 ft 6 in, on turned bulbous legs with 'H' stretcher	WE	37	0
Oak refectory table on square end supports with stretcher, 6 ft by 2 ft 8 in	L	34	0
Oak refectory table on melon supports, 6 ft 6 in	SE	32	0

Tables—Side

		£	s
Sheraton inlaid satinwood side or sewing table of semi-circular shape with drawer and wing compartments, 3 ft 6 in	M	810	0
Sheraton satinwood and crossbanded side table on taper legs, 5 ft	SE	360	0

M

		£	s
George III gilt gesso side table	L	290	0
Early Georgian mahogany side table with two frieze drawers, centre cellarette, on shaped four-splay pedestal with brass toes	M	155	0
Dutch marquetry side table, serpentine, on carved cabriole legs, claw and ball feet, six drawers	S	135	0
William and Mary marquetry inlaid table on barley twist legs with concave stretchers and fitted secretaire drawer, 2 ft 11 in	L	75	0
Sheraton mahogany, satinwood banded and inlaid side table fitted drawer with brass handle and having canted corners on square tapering legs, 3 ft 3 in wide	L	52	0
Eighteenth-century mahogany serpentine side table with single drawer	WE	42	0
Early eighteenth-century oak side table with drawer, on turned supports and stretcher base, 2 ft 6 in	SE	30	0
Early eighteenth-century oak side table, the shaped frieze containing three drawers and on circular tapering legs and pad feet, brass handle, 2 ft 8 in	M	27	0
Georgian oak side table, fitted drawers, on cabriole legs, 30 in	L	23	0
Georgian walnut fold-over side table	M	18	0
Regency mahogany side table on round tapered legs with brass mounts, black marble top, 4 ft 7 in wide	WE	16	0
Victorian mahogany side table with two drawers, on end supports	M	9	0

Tables—Sofa

		£	s
Sheraton sofa table, 57 in by 26 in extended	L	490	0
Regency mahogany sofa table	L	300	0
Sheraton inlaid sofa table, 5 ft 4 in by 1 ft 11½ in	N	220	0
Regency inlaid rosewood sofa table containing two drawers and on twin ringed and carved pedestals with turned stretcher and curved legs with brass nosings and castors, 5 ft 6 in	M	155	0
Regency rosewood sofa table with brass line inlay, fitted two mahogany lined drawers, and end flaps, on two pillar and quadruple supports with brass claw nosings, 4 ft 11 in opened	L	130	0
Walnut sofa table, crossbanded, with brass toes	NI	77	10
Banded rosewood sofa table	SE	62	0

Tables—Sutherland

		£	s
Nineteenth-century figured walnut Sutherland table	WE	34	0
Victorian walnut shaped-top Sutherland table on turned supports, 3 ft by 2 ft 10 in	WE	23	0
Figured walnut oval top two-flap Sutherland table, on turned legs and stretcher, 3 ft wide	L	22	0
Walnut Sutherland table having turned end supports and stretcher	L	15	0
Victorian mahogany oval Sutherland table on carved supports	WE	15	0
Nineteenth-century inlaid mahogany swivel-top Sutherland table with under tray, 24 in wide	SE	14	0
Sutherland inlaid mahogany table, 24 in	L	10	10

		£	s
Mahogany Sutherland tea table with oval top, turned legs and stretchers, 1 ft 9 in	L	9	0
Victorian oak Sutherland table	M	5	0

Tables—Tea

		£	s
George III semi-circular tea table, 3 ft 2 in	M	80	0
Sheraton mahogany folding 'D'-top tea table, cross banded, inlaid with boxwood and satinwood stringing, frieze drawer with brass knop handle, square tapering supports	WE	60	0
Late eighteenth-century mahogany folding-top tea table on centre pedestal with four splay legs, 3 ft wide	WE	56	0
Regency mahogany folding-top tea table on carved pedestal with four reeded splay legs having brass nosed feet, 2 ft 9 in wide	WE	40	0
Georgian mahogany fold-top tea table with turned tapering supports	WE	36	0
Circular rosewood pedestal tea table	S	24	0
Georgian mahogany folding-top tea table on square chamfered legs fitted drawer, 2 ft 9 in wide	WE	19	0
Victorian mahogany folding-top and revolving tea table on carved pedestal support, 3 ft wide	WE	16	0
Early nineteenth-century mahogany tea table with galleried top, 1 ft 10 in by 1 ft 5 in on turned column and swept tripod base	WE	8	0
Victorian mahogany tea table having dished top with slides, undertier and cabriole legs, 1 ft 10 in	L	7	0

Tables—Wine

		£	s
Hepplewhite shaped octagonal wine or reading table on barley-twist pillar and tripod base, 1 ft 5 in	SE	70	0
Red painted and lacquered Regency wine table, 18 in	SE	33	0
Circular walnut-top table on oak tripod base, 19 in	SE	24	0
Mahogany snaptop stand on pillar and tripod	SE	14	10
Victorian rosewood wine table with carved feather edge, twist pedestal and on tripod, 22 in diameter	SE	10	10
Georgian oak circular-top tripod table, 21 in	L	6	0

Tables—Work

		£	s
Sheraton mahogany work table with cross banded top and back flap; two fitted drawers and brass knob handles; on turned ring supports	SE	78	0
Lady's Regency rosewood work table	M	70	0
Hepplewhite mahogany octagonal work table on taper legs with cross stretchers	M	48	0
Georgian mahogany two-drawer work table on turned legs	M	47	0
Early nineteenth-century cross-banded satinwood worktable on turned legs, 22 in by 16 in	WE	42	0
Georgian mahogany two-flap work table with two drawers on turned legs	M	42	0
Sheraton inlaid satinwood work table with rising top, tapered supports and undertier, on original brass feet	SE	40	0
Victorian carved walnut-wood work table having shaped top on quadrant support with splay feet	L	22	0
Early Victorian black lacquer work table	SE	19	0

		£	s

Tables—Writing

		£	s
William and Mary walnut-wood and marquetry kneehole writing table, 3 ft wide, 2 ft 7 in high	L	415	0
Nineteenth-century satinwood writing table, 2 ft 10 in wide	SE	270	0
Eighteenth-century mahogany kneehole writing table with frieze drawer and six side drawers, fitted brass handles; recess cupboard and bracket feet, 2 ft 6 in wide, 31 in high	SE	175	0
Early Victorian inlaid walnut writing table	SE	85	0
Small Regency mahogany writing table	SE	72	0
Nineteenth-century inlaid mahogany enclosed writing table	SE	70	0
Georgian walnut small writing table	M	50	0
Sheraton inlaid mahogany writing table	SE	50	0
William IV mahogany writing table, the rectangular top with rounded corners and reeded edge, two drawers below on turned and fluted legs with brass castors, 3 ft 1 in by 2 ft	WE	30	0
Early nineteenth-century mahogany lady's writing table on turned bamboo legs, fitted drawer, 22 in wide	WE	16	0
Victorian rosewood writing table with leather inlaid top, two drawers, on turned and carved pillar supports	SE	11	0

Tallboys and Lowboys

		£	s
George III walnut-wood tallboy with three small and three long drawers to the top, three single frieze drawers to the base above a waved apron, supported on cabriole legs and ending in claw and ball feet	M	225	0
Eighteenth-century tallboy in walnut with sunburst inlay	M	180	0
George I figured walnut tallboy	WE	155	0
Small eighteenth-century oak tallboy	SE	80	0
Chippendale mahogany tallboy	WE	80	0
Georgian mahogany tallboy on bracket feet having dentil cornice and fret-canted corners, fitted eight drawers, 3 ft 6 in wide	WE	62	0
Eighteenth-century mahogany tallboy	WE	52	0
Queen Anne oak lowboy fitted two short and three long drawers and a further drawer to the projecting plinth, on short turned supports, the oak-lined drawers with brass pear-drop handles, 3 ft 4 in wide by 4 ft 1 in	WE	40	0
William and Mary walnut lowboy with crossbanded and herringbone inlay on top, three long and two short drawers, on cabriole legs, 3 ft 3 in	SE	33	0
Georgian mahogany straight-front tallboy, five long and two short drawers, brass swan-neck handles, 5 ft	WE	26	0
Eighteenth-century mahogany tallboy fitted two short and six long drawers with brass dropped handles, on bracket feet, 3 ft 9 in	WE	22	0
Mahogany tallboy, brass drop-ring handles, chamfered corners	WE	12	10

Torchères

		£	s
Regency *torchère*	WE	20	0
Victorian mahogany *torchère*	WE	12	0
Victorian china tall *torchère* on blue, green and yellow ground with decorations and acanthus leaves	SE	5	0

		£	s
Mahogany *torchère* with carved and spiral column, on square base	L	3	10
Two Hepplewhite-style mahogany *torchères*	L	3	0
Torchère with fluted column on tripod support	L	2	15

Trays

Set of three Victorian black *papier mâché* tea-trays in graduated sizes, decorated flowers and butterflies	L	39	0
Early nineteenth-century japanned tray	WE	28	0
Sheraton inlaid mahogany kidney-shape gallery tea-tray	L	12	0
Large *papier mâché* tray	M	8	0
Sheraton inlaid mahogany oval tea-tray	L	7	10
Large *papier mâché* tray	M	7	0
Tray inlaid design of mother of pearl	WE	6	0
Small *papier mâché* tray	M	3	10
Inlaid mahogany two-handled tea-tray	SE	3	0

Waiters—Dumb-waiters and Table Waiters

Georgian mahogany dumb-waiter formed of three diminishing tiers	M	48	0
Nineteenth-century dumb-waiter with three graduated circular tiers, on tripod supports	SE	46	0
Revolving mahogany table waiter	WE	14	0
Revolving mahogany table waiter	WE	9	0

Wardrobes

Eighteenth-century Dutch walnut wardrobe, 6 ft 2 in wide, 8 ft 2 in high	L	260	0
Gentleman's figured-mahogany wardrobe with sliding trays above and drawers below, 4 ft wide	M	24	0
Georgian mahogany two-panel door dwarf wardrobe	S	24	0
Gentleman's wardrobe or linen press, blue and gilt lacquered in the Chinese taste, the upper part fitted sliding trays, enclosed pair of drawers, two long and two short drawers under with brass drop-handles, 4 ft wide	L	21	0
Gentleman's Georgian inlaid mahogany wardrobe, enclosed pair of panelled doors, two long and two short drawers under, splayed feet, 4 ft	L	16	0
Gentleman's Georgian inlaid mahogany wardrobe, enclosed pair of panelled doors, two long and two short drawers under, on splayed bracket feet, 4 ft 6 in	L	11	0

Washstands

Sheraton mahogany enclosed washstand with lift-up top and canted corners, shell inlay, two drawers and cupboards	M	155	0
Shield-back carved washstand	S	35	0
Hepplewhite mahogany enclosed washstand	WE	32	0
Sheraton mahogany enclosed washstand, with hinged lid and fitted interior, the front with one dummy drawer, cupboard and two drawers below on turned and ringed legs, 2 ft 8 in	WE	27	0
Eighteenth-century mahogany corner-toilet-stand with inlaid stringing, one drawer and undershelf on splayed legs and complete with jug and basin	SE	21	0
Georgian mahogany washstand with splashback, two undershelves and three false drawers	SE	15	10

		£	s
Georgian mahogany two-tier square-top washstand, one drawer with brass drop handle	WE	12	0
Sheraton mahogany square washstand converted to vitrine with hinged top, glazed side panels and one drawer below	WE	12	0
Georgian mahogany bow-front corner-washstand, one real, two false drawers	WE	10	0
Georgian mahogany corner-washstand with two undershelves and drawer	SE	9	0
Eighteenth-century mahogany washstand, fitted small drawers and undershelf	WE	7	10

What-nots

Mahogany five-tier what-not	M	40	0
Pair of nineteenth-century corner what-nots of rosewood, on carved cabriole feet and serpentine to the front, in four graduated tiers on carved scroll supports, the top with fretted galleries	SE	30	0
Victorian mahogany three-tier oblong what-not	SE	7	0
Mahogany three-tier what-not with slender supports and fret top gallery, 13 in	L	5	0
Carved mahogany three-tier what-not, 21 in wide	L	4	0

Wine Coolers

Georgian 18 in inlaid mahogany octagonal wine cooler	N	135	0
Chippendale mahogany and brass-bound wine cooler (eight sides and short taper legs)	M	125	0
Hexagonal mahogany brass-bound wine cooler on stand	S	80	0
Old English mahogany wine cooler, banded with brass and having brass liner and swing handle, 15 in	L	40	0

CLOCKS, WATCHES AND BAROMETERS

Bracket Clocks

Early eighteenth-century English bracket clock by Daniel Delander, London	L	410	0
Mid-eighteenth century bracket clock, in ebonized case with leaf spandrels, by Gray and Vulliamy, London, 12 in high	SE	310	0
Bracket clock of chased design, in ebonized and ormolu-enriched case, by John Ellicott, London, eighteenth century, 16 in high	SE	180	0
Striking, early arch-dial bracket clock of excellent quality, in red and gilt lacquer case, by William Gatford, Uxbridge, mid-eighteenth century, 22 in high	SE	160	0
Regency bracket clock, by Recordon and Dupont, London, in ebony case mounted in ormolu, the domed-hood with vase finial, 28 in high overall	M	145	0
Early eighteenth-century striking bracket clock in oak case, with ormolu enrichments and double bracket top, pierced side grills, etc., engraved face with Roman numerals, by John Berry, London. Engraved back plate and repeater movement, 20 in high	SE	130	0
Georgian bracket clock movement by William Challoner, London	SE	130	0

		£	s
George III bracket clock by F. Swindon, Brentford	SE	130	0
Small eighteenth-century bracket clock by Stephen Rimboult, London	M	110	0
Bracket clock by Wachter, in walnut case	SE	60	0
Bracket clock, gilded and silverized dial, by Barrie, Edinburgh	S	54	0
Mahogany bracket clock by Joannes Mondehare of London	SE	49	0
Eighteenth-century striking bracket clock, with barrel and verge escapement in ebonized case, 12 in high, believed to be by Henry Jones	SE	46	0
Eighteenth-century steel-faced quarter striking bracket clock in ebonized case, 7 in high	W	42	0
Early nineteenth-century eight-day chiming and striking bracket clock in ebonized brass-mounted case	SE	40	0
Nineteenth-century Louis XVI-style walnut and ormolu-mounted bracket clock with enamel dial. In perfect working order	SE	30	0
Mahogany-cased and brass-mounted eight-day bracket clock by Finnigans, Manchester, with round steel dial	SE	7	0

Carriage Clocks

Brass-cased carriage clock with fine porcelain panels of Eastern beauties, 5½ in	SE	115	0
Engraved brass carriage clock with repeater movement and enamel dial, in carrying case	SE	80	0
Brass carriage clocks, strike and repeat, recently overhauled, with case	WE	35	0
French carriage clock with repeater movement in gilt brass frame, height 6 in	SE	31	0
Brass carriage clock in travelling case	M	25	0
Brass lever movement carriage clock by Z. Barraclouch & Sons, Paris, in leather case	SE	13	0

Lantern Clocks

Miniature brass lantern clock, engraved and signed by Joseph Knibb, seventeenth century	SE	260	0
Mid-seventeenth century brass lantern clock, signed Jeffrey Bayley, at the Turnstile in Holburn, 12 in high	SE	125	0
Brass striking lantern clock by Charles Goode, late seventeenth century	SE	105	0
Dutch painted dial Friesland lantern clock, 16 in high, on contemporary bracket with canopy and mermaid side frets	SE	80	0
Nineteenth-century brass lantern clock having embossed brass dial with enamel numerals and figure surmount	L	53	0

Long-case Clocks

Eighteenth-century marquetry-inlaid long-case clock, with striking movement, by John Clowes, London, 1672-1713	SE	520	0
Inlaid walnut long-case clock, with pendulum beating 1¼ seconds, by John Davies of Windsor, the front of the base forming a door giving access to the pendulum for regulation, and containing a bull's-eye of glass through which the fob can be seen	SE	350	0
Walnut marquetry long-case clock by Edmund Card, London. Seventeenth century	SE	300	0

		£	s
Early eighteenth-century long-case clock by John Finch, London	L	250	0
Early eighteenth-century marquetry long-case clock with eight-day movement by George Bayford, Upper Shagwell	SE	190	0
Old English small long-case clock by Charles Gretton, Fleet Street, London, 6 ft 6 in high	SE	180	0
Eighteenth-century marquetry-inlaid long-case clock with eight-day movement by Charles Gretton, London	SE	150	0
Oak long-case clock by Gilbert Kidd, Malton	N	74	0
Oak grandmother clock, with brass and silvered dial, with Westminster chimes	NI	65	0
William and Mary long-cased lacquered clock by Elisha Curtis	SE	62	0
Grandfather clock with brass dial, inscribed Sam Townson of London, the case in figured walnut wood	L	58	0
Eight-day grandfather clock, by John Brown, Kirkaldie	N	50	0
Nineteenth-century year clock in mahogany grandfather case with steel dial, signed B. Russell, Norwich	SE	44	0
Grandfather clock in inlaid mahogany case with silverized dial by William Ballantyne, Edinburgh	S	44	0
Early eighteenth-century grandfather clock with eight-day striking movement by John Jackler, Kilkenny (apprenticed London 1697) in finely figured mahogany case, 13 in square brass dial with very finely engraved spandrels, cherub and crown design on dial, standing on ogee bracket feet	SE	36	0
Grandfather clock, oak case brass dial, by T. Haye of Melrose	S	32	0
Grandfather clock in mahogany case with painted dial	S	32	0
Oak-cased grandfather clock with brass dial by Samuel Buxton, Diss	M	25	0
Oak long-case clock with reeded pilasters, shaped hood, eight-day striking movement with embossed and engraved brass dial with date and luna panels by Kirkham, Holywell	WE	21	0
Carved oak long-case clock, eight-day striking movement, by Daniel Dalton, Church Lanford	WE	20	0
Oak miniature grandfather clock case, fitted with a movement by Henry Harper, London, having Roman face and cherub spandrels. Seventeenth century	SE	18	0
Eighteenth-century long-case clock by William Nicholson, Whitehaven	M	14	0
Oak-cased grandfather clock with eight-day striking movement and arched brass dial by McCabe, Belfast	SE	11	0
Oak-case 36-hour grandfather clock with square dial, Bromley, Horsham	SE	9	0
Oak-cased grandfather clock with painted dial and eight-day striking movement	SE	8	0
Oak-cased grandfather clock with 36-hour movement by J. Pearson, Towcester	SE	5	0

Mantel Clocks

		£	s
Seventeenth-century lantern striking mantel clock in engraved brass case and having steel movement, etc., German, 7 in high	SE	353	0

		£	s
Large Regency balloon mantel clock	SE	75	0
Louis Philippe ormolu mantel clock, modelled with a cupid painting a picture and inset with Sèvres porcelain plaques painted with flowers and cupids in brilliant colours, 12 in wide	M	60	0
Late eighteenth-century mantel clock with jewelled movement, by John Holmes, Strand, in brass case, 5 in high	SE	32	0
Early Victorian mantel clock by Payne of New Bond St, London, in carved walnut case	SE	24	0
Brass-cased mantel clock with painted enamel dial and mahogany side pilasters and top, 11 in	SE	12	0

Ormolu Clocks

Gilt ormolu timepiece, by Charles Frodsham, London, in ornate vine-decorated case with bronze recumbent child surmount, 17 in long, 14 in high	M	34	0
Small ormolu mantel clock with china face under glass shade	M	28	0
French gilt ormolu clock under glass shade	M	26	0
French eight-day ormolu mantel clock, the baroque case with flame motifs and satyrs by Ad Moudin	WE	12	0

Wall Clocks and Act of Parliament Clocks

Weight-driven wall clock with pendulum and brass dial, by Barden of Boreham	SE	70	0
Large Act of Parliament clock, with painted dial, in oak case	SE	30	0
Vienna wall clock in glazed oak case, 30 in by 12 in	SE	10	0
Mahogany and inlaid Act of Parliament clock	SE		15
Mahogany Act of Parliament clock by Wyatt of Blandford	SE		10

Watches

Silver-cased verge movement pocket watch by Edward Bax, Chichester	SE	35	0
Gentleman's pocket watch by John Walker of Cornhill, in 18-carat gold case	L	12	10
Gold half-hunter pocket watch, 18 carat	WE	9	0
Watch by Edward Roffey, London, silver case, London 1815	M	3	10

Banjo Barometers

Sheraton inlaid mahogany banjo barometer	WE	36	0
Regency rosewood banjo barometer	WE	20	0
Nineteenth-century mahogany banjo barometer	M	8	0
Mercury barometer and thermometer in mahogany banjo case by Coates, Devizes	WE	8	0
Nineteenth-century banjo-cased barometer and thermometer	SE	6	0

Stick Barometers

Walnut-cased stick barometer by Newton & Co	WE	70	0
Regency stick barometer in rosewood case inlaid with mother-of-pearl, height 38 in	SE	56	0
Stick barometer in mahogany case with herringbone inlay	WE	31	0

SILVER

(Troy weight: 20 pennyweights [dwt]=1 ounce [oz])

Baskets for Cakes or Fruit

George III rococo basket, London 1766, *28 oz*	M	215	0
George III pierced cake basket with foliated rim, the ground decorated with ears of wheat, by Charles Albridge and			

		£	s
Henry Green, London, *circa* 1769, *21 oz 10 dwt*	M	115	0
George III engraved cake basket with over-hang handle, 7 in diameter, by John Crouch and Thomas Hannan, London 1777/8, *34 oz*	WE	62	0
Victorian pierced and embossed cake basket with over-hang handle, 10 in diameter, London 1856/7, *24 oz*	WE	23	0

Brandy Saucepans

George III brandy saucepan and lid, engraved crest, by John Emes, London, *9½ oz*	SE	90	0

Butter Dish

William IV butter dish, cover and stand, the dish of circular form with reeded girdles, and square handles; moulded glass liner, by Charles Fox, London 1836, *17 oz*	SE	52	0

Candlesticks

Set of four George II table candlesticks, by John Priest, London 1752	L	1,500	0
Pair of George II 10 in cast candlesticks with twist columns, shell mounts and square bases, crested, by John Innocent, London 1755, *43 oz 10 dwt*	S	560	0
Pair of William IV square-base candlesticks, moulded and chased acanthus leaf decoration with matching sconces, by Henry Wilkinson, Sheffield 1832-1835, 9 in	WE	100	0
Pair of William IV candlesticks, *repoussé* with acanthus and plain cylindrical stems, by Henry Wilkinson, Sheffield 1832	M	80	0
Pair of George III square-base column candlesticks, by John Roberts, Sheffield, 1773	WE	65	0

Coffee Pots

George II coffee pot, Paul de Lamerie, London 1735, *30 oz*	L	1,000	0
Georgian plain-shaped coffee pot, by Richard Morton, Sheffield 1778	L	280	0
George II *repoussé* baluster coffee pot on fluted circular foot, the cover with vase finial, wood handle, London 1759, all in *26½ oz*	SE	165	0
George IV coffee pot, the ground embossed with floral swags and flower heads, the lid with floral and ivory knop, by John, Henry and Charles Lias, London 1825, *28 oz*	M	140	0
George III baluster coffee pot with *repoussé* body of flowers, scrolls and pineapples; domed lid and circular foot; wooden scroll handle, by Alice and George Burrows, London 1816, *19½ oz*	SE	92	0
Early Victorian hexagonal coffee pot, by Joseph and John Angell, London 1843, *28 oz 10 dwt*	WE	60	0

Cream Jugs

George III cream helmet engraved to rim and cartouche by Richard Ferris, Exeter, *circa* 1800, *3 oz 10 dwt*	SE	32	0
George III oviform cream jug embossed with swags and drapes, on circular foot, by Thomas Smith, London 1773, *2 oz 15 dwt*	SE	30	0
George III cream jug, flatly chased with girdles of festooning, by Robert Salmon, London 1793, *4 oz 5 dwt*	M	27	0
George III engraved cream jug, London 1807, *4 oz*	M	26	0

		£	s
Regency feather-edge cream jug, concave banding, on four ball feet, attributed to William Bateman, London 1819	WE	20	0

Cups

		£	s
Queen Anne cup and cover, Pierre Platel, London 1707, 90 oz	L	2,100	0
William III two-handled cup and cover, William Fawdery, London 1698	L	750	0
Charles II tumbler cup, Marmaduke Best, York 1674, 4 oz	L	300	0
George III 7 in plain two-handled loving cup, Newcastle 1769	N	80	0
George II plain two-handled cup with ogee-shaped body and reeded handles, possibly by John Langlands, Newcastle 1757, 6 oz	SE	55	0
George III loving cup with two scroll handles by Langlands and Robertson, Newcastle 1778, 10 oz	SE	46	0
George III plain two-handled loving cup on circular foot by George Culer, London 1791, 12¼ oz	SE	42	0

Jugs

		£	s
George I lidded jug, John White, London 1720, 44 oz	L	4,600	0
George III pear-shaped hot-water jug, with leather-cased handle, by J. Young, London 1776, 25 oz	WE	275	0
George III square-base pedestal hot-water jug, rising lid with pineapple finial, classical urn shape, London 1773, 11¾ in high, 27 oz	WE	250	0
George III pear-shaped hot-water jug by John Parker, London 1775, 24 oz 10 dwt	M	210	0

Knives

		£	s
Sheraton mahogany knife case, inlaid with star motifs in coloured woods and fitted with a set of twelve George III table knives and forks and twelve dessert knives and forks, with silver handles, by John Sykes & Co., Sheffield 1782	M	210	0

Dishes

		£	s
Set of four George III oblong octagonal entrée dishes and covers by Robert Makepeace, London 1795	M	850	0
Set of four George III kidney-shaped supper dishes, by William Bateman, London 1817, 81 oz 10 dwt	M	400	0
Pair of George IV octagonal-shaped entrée dishes by Alexander Edmunston, Edinburgh 1824	S	290	0
Pair of George III octagonal-shaped entrée dishes by John Edwards, London 1800	S	95	0
William IV oval cake or dessert dish, well pierced and chased, by Charles Fox, London 1835, width 10 in, 22½ oz	SE	58	0
Victorian double-handled oval entrée dish and cover, maker 'W.W.W.', London 1860, 36 oz 10 dwt	WE	42	0

Forks

		£	s
Set of six George III three-prong forks by Hester Bateman, London 1783	M	180	0
Set of seven George IV forks by R. Rutland, 1823, 16 oz 10 dwt	M	16	0
Six fiddle-pattern table forks engraved crest, London 1837, 14 oz	N	6	10

		£	s

Marrow Scoops

		£	s
George III plain marrow scoop by Peter and William Bateman, London 1809, *1 oz 10 dwt*	SE	15	0
Marrow scoop, London 1823, *1 oz 8 dwt*	WE	12	0

Mote Skimmers

Georgian mote skimmer by Hester Bateman	SE	21	0
George III mote skimmer by 'I.D.'	SE	15	0
George III mote skimmer by 'W.T.'	SE	18	0

Mugs

George II baluster half-pint mug, later chased with flowers and scrolls in Victorian times, *5 oz*	SE	36	0
Victorian shaving mug with engraved crest, interior compartment and small ivory handle, London 1865, *31 oz nett*	M	31	0
George III christening mug, with hooped body by Charles Chesterman, London 1803, *4 oz*	SE	23	0
George IV christening mug on circular foot, gilt inside, by R. Hemmell, London 1820, *3 oz 5 dwt*	SE	20	0

Mustard Pots

Georgian mustard pot with blue glass liner, *7 oz nett*	M	48	0
Circular 2¼ in mustard pot and cover engraved and thread bands with pierced thumb piece and scroll handle, 4 in high, engraved crest and initial, by Hester Bateman, London 1785 (no glass lining), *2 oz 10 dwt*	N	40	0
Oval mustard pot, 1810, *3 oz 15 dwt*	M	35	0
George III circular mustard pot with embossed rim; half gadrooned on three paw feet, London 1817, with blue glass liner, *6 oz*	WE	32	10
George III gadrooned cylindrical mustard pot with scrolled billet and sapphire glass liner. London *circa* 1820, *4 oz 10 dwt*	M	28	0

Porringers

Charles II porringer and cover, London 1664, *20 oz*	M	670	0
Commonwealth porringer, 'E.T.', London 1657, *16 oz*	L	500	0
Queen Anne porringer, punched banding, spiral fluted and gadrooned, twist cable handles, by Richard Freeman, Exeter 1706	WE	175	0

Salt Cellars

Four George III oval salts, by William Abdy, London 1780	SE	70	0
Pair of small oval salts, London 1784	M	35	0
Pair George II salts on hoof feet, maker 'L.R.M.', *circa* 1744, *3 oz*	SE	26	0
Pair George II circular salts by Edward Wood, 1737, *3 oz 15 dwt*	SE	24	0
George III oval salt cellar on raised foot by Robert and Samuel Hennell, London 1804, *2 oz*	SE	13	0
Set of four 2¼ in circular salt cellars with bead borders and engraved bands, on trio scroll feet, engraved initials, London 1867, *8 oz*	N	8	0

Salvers

Set of four George II circular salvers, maker William Peaston, London 1749, *99 oz*	M	900	0

		£	s
James II salver (tazza), maker's mark 'T.A.' in monogram 1688, *28 oz*	SE	785	0
George II circular salver with engraved floral ground, the foliated rim with shell medallions, by Robert Abercrombie, London, *circa* 1773, *27 oz*	M	205	0
George II circular salver, London 1749, *49 oz*	M	180	0
Salver by Edward Jay, 1786, *39 oz 10 dwt*	M	98	0
George III engraved circular salver with bead border on three scroll feet by Peter and Ann Bateman, 11¾ in, London 1796, *24 oz*	N	82	0
George IV salver with a raised chased border and engraved with flowers and a crest by Joseph Craddock and William Reed, London 1823, *17 oz 10 dwt*	M	68	0
George III salver, engraved with monogram in chased surround of scrolls and flowers, on three feet, 7½ in diam, by William Doyle, Dublin 1803, *11 oz*	L	25	0

Sauceboats: Gravyboats

		£	s
Pair of gravyboats by Thomas Evans, 1780, *19 oz 15 dwt*	M	142	10
Pair of small George II sauceboats by William Bagnell, 1739, *10 oz*	M	81	0
George II plain tripod sauceboat by Robert Cox, London 1754	SE	44	0

Snuff Boxes

		£	s
William IV rectangular snuff box with oval panel on lid, London 1827, 4 in, *5 oz*	SE	36	0
George III snuff box by William Pitts, London 1798	SE	30	0
George III oval plain snuff box by 'WW' and 'PK.', Birmingham 1812, *1 oz*	SE	20	0
George III concave-shaped snuff box by 'W.B.', Birmingham 1805, 2½ in	SE	11	10
George III engine turned snuff box by Joseph Taylor, Birmingham 1817	SE	11	0
George III double crown 1821 circular snuff box engraved Henry Day, 1822, 1½ in, *2 oz 5 dwt*	SE	10	0

Spoons—Caddy

		£	s
Irish fluted caddy spoon by T. Carden and Jane Williams, Cork, *circa* 1807	SE	11	0

Spoons—Dessert

		£	s
Six Georgian old English dessert spoons, *8 oz 15 dwt*	M	47	0

Spoons—Table

		£	s
Three George III Hanoverian-pattern double drop tablespoons by Richard Paigiter, London 1735, *5 oz*	SE	20	0
Set of four George III old English pattern tablespoons, Dublin 1774, 7½ oz	SE	20	0
Pair of George II Hanoverian-pattern tablespoons, Edinburgh, 1732, 4½ oz	SE	14	0
Four George III tablespoons with cut design borders, London 1800	L	14	0
Four George III tablespoons, 1801, *8 oz 10 dwt*	M	12	0
Four George III tablespoons, by John and Henry Lias, London 1818, *7 oz 10 dwt*	L	9	0

		£	s
Four William IV Irish tablespoons, the fiddle-pattern handles with stag crests, by Thomas Farley, Dublin 1830, *9 oz 10 dwt*	L	8	10
Pair of George III Hanoverian-pattern tablespoons, London 1765, *4 oz*	SE	6	0
Two William IV old English thread-pattern tablespoons, London 1833/36, *5 oz*	SE	5	0
Two Victorian tablespoons, Exeter hallmark, *4 oz*	M	3	0
Two Georgian tablespoons, London hallmark, *3 oz 10 dwt*	M	3	0
Two tablespoons, maker 'W.B.', London 1839, *4 oz*	M	2	10
George IV tablespoon, 1820, *1 oz 10 dwt*	M	2	0
Two fiddle-pattern tablespoons, engraved initials, Edinburgh 1817	N	2	0

Spoons—Tea and Coffee

		£	s
Set of six George III old English-pattern coffee spoons, London 1807, *3 oz 5 dwt*	SE	15	10
Set of twelve Victorian fiddle-pattern teaspoons decorated with a shell pattern, Edinburgh 1839/43/44	M	14	10
Twelve teaspoons with beaded borders, engraved initials, London 1867, *11 oz 5 dwt*	N	12	0
Set of George II old English-pattern teaspoons, maker's mark 'T.S.', London 1799, *2½ oz*	SE	8	0
Six George III teaspoons, 1805	SE	8	0
Six George IV teaspoons, 1826, *5 oz*	M	5	10

Spoons—Ladles—Various

		£	s
Elizabethan seal-top spoon, hallmark 1570, *1 oz*	M	80	0
Soup ladle by Hester Bateman, London 1778, *5 oz*	WE	42	0
Shaped toddy ladle, 1819	WE	21	0
Two George III old English-pattern sifting spoons with pierced bowls, London 1799/1807	SE	20	0
George III punch ladle with shaped bowl and turned wood handle, by Dorothy Mills, London 1770	SE	19	0
George III punch ladle, the base inset with 1787 coin, whalebone handle	SE	11	10
George III gravy spoon with bird crested handle, maker's mark 'G.S.' (George Smith), London 1784, *4 oz*	L	7	10
Two George III serving spoons 1801 and 1803, *3 oz 10 dwt*	M	6	10
William IV fiddle-pattern basting spoon, Edinburgh 1837, *3 oz*	SE	6	0
Fiddle, thread and shell pattern soup ladle, Newcastle 1860, *9 oz 10 dwt*	N	6	0
Eight Georgian silver condiment spoons, *2 oz 5 dwt*	M	2	10

Strainers

		£	s
Strainer, bead border and handle, by Hester Bateman, 1782, *2 oz 12 dwt*	WE	54	0

Sugar Basins and Casters

		£	s
Set of four George III casters, *22 oz*	SE	210	0
George III urn-shaped sugar basin, London 1769, *12 oz 10 dwt*	M	100	0
George III plain oval two-handled sugar basin, *7 oz 5 dwt*	M	70	0
George III baluster caster with pierced top by Hester Bateman, London 1780, *4 oz 10 dwt*	M	65	0

		£	s
Richly-decorated Queen Anne sugar caster with elaborately-pierced cover on bayonet fitting, London hallmark, *7 oz 10 dwt*	M	60	0
George II pyriform caster with moulded girdle by Samuel Wood, London 1734, height 6½ in, *7 oz*	SE	60	0
Two-handled Irish George III sugar basin by Le Bross, 1818, *8½ oz*	M	24	0

Sugar-scissors

George III sugar-scissors by Robert Makepiece, *circa* 1795	SE	12	0

Sweetmeat (or Bon-bon) Trays

George III shell sweetmeat dish, *3 oz 15 dwt*	M	36	0
Circular fluted bon-bon dish engraved crest, 4¾ in Sheffield 1835, *4 oz*	N	8	0

Tankards

Charles II covered tankard 1672/3, *24 oz 10 dwt*	SE	560	0
George III lidded tankard, the plain ground with single girdle, and engraved coat-of-arms with motto: *Si Je Puis*, by Louis Black, London 1764, *24 oz*	M	200	0
George III lidded tankard, the ground later embossed with cupids upon a ram with fruiting vines, the lid with vine decoration, by Peter and Anne Bateman, London 1793, *27 oz 10 dwt*	M	170	0
George I pint tankard of plain design, by Joseph Clare, London 1719, *10 oz*	M	112	0
George II plain domed-top lidded tankard, 1773, *19 oz 10 dwt*	M	75	0
George III embossed tankard by Robert Harper, London 1867 (crested), *12 oz*	SE	52	0
George III plain tankard with scroll handle, 5 in high, London 1778, *11 oz*	N	44	0
Victorian lipped tankard with cover, 1863, *76 oz 10 dwt*	SE	44	0
Victorian bell tankard with double scroll handle and acanthus thumb piece, *10 oz 10 dwt*	SE	29	0
William IV *repoussé* tankard, *4 oz 15 dwt*	SE	19	0
Victorian monogrammed tankard, *4 oz 10 dwt*	SE	16	0

Tapersticks

George II taperstick with turned knopped stem and shaped square base, by Jos. Steward, London 1739, height 4½ in, *4 oz*	SE	140	0

Teapots

George III teapot and stand by George Baskerville, 1792, *16 oz*	M	192	0
George III teapot of oblong form, richly chased with a girdle of scrolling flowers issuing from fluting and supported on ball feet, by Robertson and Walton, Newcastle *circa* 1795, *30 oz 10 dwt*	M	160	0
George III teapot with raised gadroon band, silver knob and handle with ivory insulators, on four ball feet, by Alice and George Burrows, London 1807, *20½ oz*	SE	82	10
George III chased and embossed teapot with flower finial, by C. Wright, London 1777, *27 oz*	WE	70	0

	£	s
George II gadrooned teapot, crested, probably by William Fearn, London 1799, *18 oz*	WE	52	0
George III teapot, engraved with a crest and supported on claw feet, by Alice and George Burrows, London 1810, *22 oz*	M	52	0
George III circular teapot, richly *repoussé* with scrolling flowers, the cover with floral knop, by Alice and George Burrows, *29 oz*	M	50	0
Regency gadrooned teapot on four ball feet, by John Angell, London 1816, *17 oz*	WE	45	0
William IV teapot, by Charles Fox, London 1830, *23 oz 10 dwt*	WE	45	0
William IV teapot with presentation engraving, *25 oz 15 dwt*	M	40	0
George III oval teapot, possible maker Daniel Ponifex, London 1800, *16 oz*	M	38	0
George III small oval teapot, with melon-fluted ground, the cover with bold eagle knop, by Charles Hogham, London 1808, *11 oz*	M	26	0

Tea and Coffee Services

George IV four-piece tea and coffee service, by Joseph Craddock and Peter Reid, London 1825	SE	360	0
George IV tea and coffee set, London 1852, *50 oz*	SE	260	0
George III half-fluted tea service with engraved girdle and beaded rim, comprising teapot with fruit knop, sugar basin and cream jug, by Peter, Ann and William Bateman, London 1804, *32 oz 10 dwt*	M	205	0
William IV pumpkin-shaped tea service, London 1830	M	190	0
Three-piece tea set probably by Thomas Dexter, *circa* 1818, *33 oz*	M	159	0
Georgian three-piece tea service, *44 oz*	SE	130	0
Victorian three-piece tea service with engraved and *repoussé* floral decoration and raised on scroll supports, comprising teapot, with bird knop, two-handled sugar bowl and milk jug. Maker's initials 'R. and H.', Sheffield 1852, *50 oz*	SE	115	0
Victorian three-piece tea set, 1848, *41 oz 10 dwt*	SE	76	0

Trays

George III rectangular tea tray, by Phillip Russell, London 1819	M	460	0
George II two-handled tea tray by John Crouch and Thomas Hannon	S	250	0
George II circular card tray with chased border, on claw and ball feet, by John Carter, London 1759, *11 oz 10 dwt*	M	61	0

Tureens

George II oval soup tureen and cover, John Elkford, London 1746, *134 oz*	L	2,500	0
Pair of George II circular tureens and covers by Paul Storr, London 1805	M	920	0
Set of four George III oblong gadrooned sauce tureens and covers, by John Graddock and William Reed, total weight *102 oz 10 dwt*	M	840	0
George III soup tureen by Paul Storr, London 1796	M	680	0

		£	s

Vinaigrettes

| Early Victorian vinaigrette, silver gilt interior, pierced and embossed design | WE | 20 | 0 |
| Early Victorian vinaigrette, Birmingham | M | 5 | 0 |

Wine Coasters

| Set of George III circular wine coasters, London 1808 | M | 310 | 0 |
| Pair of George III silver coasters, maker's mark 'W.T. & Co.', Sheffield 1809 | L | 89 | 0 |

Waiters

| George II circular waiter with engraved floral ground, the foliated rim with shell medallions, by Robert Abercrombie, London 1750, *7 oz* | M | 140 | 0 |
| George III circular waiter with plain ground and shell and scroll rim, supported on three volute feet, by Edward Capper, London 1767, *22 oz* | M | 135 | 0 |

Wine Cistern

| George III silver gilt wine cistern by Paul Storr, London 1818, 11¾ in height, 15 in diameter, *275 oz* | M | 2,150 | 0 |

Wine Coolers

| Pair of George III vase-shaped crested wine coolers by Paul Storr, London 1816 | S | 1,800 | 0 |

Wine Labels

| Four various Georgian decanter labels with hanging chains, 'Port', 'Port', 'Sherry', and 'Madeira', *1 oz 5 dwt* | SE | 17 | 0 |

SHEFFIELD PLATE

Candlesticks

Set of four Georgian Corinthian column candlesticks, maker Thos. Law, *circa* 1758	WE	40	0
Pair of 21 in three-light candelabra	M	31	0
Pair of cluster column pillar candlesticks with husk decoration on square base, 12½ in	SE	31	0
Set of four telescopic candlesticks	M	26	0
Pair of 12 in candlesticks	NI	25	0
Pair of candlesticks	M	8	0

Coasters

Pair of eighteenth-century pierced coasters decorated with crests and bead edges, wood bases, 4¾ in	SE	18	0
Pair of Crown Mark wine coasters with vine embossed borders	SE	16	0
Pair of nineteenth-century coasters with wood bases	SE	14	0
Pair of nineteenth-century coasters with wood bases and crests	SE	12	0
Pair of Georgian gadrooned coasters with wood bases	SE	9	0
Pair of wine coasters with gadroon borders	WE	7	10
Pair of nineteenth-century gadrooned coasters with wood base	SE	5	10
Pair of pierced-edge wine coasters	SE	5	15

Cream Jugs

| Eighteenth-century helmet-shaped gadrooned cream jug | SE | 6 | 0 |

N

		£	s

Cups

Nineteenth-century embossed two-handled cup with initials 'E.G.'	SE	13	0

Entrée Dishes

Pair of entrée dishes with covers and handles	BI	25	0
Nineteenth-century entrée dish and cover with acorn handle and crest, 13 in	SE	11	0
Oval dish with vine-decorated edge, 16 in	SE	3	0

Hot-water Jugs

Eighteenth-century hot-water jug with eagle spout on four feet, 10 in	SE	8	0
Large hot-water jug with boxwood handle	M	4	10

Inkstands

Oval inkstand with pierced gallery, taperstick and two blue glass pots on chased feet, 9 in	SE	23	0
Inkstand with pierced gallery, two pots and taperstick, crested 8½ in	SE	11	0

Snuff Box

Nineteenth-century snuff box inset with George coin, 3½ in	SE	4	0

Sweet Stands

Pair of gadrooned and pierced sweet stands, 7 in by 4½ in height	SE	6	0

Tankard

Old half-pint tankard with turned wood base	M	1	5

Tea Caddies

Tea caddy with lion-head ring handles, 4 in	SE	7	0
Nineteenth-century octagonal tea caddy	SE	4	15

Trays

Circular two-handled engraved tray with crest, 27 in	SE	10	0
Nineteenth-century oval tea tray	SE	6	0
Oval gadrooned tray	SE	3	0

Tureens

Oval soup tureen and cover with acorn handle on scroll feet, 5 in	SE	78	0
Oval gadrooned soup tureen with scrolled handles and richly foliated feet	M	60	0

Waiter

Nineteenth-century gadrooned and crested waiter, 8⅜ in	SE	2	5

Wine Coolers

Pair of Regency wine coolers, the borders chased with foliage, 10½ in high	SE	27	0

NON-PRECIOUS METALS

(The prices given below for brass and copper are the highest we have recorded for each particular type of item.)

Brass

Early nineteenth-century brass lantern	M	125	10
Pair of brass carriage lamps with eagle surmounts, bevelled glass octagon panels, 34 in high overall	M	38	0

		£	s
Charles II brass warming pan with wrought iron handle	SE	32	0
Pair of brass carriage lamps each surmounted by an eagle, 29 in high overall	SE	26	0
Brass standard lamp with oil lamp	M	21	0
Brass Corinthian column table lamp with cut-glass bowl and shade	SE	17	0
Heavy brass *jardinière* (two handles)	NI	15	0
Solid brass fire companion with beaten shield panel	SE	13	0
Pair of seventeenth-century fire dogs and two brass-topped steel irons	SE	11	10
Brass kettle on tall stand	SE	11	0
Embossed brass alms dish	WE	9	10
Brass two-handled kettle stand	M	9	10
Brass footman with pierced top and bowl	SE	9	0
Set of large brass scales with pan and five weights	WE	7	0
Brass chestnut roaster	WE	6	5
Brass helmet-shaped coal scuttle	M	6	0
Brass rail fender	WE	6	0
Brass cream skimmer	SE	5	10
Brass warming pan with wooden handle	SE	5	10
Brass kettle on four feet	M	5	0
Georgian pierced brass fender on paw feet	M	5	0
Pierced brass fender and set of fire irons	M	4	10
Corinthian column table oil lamp, 24 in	N	4	10
Pair of brass candlesticks	WE	3	10
Engraved brass oval tray	M	3	10
Brass preserving pan	SE	3	5
Embossed *jardinière* with lion-mask ring-handles on three claw feet	N	3	0

Bronze

Italian bronze figure of a stallion	L	880	0
Pair of French bronze figures of bulls, stamped I. Bonheir	L	260	0
Pair of Italian bronze centaur figures	WE	220	0
Pair of nineteenth-century bronze lamps	M	160	0
Bronze figure of a musician Improvisatore by Duret, 22 in	M	53	0
Pair of bronze ewers	M	32	0
Bronze figure of Narcissus, 24 in	M	30	0
Bronze ecclesiastical candlestick, 4 ft 2 in	SE	25	0
Pair of bronze figures—Charles II and Cromwell—signed A. Carrier, 16 in high	SE	23	0
Pair of nineteenth-century Italian bronze classical figures on ebonized bases with frieze decoration, signed J. Bologne, 32 in high	WE	20	0

Copper

Coal drum with lion feet	M	26	0
Victorian tea urn	WE	13	0
Four-gallon measure, 17 in	N	13	0
Warming-pan	NI	11	10
Helmet-shaped coal scuttle, 17 in	N	9	0
Two-handled log-pail, 12½ in	N	7	0
Coal bucket, heavily studded, with swing handle	WE	7	0
Oval coach footwarmer	SE	6	10

		£	s
Preserving pan	WE	6	15
Long-handled copper skillet	SE	6	10
Kettle	SE	6	10
Warming flask	SE	5	10
Hot-water jug with flat top	SE	3	10
Jelly mould	WE	3	10
Water-can	SE	3	10
Embossed two-handled *jardinière,* 12 in	N	3	5

Iron

		£	s
Cast-iron dog grate with wrought-iron finials having brass ball terminals	WE	28	0
Seventeenth-century Sussex wrought-iron fireback, with decoration of arms and supporters, 32 in by 33 in	SE	22	0
Pair of massive seventeenth-century andirons decorated with figures and birds	SE	22	0
Pair of heavy wrought-iron firedogs with shield decoration	SE	14	0
Wrought-iron fireback with the initials 'A.W.' and dated 1665, 29 in by 22 in	SE	13	0
Black wrought-iron fire-basket	M	13	0
Sussex iron fireback, 22 in	SE	8	0
Wrought-iron three-branch candle standard with coronet sconces on twist pillar supports and tripod (fitted for electricity)	SE	7	0
Wrought-iron rectangular fire-basket, 19½ in	WE	3	0

Lead

		£	s
Pair of lead garden urns	M	174	0
Lead bird-bath	M	102	0
Early lead tobacco-box with cover, lion mask and flower decoration	SE	6	10

Pewter
Candlesticks

		£	s
Pair of pewter candlesticks on square bases	L	14	0
Two pairs of pewter candlesticks	SE	13	0

Dishes and Plates

		£	s
Early pewter wide-rimmed well dish (three touchmarks), 18 in	SE	44	0
Pewter dish, 13 in, and four London-made pewter plates, 7 in	SE	20	0
Pair of 9½ in pewter plates, having gadrooned borders, and 13 in embossed pewter bowl	SE	17	0
Pewter shallow dish, 15 in diameter, London marks	WE	6	10
Pewter side plate	SE	4	10

Flagons

		£	s
Pewter flagon, inscribed Duke of Cumberland, *circa* 1760, 11 in	SE	60	0
Pewter flagon with double-acorn thumb-piece to lid, 9 in (and sundries)	SE	24	0

Pepper-Pots

		£	s
Set of three pewter pepper-pots, 4½ in	SE	4	0
Pewter pepper-pot in form of a hand holding an acorn	M	3	15

£ s

Tankards

Early eighteenth-century quart domed-lid tankard, the
handle with 'fish tail' finial, made by Richard Going,
Bristol, 5⅝ in to lip, *circa* 1730   L   34   0
German pewter tankard   SE   35   0
Heavy pewter quart tankard   WE   4 10

PORCELAIN

EIGHTEENTH-CENTURY FACTORIES

(For figures and groups see pages 202-4)

Bow

Two candlestick groups formed as nymphs seated in flowered
robes and blue and pink cloaks, with putti standing on
their laps, supporting wave scrolls terminating on candle
nozzles with foliage canopies, the spreading bases enriched in blue and puce, 12½ in high   L   115 10
Bouquet of garden flowers, naturally modelled and decorated in colours and tied with a puce ribbon including a
daisy, a carnation, a dahlia and a poppy on triangular
base, 6¼ in high   L   63   0
Pair of oval sauce boats, enamelled in colours with flowering chrysanthemums and hurdles in the Oriental style, on
three lions' masks and paw feet, 8½ in wide   L   39 18
Baluster frill vase, with mask handles to the sides, encrusted
with garlands of flowers in colours, and painted in
colours with insects, the pierced shoulders with rosettes,
7½ in high   L   31 10
Pair of circular plates, painted in colours in the *famille rose*
style, the centres with flowering peonies issuing from blue
rockwork, the borders with trailing peony branches, 9 in
diam   L   29   8

Bristol

Floral hand-painted posset pot   WE   16   0

Caughley

Blue and white cylindrical mug, transfer-printed with a
Chinese lady in a boat in river landscape, 5¼ in high. Blue
'S' mark   L   18 18
Blue and white cabbage leaf mask jug, with scroll handle
and mask spout, transfer-printed with pagoda buildings in
river landscape, 9 in high   L   17 17
Blue and white cabbage-leaf jug with mask spout and scroll
handle, transfer-printed with figures in sampans in Chinese
landscapes, 9½ in high   L   14 14

Chelsea

Hans Sloane plate, painted in colours, with a large iris spray
occupying the centre of the plate and with a small red
chrysanthemum to the right, with waved chocolate rim,
9 in diam. Red anchor mark   L   287   0
Three Chelsea circular saucer dishes, painted in colours with
bouquets of flowers and flower sprays, with waved chocolate rim, 9½ in diam. Red anchor mark   L   94 10

£   s

Oval basket, with tied branch handles, the terminals encrusted with flowers, the centre painted in colours with flower-sprays, the pierced sides with applied rosettes to the exterior, 11¾ in wide. Red anchor mark   L   54   12

Circular plate, moulded with basketwork, with pierced basketwork borders, painted in colours with a bouquet of flowers, with chocolate rim, 9½ in diam. Red anchor mark   L   42   0

Two circular soup plates, moulded in relief and painted with flower-sprays, the borders with alternate moulded and painted flower-sprays, with lobed chocolate rims, 9½ in diam. Red anchor period   L   31   10

Sunflower tureen, the lower part moulded with overlapping leaves in shades of green, the everted lip with overlapping petals edged in yellow, 5 in diameter. Red anchor period   L   27   6

Oval dish of silver shape, with puce shell handles, moulded with shell flutes and painted in colours with flower-sprays, with pale turquoise *feuill-de-choux* rims, 9¾ in wide. Gold anchor mark   SE   15   15

Chelsea-Derby

Cylindrical mug, painted in the Worcester style with vertical panels of the Jabberwocky pattern and with birds perched among flowering chrysanthemums on *gros bleu* grounds reserved with white flowers and enriched with gilt scrolls, 4¾ in high. Gilt anchor and 'D' mark   L   63   0

Shaped oval dish, the centre painted in colours with an urn enriched with roses, the border with scrolling, floral swags suspended from gilt rosettes, with gilt dentil rim, 10¼ in diam. Gilt anchor and 'D' mark in gold   L   39   18

Cylindrical pomade pot and cover, decorated in royal blue and gold with diagonal bands of flowers and gilt oat swags, the cover with fruit finial, 3-in high. Gilt anchor and 'D' marks   L   25   4

Derby

Pair of oval sauce boats, with scroll handles, painted in colours with bouquets of flowers and moulded in relief with C-scrolls and flower-sprays and buds enriched in colours, with gadrooned borders and iron-red rims, 8 in wide   L   94   10

Cylindrical mug, the rectangular panel painted in colours with a ship offshore in a fresh gale, the reverse with gilt foliage scrolls, 4¾ in high. Iron red crowned crossed batons and 'D' marks   L   60   18

Bloor miniature watering can, the cylindrical body encrusted with flowers in colours on a turquoise ground, the cover with bouquet finial, 3½ in high   L   44   2

Pair of two-handled vases of urn shape, with scroll handles, painted in colours each with a panel of garden flowers within a gilt foliage scroll cartouche on royal blue grounds, on square bases, 8¾ in high. Iron red crown 'D' marks   L   39   18

Bloor period teacup and saucer with *gros bleu* ground and narrow gilt border, each with a single richly gilded panel

£   s

painted with exotic birds in a landscape setting. Red
crown and 'D' mark   M   20   0
Cylindrical coffee cup and saucer, painted in colours with
views near Breadsall, Derbyshire and in Staffordshire, the
border with gilt scrolling foliage. Iron red crowned crossed
batons and 'D' marks   L   16   16
Twenty Bloor soup plates decorated in red, blue and gold
with flowering plants issuing from rockwork in the Oriental style, the borders with scrolling flowers, with gadrooned gilt rims, 10¼ in diam   L   14   14
Pair of early dishes painted in Japanese style with bright
enamel colours   M   8   0
Seven Bloor plates with gadrooned rims, painted in red,
blue, pink and gold, with flower sprays in Oriental style.
10 in diam   L   5   5

Longton Hall
Strawberry-leaf plate, the centre painted in colours by the
Trembly Rose painter, the border moulded in relief and
painted in colours with strawberry sprays and leaves, 9¼ in
wide   L   147   0
Oval sauce boat, with branch handle, modelled with overlapping leaves, and painted in colours with three flower-
sprays, the edges and foot rim in green, 7 in wide   L   29   8

Lowestoft
One large and four smaller armorial plates   M   100   0
Oriental mug   M   43   0

New Hall
Lozenge-shaped teapot and cover, painted *en grisaille* with
baskets of flowers and flower-sprays, the cover with vase
finial, 9 in wide   L   10   10

Plymouth
White glazed triple sweetmeat dish, encrusted with shells,
7 in   SE   42   0

Worcester—Dr Wall
Pair of leaf-shaped dishes, painted in colours with floral
swags within vase and mirror-shaped gilt scroll cartouches on scale blue grounds, with pale green branch
handles, 7¾ in high. Blue square seal marks   L   147   0
Pair of shell-shaped dishes, painted in colours with floral
swags within vase and mirror-shaped gilt scroll cartouches
on scale blue grounds with gilt rim, 7¾ in wide. Blue
crescent marks   L   99   15
Pair of kidney-shaped dishes, en suite to the preceding lot,
with gilt rims, 11 in wide. Blue script mark   L   75   12
Pair of lobed oval dishes, painted in colours with bouquet
of flowers and flower-sprays, the royal blue borders edged
with gilt C-scrolls, 11 in wide. Blue crescent marks   L   60   18
Pair of fluted circular dishes, with chrysanthemums in
shaped panels on blue scale grounds, 9 in diam. Blue
square seal marks   L   47   5

		£	**s**
Blue and white tea poy and original cover, decorated with bouquets of garden flowers and butterflies, 6½ in. Crescent mark	M	42	10
Oval dish decorated with chrysanthemums on a blue scale ground, 10¼ in wide. Blue square seal mark	L	36	15
Plate painted with blue and gilt border and flowers, 9 in. Open crescent mark	SE	36	0
Fluted saucer dish decorated with sprays of garden flowers, diam 7¼ in. Square mark	M	32	10
Hexagonal teapot stand, with large central spray of flowers and smaller sprays around the fluted edge	M	30	0
Gilt-framed porcelain plaque, oval-shaped, with narrow gilt border, depicting cock and hen pheasants standing and in flight in a woodland setting, painted by J. Hancock (signed), 8 in by 10 in	M	27	10
Rare dry blue saucer dish, fluted, with gilt dentil edge, the sole decoration being dry blue bouquets and flowers, diam 7 in. Square mark	M	25	0

Worcester—Flight, Barr and Barr

Two porcelain dishes, biscuit and gilt ground. Impressed mark	WE	27	0
Large botanical plate with shaped and gilded edge, decorated with large sprays of leaves and blossom, several smaller sprays around the rim, and with one large and four smaller butterflies in brilliant colours, 10 in diam. Impressed mark	M	22	0
Plate with gold and apple green border and armorial crest	SE	4	15

Worcester—Chamberlain

Rare mug with loop handles, gilt rim and base, and delicate pink ground. Large square panel with beautifully-painted landscape depicting Eastnor Castle, Worcs., seat of Lord Somers, and inscribed as such on base, 3½ in high	M	55	0
Two-handled vase and stand, the arched gilt handles with squirrel finials, the sides painted in colours with roses, convolvulus and other garden flowers reserved on gilt grounds, 5½ in high	L	42	2
Pair of oval dishes, each painted with seven specimen flower-sprays, within oval gilt cartouches on royal blue grounds, 10 in wide. Script marks	L	35	14
Basket painted with blue border and flowers and fruit in the centre, rustic handle with acorns in gilt, 10½ in by 9 in	SE	34	0
Cup and saucer of flared bucket shape, the octagonal panels finely-painted with branches of fruit on ledges, the royal blue grounds with gilt marbling, the interiors with pink grounds. Script marks in puce	L	29	8
Botanical plate with a scalloped border in turquoise and gilt. In the centre of the plate is a large, finely-painted ivy-leafed geranium, 8¾ in diam. Printed mark	M	27	10
Blue scale plate with rococo gilding encircling three large panels with exotic birds in flight and standing, and several smaller reserves with moths and insects. There is a central circular medallion finely gilded, 9 in diam	M	22	10

£   s

Two-handled vase of campana shape, the loop handles with
   dogs' masks below, painted in colours with landscape
   panels, the lower part with gilt trailing branches and with
   lilac marbled foot, 6 in high   L   16 16
Plate painted in blue and gilt border of flowers, 9 in   SE   7   0

NINETEENTH-CENTURY FACTORIES

Coalport (Coalbrookdale)

Circular pot-pourri vase and cover, with branch handles, the
   sides encrusted with flowers and painted in colours with
   floral bouquets, the borders with gilt C-scrolls, on four feet,
   4½ in high   L   42   0
Vase of cornucopia shape, encrusted with flowers and edged
   in turquoise and gilt on shaped oval base. 6½ in high   L   31 10
Pair of two-handled baluster vases with gilt scroll handles,
   the sides painted in colours with bouquets of flowers reserved on turquoise grounds, with frilled lips, 8 in high   L   23   2
Oval basket, the centre painted in colours with a bouquet of
   flowers, the border encrusted with trailing flowers, on four
   gilt paw feet, 8 in wide. Blue crossed-swords mark   L   16 16
Two-handled pot-pourri bowl and cover of bucket shape, the
   handles with gilt ribbons, the sides encrusted with flowers,
   the flared rim similarly decorated, the pierced cover with
   loop handle, 7½ in high   L   12 12
Two-handled loving cup   M   9   0
Small pot and cover encrusted with white flowers and with
   flowers and fruit on the cover, 3½ in   SE   6   0

Davenport

Circular pot-pourri bowl and cover, the flared sides painted
   with garden flowers on a gilt ground, the pierced cover
   with gilt flammiform finial, on four gilt paw feet, 5 in high   L   26   5
Five plates, the centres painted in colours with named views
   of Dunolly Castle near Oban, Loch Lomond from Tar-
   bet, Loch Ard, Loch Leven Castle and Loch Katrine, and
   Ellens Isle, the green borders with cream and gilt foliage
   scrolls, 9 in diam   L   16 16
Two-handled semi-circular *jardinière*, the border painted
   with garden flowers, 5¼ in high. Impressed mark   L   14 14

Minton

Two-handled vase in the Sèvres-style, the beaded handles
   springing from the base of the body enriched with gilding
   and suspending fixed rings, the sides painted in colours
   with bouquets of flowers within beaded quatrefoil cartouches on pale turquoise grounds with marbled neck,
   spreading stem and square base, 13½ in high   L   42   0
Pair of slender oviform ewers, with gilt handles, the sides
   painted in colours with primroses, bluebells and ferns, the
   pinched lips and spreading bases with lilac grounds and
   gilt borders, 12½ in high   L   18 18

Rockingham

Puce griffin-marked vase with flared rim, the blue ground
   with gilt and a reserve painted with a parakeet, 14½ in
   high   M   55   0

£   s

Circular two-handled sauce tureen, cover and stand, the centre painted in colours with bouquets of flowers, the buff borders reserved with flower-sprays in white. The stand, 9 in wide   L   26   5

Square dish, the centre painted in colours with the Descent into the Valley of Wyoming, Pennesylvania (*sic*) America, the green border enriched with formal patterns in white and gold, 11 in wide   L   23   2

Spode

Pair of gold ground beakers of flared form, painted with scattered garden flowers on gold grounds, $4\frac{3}{4}$ in high. Pattern No. 711 in red   L   99   15

Set of four oval dishes, painted with botanical flowers on a grey ground, pattern 2424. Marked in red 'Spode.'   M   50   0

Garniture of a two-handled baluster vase and two ewers, the buff scroll handles enriched with gilding, painted in colours in the Oriental style with flowering branches and butterflies reserved on pink grounds, on square bases, 12 in and 9 in high   L   38   18

Pair of square quatrefoil plates, $8\frac{1}{2}$ in wide. Marked Spode 3838 in red   L   27   6

Oblong two-handled dish with branch handles, painted in colours with four bouquets of garden flowers in gilt dentil rims, $11\frac{1}{2}$ in wide. Marked Spode 3838 in red   L   26   5

Oval pierced basket and stand painted with Chinese flowers on a green and white stand, 9 in. Impressed mark   SE   18   0

Two-handled vase of Barberini form, with gilt handles, the sides painted in colours and gilt in the Oriental style with flowering plants issuing from rockwork, 10 in high. Red 967 mark   L   16   16

Tulip cup, the six-petalled flower enriched in red, on gilt base with canted corners, $2\frac{3}{4}$ in high. Marked Spode in black   L   8   8

Swansea and Nantgarw

Nantgarw porcelain gilt rim floral- and gilt-decorated oval dish, 11 in diam   WE   110   0

Swansea porcelain gilt rim floral-decorated oval dish, 11 in diameter. Marked Swansea and trident impressed   WE   75   0

Swansea square dish with moulded decoration and painted with flowers, 8 in. Marked in red   SE   52   0

Pair of Swansea campana-shaped vases with gilt lion-head ring handles, painted with flowers, on square bases, $5\frac{1}{2}$ by 6 in high   SE   50   0

Swansea oval dish, painted with gilt decoration and flower-sprays, 12 in. Marked in red   SE   40   0

Pair of Swansea gilt-rimmed plates painted with flowers, 8 in. Impressed mark   SE   32   0

Swansea bowl with moulded basket pattern border painted with flowers, $5\frac{3}{4}$ in. Marked in red   SE   20   0

Bow   EIGHTEENTH-CENTURY FIGURES AND GROUPS

Italian comedy white musical group, of Scaramouche and Isabella, after the Meissen original, seated on a tree stump,

£   s

Scaramouche leaning back and singing, whilst Isabella
accompanies him on a guitar, on rectangular rockwork
base, 7¾ in high   L   483   0
Companion figure of a Turkish lady, standing before a tree
stump, raising her veil with her right hand and holding
the skirt of her coat in her left, in lilac veil, flowered coat,
pink sash and yellow trousers, the circular white mound
base with applied flowers in colours, 7 in high   L   252   0
Sportswoman, standing before a tree stump holding a falcon
and with a dog at her feet, in yellow hat and pink-lined
yellow bodice and flowered skirt on circular white base,
6¼ in high   L   178   0
Early figure of Una and the lion, formed as a standing
female figure crowned and wearing a flowing, flowered
robe and blue sash, holding a cornucopia in her left hand
and with lion recumbent at her feet, 6½ in high   L   126   0
Group of a goat and a kid, standing before a brightly-
coloured flowering tree, naturally modelled and painted
with hair markings in brown, the kid recumbent on the oval
flowered base, 4½ in high   L   115 10
Neptune, standing holding a helmet, in yellow-lined pink
cloak, a green and red dolphin at his feet, among blue
waves, the high base with four scroll feet enriched in puce
and gilding, 9¾ in high   L   65   2
Miniature figure of a dismal hound, seated, its head turned
and its tail curled over its hind legs, decorated with
patches of hair markings in brown, the scroll base en-
riched in purple, 2¼ in high   L   35 14
A seated boy, turning to one side, in blue hat, flowered coat
and breeches, a mug of beer to his left, on grasswork base,
4¾ in high   L   31 10

Chelsea

Figure of a smuggler, standing before a flowering tree stump,
with a sword, a gun and a barrel of powder, with iron-
red fur-lined cap, cream-lined lilac cloak, turquoise coat
and iron-red breeches, the wave scroll base enriched with
gilding, 8 in high. Gold anchor mark   L   147   0
A pair of groups emblematic of the seasons, formed each as
two putti before a flowering tree and a vine, partly clothed
in coloured drapery. Spring with a basket of flowers,
Autumn picking a bunch of grapes, Winter warming his
hands at a brazier, and Summer formally holding a cornucopia, the high scroll bases encrusted with flowers on four
shell and wave scroll feet enriched with gilding, 7 in high.
Gold anchor period   L   89   5

Derby

A pair of musicians, seated in pierced gazebos, encrusted
with blue flowers and enriched with gilding, the lady playing the guitar and wearing feathered headdress, green
bodice, yellow apron and flowered skirt, her companion
playing the bagpipes, with feathered iron-red hat, green
waistcoat, his flowered shirt matching her skirt, and with

£   s

yellow flowered breeches, on stepped scroll bases, enriched
in green and gilding, 12 in high   L   157   10

A Ranelagh dancer standing before a tree stump, holding a
bouquet of flowers and wearing ermine-lined cream cloak,
turquoise bodice, her patterned skirt with red fringe, on
gilt turquoise and pink scrollbase, 9½ in high   L   81   18

A lady, standing before a flowering tree stump, playing the
triangle, her head turned and wearing flowered shawl,
yellow bodice, white apron and flowered skirt, the wave
scroll base enriched in gilt and turquoise, 10 in high.
Patch marks   L   71   8

A sailor, standing before a flowering tree stump, in black tricorn hat, yellow-lined blue coat, gilt-spotted waistcoat and
striped trousers, three gold coins in his left hand, on
pierced and gilt wave scroll base, 10 in high. Incised No.
316   L   57   15

John Milton, standing, leaning on a pile of books on a
pedestal, his head turned and his right foot forward, in
yellow-lined lilac cloak and iron-red breeches, the wave
scroll base enriched in pink and green, 11½ in high   L   47   5

A boy, emblematic of winter, kneeling on a berried tree
stump, holding a bundle of kindling and wearing fur-lined
iron-red coat, flowered waistcoat and pale turquoise
breeches, on circular base, 9¾ in high. Incised marks   L   44   2

A girl, standing before a flowering tree stump, holding a
basket of eggs, wearing a blue and iron-red hat, turquoise
bodice, flowered skirt and a pink apron with flowers, on
turquoise and gilt wave scroll base, 10 in high   L   42   0

A boy seated in a chair, a cat beside him, in turquoise-lined
pink coat and white nightshirt, a basket of flowers on the
square grasswork base, 6 in high   L   23   2

POTTERY

Slipware

Eighteenth-century dish, the pale honey-coloured ground
with horizontal dark stripes and with piecrust rim, 13½ in
diam   L   7   7

Delftware

Pair of Lambeth blue and white wall pockets of stepped
semi-bucket shape, terminating in knops below, painted
each with a Chinaman holding a bird on a terrace, with
pine trees and rockwork, with formal patterns below, 8 in
high   L   252   0

Bristol Adam and Eve charger, naively decorated with Adam
to the right and Eve to the left of the tree, all in blue,
pricked out in manganese, the ochre serpent reaching
down from the branches and with orange fruit among pale
green foliage, with two trees to either side within a double
manganese band, 13 in diam   L   94   10

Lambeth blue dash oakleaf charger, painted in blue, turquoise and yellow with a formal arrangement of leaves
and onions, with blue dash rim, 13¾ in diam   L   47   5

£ s

Bristol blue and white pap warmer in two parts, the bowl
   with shell handles, the almost cylindrical stand with scroll
   handles painted with leaf scroll patterns, 8¼ in high   L   44   2
Pair of Bristol polychrome circular dishes, painted in manganese, iron-red, blue, green and yellow, the centres with
   formal medallions, the borders with flower-sprays, 12 in
   diam   L   44   2
Bristol charger of farmhouse type, the centre with a peacock
   standing among sponged trees, the border with formal patterns in blue, 13 in diam   L   36 15
Lambeth blue and white two-handled posset pot, with blue
   dash scroll handles to the sides, painted with Chinese
   figures seated in landscapes, 8½ in wide   L   33 12
Bristol punch bowl with Chinese figures and landscape in
   blue, 10½ in diam   SE   32   0
Large Lambeth blue and white two-handled posset pot and
   cover of almost cylindrical form, the spout with scroll pattern, the sides painted in colours with pagoda buildings in
   a Chinese landscape, 11 in high   L   31 10
Pair of Liverpool polychrome circular dishes, painted with
   birds perched on trees, 14¼ in diam   L   25   4
Bristol blue and white circular dish, painted with a Chinese
   lady standing on a terrace holding a vase, with a flying
   duck and a pagoda, the border with lobed oval panels,
   13 in diam   L   23   2
Bristol blue and white flower brick with silver mounts, painted with Chinese figures in river landscapes, the cover
   with twelve circular and one square aperture, fitted with
   a hinged inkwell and cover, and foot rim in silver, 5¾ in
   wide   L   23   2
Lambeth drug jar on foot and labelled M. Commun, 8½ in   SE   21   0
Six Bristol blue and white circular plates, painted in Oriental
   style with storks standing among flowering chrysanthemums issuing from rockwork, the wells with cell pattern
   and the borders with trailing flowers, 9¼ in diam   L   10 10

Liverpool Ware
Slender oviform jug, transfer-printed in colours, one side
   with British liberty, the reverse with French liberty, with
   accompanying inscriptions, 9 in high   L   21   0
Blue and white oval sauce boat, decorated with pagoda
   buildings beneath pine trees in Oriental style, 6¾ in wide L   16 16

Leeds Creamware
Pair of Dutch decorated creamware plates, the centres painted in colours each with a bird perched on a branch, the
   borders with exotic birds, on branches of honeysuckle
   suspended from rings, 8¼ in diam   L   48   6
Creamware mug with ribbed handle, transfer-printed in
   black with the Apotheosis of Bonaparte, Napoleon hanging
   on a gibbet with John Bull kneeling in prayer with repre-
   sentatives of the nations of Europe exclaiming in the
   background, 4½ in high   L   29   8
Circular two-handled basket, the interlaced handles with
   floral terminals, with a border of pierced rosettes and

	£	s
pierced with vertical apertures below, 8 in diam. Impressed Leeds Pottery mark	L 23	2

Lustreware

Large Sunderland lustre punch pot, transfer-printed with a west view of the Iron Bridge, figures, inscriptions and masonic emblems, within iron-red, green and yellow cartouches and mottled pink lustre ground, 9 in high — L 36 15

Silver-resist oval jug, moulded in relief with arched panels and reserved with flower-sprays on a silver lustre ground, the rim with circular medallions, 6½ in wide — L 21 0

Silver-resist lustre Parliamentary portrait jug, commemorating the commital to the Tower in 1810 of Sir Francis Burdett, M.P., 4 in — SE 16 0

Martin-ware

Bird jug and cover, standing, naturally modelled with curved beak and small eyes and incised with feather markings under a dull mottled brown glaze, with touches of blue to the wings and tail, 15 in high. Signed on the cover and base R. W. Martin & Bros. London & Southall, 21.4.1903. Wood stand — L 52 10

Pair of vases — SE 40 0

Pot Lid Collections

Twelve black-framed pomade pot lids — WE 30 0

Four pot lids: 'The Enthusiast', 'Wimbledon, July 2nd, 1860', 'Fishing boats at Sea', and 'Coral and Shells', 14 in diam — L 14 14

Three shaped oval pot lids, two with horsemen in battle and in a landscape after Wouvermann, the other with Queen Victoria's carriage before the Crystal Palace, 5½ in wide — L 14 14

Three pot lids: 'On Guard', a letter from the Diggins, and two girls and a wounded soldier drinking, 4 in diam. Wood frames — L 14 14

Four pot lids: 'Pegwell Bay, established 1750', 'Pegwell bay', 'the Belle Vue Tavern', and 'Peace', 4½ in diam. Wood frames — L 14 14

Four pot lids: lovers in a rocky arbour, two girls and a drinking soldier, the room in which Shakespeare was born, and Shakespeare house, 4¼ in diam. Wood frames, — L 14 14

Three pot lids depicting Shakespeare's house, Henley Street, Stratford-on-Avon; the residence of Anne Hathaway, Shakespeare's wife, Shottery, near Stratford-on-Avon; the room in which Shakespeare was born, 1564, Stratford-on-Avon, 4 in diam. Ebonized wood frames — L 13 13

Three pot lids, transfer-printed with Strasbourg, the Trooper, and Peace, 4¾ in and 4¼ in diam — L 12 12

Four pot lids: a Pair, a Fish Market, The Best Laid, and the Swing. 4½ in diam. Wood frames — L 12 12

Prattware

Stirrup cup, formed as a rabbit's head with fluted trumpet neck and crabstock handle, naturally modelled, and splashed in a mottled brown glaze, with yellow eyes, and with blue border to the lip, 5¾ in wide — L 60 18

£   s

Figure of a boy, standing holding a dog on a tree stump at
his side, in spotted cloak and blue breeches, on grasswork
mound and shaped base, 7¼ in high   L   35 14

Cow creamer, formed as a cow standing hobbled and being
milked by a milkmaid, its body splashed in black and
puce, on grasswork base, 6½ in wide   L   35 14

Toby jug, with caryated handle. Sir Toby standing holding
a bottle and a glass of beer, in buff-lined blue coat, with
striped waistcoat, the base and his hat splashed in blue,
black and ochre, 7½ in high   L   31 10

A fisherwoman, seated holding a basket of fish, her dress
with yellow spots, on grasswork mound and green base,
4¾ in high   L   23   2

Recumbent sheep naturally modelled and splashed in brown
and ochre, on grasswork base, 3 in wide   L   21   0

A girl standing before a tree stump, holding a bird, splashed
in blue and ochre, on rockwork base, 7¼ in high   L   18 18

Wedgwood—Black Basalt

Pair of black basalt wine and water ewers after the models
by Flaxman, the spouts with a triton and satyr holding a
goat and a porpoise suspending swags of seaweed and vines,
on gadrooned stems and square bases, 17½ in high   L   110   5

Pair of black basalt oval medallions with Hercules slaying
the Nemean lion and carrying Erymanthean boar, 7 in
wide. Gilt and wood frames   L   73 10

Black basalt oval portrait medallion of Oliver Cromwell, the
raised rim modelled with berried laurel leaves, 6½ in wide   L   14 14

Basalt ware teapot, cream jug and sugar basin with raised
ornamentation   N   5   5

Black basalt milk jug, moulded in relief with scrolling thistles,
roses and shamrocks and Welsh shamrocks, emblematic of
Scotland, England, Ireland and Wales, 4 in high   L   4   4

Wedgwood—Creamware

Pair of creamware handled vases and cover, with slender
bodies, painted with dancing classical and contemporary
figures, the shoulders with bands of formal patterns, the
concave necks, spreading bases and domed covers in bright
blue, 16 in high. Impressed marks   L   47   5

Pair of creamware blue and white candlesticks, formed as
fluted pillars, with flared wax pans and spreading square
bases, with fluted concave sides, enriched with scroll patterns in blue, 7 in high. Impressed mark   L   25   4

Wedgwood—Jasper

Blue and white jasper oval plaque, the solid blue ground
decorated in white relief with a nymph standing partly
draped in a lion's skin and holding a club, 3½ in high.
Impressed lower case 'Wedgwood & Bentley'. Wood frame   L   189   0

Blue and white jasper gold-mounted plaque, the blue ground
moulded in white relief with 'Poor Maria', the reverse with
a shepherd and his dog, mounted as a locket in gold, 2½ in
high   L   60 18

£   s

Pair of blue and white jasper oval portrait medallions of
Admirals St Vincent and Duncan in profile to the right
and left, with raised white borders, 5 in high. In plush
mount and glazed and ebonized frame   L   57 15

Pair of blue and white jasper oviform vases and covers, with
satyrs masks to the shoulders, the pale blue ground
modelled in white relief with 'The Dancing Hours' after
Flaxman, the shoulders, lower parts and covers moulded
with stiff leaves, the square bases moulded with anthemion,
9 in high. Impressed marks   L   44 2

Pair of blue and white jasper oblong plaques, each with five
dancing nymphs after Flaxman, 5½ in by 2 in. Gilt and
wood frames   L   27 6

Two-handled vase in pale blue and white jasper   M   15 0

Blue and white jasper oviform vase, cover and liner, the
solid blue ground decorated with ladies and cupids in
white relief, the pierced domed cover with pine cone finial,
13¼ in high. Impressed mark   L   14 14

Pair of Wedgwood blue and white jasper oval portrait
medallions of William Pitt and Charles James Fox, almost
full face, their names incised on the reverses, 4 in high   L   6 6

Whieldon

Pig, naturally modelled, standing with its head slightly low-
ered, its tail curled forward on its rump, covered in a
splashed tortoiseshell glaze, 10¾ in wide. Wood base   L   231 0

A putto, emblematic of autumn, standing holding a bunch
of grapes, on square mound base covered in a green glaze,
4¼ in high   L   57 15

Cow creamer, naturally modelled as a cow, standing, her
curled tail forming the handle and with a milkmaid seated
milking her, splashed in grey and ochre, on oblong
octagonal green base, 6¼ in wide   L   44 2

Red stoneware oblong octagonal teapot and cover, with serpent handle, the spout moulded with stiff leaves, the sides
with reliefs in the Oriental style, the central panels with a
naked Chinaman holding a spray of scrolling leaves, 6 in
wide   L   44 2

Cow creamer, the cow horizontally striped in ochre and
sepia, the milkmaid with brown and green coat, on shaped
green base, 7 in wide   L   37 16

Circular plate, splashed in yellow, green, grey and tortoiseshell glazes, with waved gadrooned rim, 9¼ in diam   L   21 0

Ralph Wood Figures

Equestrian figure of Hudibras, leaning back and drawing his
sword, with brown hat and beard and blue suit, his horse
with brown mane, tail and saddle cloth, its body covered
in a splashed greenish glaze, the rectangular pedestal base
splashed in blue and green, 9 in wide   L   945 0

Toby jug and cover, Sir Toby seated, holding a jug, in dark
brown tricorn hat, pale brown face and splashed brown
coat, the blue shield to one side impressed—*It is all out
then fill him again*—with pale brown cover, 10 in high   L   262 10

	£	s
Lord Howe Toby jug, with greenbranch handle, Sir Toby seated on a grey barrel, his right foot resting on a dog, pipe at his side, and holding a foaming jug of beer, with brown tricorn hat, grey hair, buff coat and yellow breeches, the rectangular base with canted corners, 9½ in high	L 150	0
Figure of a blacksmith standing beside an anvil, wearing black hat, sepia coat, blue apron and green breeches the base splashed in green and brown, 8 in high	L 89	5
Toby jug, Sir Toby seated, holding a glass and a jug frothing with ale, in brown tricorn hat, grey wig, buff coat, green waistcoat and yellow breeches, the square base with canted corners, 9¾ in high	L 68	5
Figure of a man emblematic of winter, standing over a brazier, wrapped in a cloak and decorated in blue and ochre, on a grassy mound, the square base moulded with stiff leaves, 9 in high	L 42	2
Figure of Flora standing, holding a cornucopia of fruit in one hand and a bunch of fruit in the other, partly draped in a flowing spotted robe, on grasswork mound base, 8 in high	L 29	8

Staffordshire Single Figures and Groups

	£	s
Jenny Jones, standing wearing black hat, green shawl and blue bodice, with checked apron, the oval base inscribed 'Jenny Jones' in gilt script, 10¼ in high	L 94	10
Louis Antoine Jullien, standing holding a score and singing, bearded, with blue tail coat, yellow waistcoat and striped trousers, the base impressed 'Jullien', 7¾ in high	L 75	12
Robert Burns, standing on a high cylindrical pedestal and square base, inscribed 'R. Burns born January 25th 1759 died July 21st 1796', 15¾ in high. Sampson Smith's factory, Longton, unmarked	L 68	5
Napoleon Bonaparte, standing before a pile of shot, his uniform enriched in black, green and pink, the square pedestal base with a gilt 'N', 13¼ in high	L 57	15
Jenny Lind, as Alice in *Robert le Diable* by Meyerbeer, kneeling in blue bodice and tartan skirt, clutching a pedestal surmounted by a Maltese cross, on oval grasswork base, 8¼ in high	L 57	15
Christ at the column, standing, His head bent to the right, with red loin cloth, the base with gilt scrolls, 15½ in high	L 52	10
Giuseppe Garibaldi, standing beside his horse, in a red shirt, holding a sword, 14½ in high	L 33	12
William Gladstone, standing before a tree stump, holding a piece of paper in his left hand, his clothes slightly gilt, the base inscribed 'Gladstone' in script, 15¼ in high	L 33	12
Group of Highland Jessie and her husband Corporal Brown with his arm in a sling, their coats in blue and their sashes in pink and green, named on the base in raised capitals, 14½ in high	L 29	8
Lord Byron standing in Greek dress, a pink cloak over his shoulder, the scroll base named 'Byron' in raised capitals, 16 in high	L 26	5

o

	£	s
Seated figure of Richard Cobden, in long blue coat and striped trousers, a cornucopia to his right, the base inscribed 'R. Cobden', 7½ in high	L	25	4
Shepherd and shepherdess, with sheep and floral bocage at rear, 7½ in high	SE	22	0
Jemmy Wood, standing in black suit, named in raised capitals on the black base 'Jemmy Wood', 10¾ in high	L	21	0
Leeds group of Charity wearing blue coloured dress on oval base, 7 in	SE	21	0
Florence Nightingale standing in black shawl and pink skirt, 5½ in high	L	16	16
Duke of Wellington, standing beside a tree stump covered in a pink cloak, his coat and waistcoat enriched with gilding, his name on the base in script, 13½ in high	L	16	16
William Tell, standing, with red-lined green cloak and blue tunic, the base with 'Wm. Tell' in script, 9¼ in high	L	16	16
Emperor Napoleon and Empress Eugenie	WE	13	0
David Garrick as 'Richard III', after the painting by Hogarth, seated beneath a red and blue tent in green cloak, blue tunic, 9¾ in high	L	12	12
Prince Albert, standing holding a sceptre, in green lined iron-red cloak and puce trousers, 6½ in high	L	9	9
The Cobbler's wife, a cat looking through her chair, on square base, 6½ in	SE	7	0
Figure with dead tiger, seated on an elephant, 8¼ in	N	6	0
King William III on horseback, 10 in high	N	6	0
The Lovers—two figures seated, on rustic background, 9 in	N	6	0
Scottish hunter with dog and deer	SE	4	10
Returning Home—two figures on horseback, 8½ in	N	4	0
The woodcutters with painted waistcoats	SE	4	0
Robin Hood, oval base, 15 in	SE	3	10

Staffordshire Figures in Pairs

Queen Victoria and Prince Albert, standing, the Queen with ermine-lined cloak, her dress with bands of flowers, the Prince beside a pillar, with ermine-lined cloak, tartan sash and yellow gloves, named in raised capitals, 'Queen and Albert', 10½ in high	L	43	1
Elijah and the Widow seated before flowering trees, named on the bases with four feet, 12 in high	L	33	12
Ira B. Sankey and Dwight L. Moody the American Evangelists, standing in black suits and white waistcoats beside red and green columns, named in raised capitals 'Moody and Sankey', 13½ in high	L	29	8
Equestian figures of King William III and Queen Mary, the King in red uniform, the Queen in pink bodice and flowered skirt, named in raised capitals below, 10 in high	L	26	5
William Gladstone and his wife, decorated in white and gold, the bases inscribed 'Mr. Gladstone and Mrs. Gladstone', 9½ in high	L	23	2
Admiral Lord Nelson and Field-Marshal the Duke of Wellington, each in uniform beside a column draped in a cloak and holding a despatch, 8 in high	L	23	2

		£	s
William Shakespeare and John Milton, standing leaning against pedestals, Shakespeare holding a scroll and wearing buff cloak, blue waistcoat and puce breeches, Milton holding a book and similarly dressed with green breeches on shaped bases, 8½ in high	L	21	0
Equestrian figures of General Sir Colin Campbell and Sir Henry Havelock, on chestnut horses, in blue uniform, the bases inscribed 'Havelock and Campbell' in raised capitals, 9 in high	L	18	18
Equestrian figures of Count Von Moltke and Prince Bismarck, enriched in black and brown, named in raised capitals 'G. Moltke and G. Bismarck', 13 in high	L	16	16
Equestrian figures of general officers, with pink and blue saddle clothes and enriched with gilding, 12 in high	L	14	14
A blind musician and his wife, the musician with a violin and a dog, with blue coat, hatched waistcoat and pink breeches, his wife with red cloak, 11 in high	L	14	14
Dick Turpin on Black Bess and Tom King on a white horse, with blue coats, red scarves and turquoise waistcoats, named in gilt capitals on the bases, 9 in high	L	12	12
Spaniels, seated erect, naturally modelled, with black ears and tails, their bodies with black patches, holding baskets of flowers in their mouths, 7¾ in high	L	10	10
Equestrian figures of Queen Victoria and Prince Albert, slightly decorated in iron-red and brown, 8¼ in and 9¾ in high	L	8	8
King Charles spaniel dogs, decorated and black	SE	8	0
Prince of Wales and the Princess Royal, each riding on a goat, dressed in blue, the goat with hair markings in black and iron-red, 6 in high	L	7	7
Falconers, each standing beside a chair, holding a bird on a glove and with a basket of dead birds below, with feathered hats, the man with red cloak and blue tunic, his companion with red cloak, blue tunic and tartan skirt, 9¾ in high	L	5	5
Pair of recumbent lions, 9½ in	N	6	0
Pair of seated spaniels, 6 in high	N	3	10

CLEAR GLASS

Ale Glasses

Ale glass with small drawn-funnel bowl and plain stem containing a small tear, terminating in a domed and folded foot, 8½ in	L	50	0
Pair of tall ale glasses with funnel bowls, supported on columnar corkscrew opaque-twist stems terminating in conical feet, 8¼ in	L	28	0
Engraved ale glass with funnel bowl, decorated with sprays and hops and barley, on a double-knopped air-twist stem terminating in a conical foot, 7⅞ in	L	26	0

Bowls

Turn-over bowl, cut with diamonds and flutes on the rim, a narrower band around the base, which is ornamental

		£	s
with a spiral whorl and supported on a plated stand, 10¼ in diam	L	50	0
Punchbowl with large bowl on a massive plain stem and wide circular foot, 9⅝ in high, 5½ in diam	L	26	0
Cut-glass covered bowl, the depressed globular body and the cover cut with convex diamonds and slanting blazes, surmounted by a mushroom knop supported on a short stem and star-cut square base, 8½ in	L	15	0
Armorial punchbowl supported on a short plain stem and massive circular foot, the large ovoid bowl engraved with a Continental coat-of-arms on one side and bold sprays of flowers on the reverse, 9¾ in	L	14	0

Candlesticks and Candelabra

Pair of candlesticks, with ribbed double-ogee nozzles, on columnar stems with plain knops at the top and base, supported on domed feet, 8½ in	L	110	0
Pair of Victorian twin-branch candelabra with drops, sconces and moulded columns	SE	46	0
Candlestick with plain moulded nozzle, on a tall columnar spiral air-twist stem, supported on a high domed and wide foot, 9½ in	L	32	0

Cordial Glasses

Cordial glass with ogee bowl, supported on a colour-twist stem composed of a multiple opaque white corkscrew encircled by a single wine-red spiral thread, terminating on a conical foot, 5¾ in	L	65	0
Cordial glass with ogee bowl, supported on an opaque-twist stem composed of a green-edged corkscrew enclosed within a single broad white tape, terminating in a conical foot, 5½ in	L	62	0
Engraved cordial glass, the drawn-trumpet bowl decorated with the Jacobite emblem of six-petalled rose with open and unopen buds, an oak leaf and six-rayed star, supported on a columnar air-twist stem and conical foot, 6⅛ in	L	52	0
Cordial glass, with short flared bowl and solid base, supported on an inverted baluster stem containing a tear and terminating in a folded foot, 4¾ in	L	45	0
Williamite cordial glass with small cylindrical bowl, on a faceted columnar stem and conical foot, the bowl engraved with a profile bust portrait of King William, to sinister, as an emperor, within the legend: 'The Immortal Memory', the reverse with a crowned harp, flanked by fruiting vine, 6½ in	L	40	0
Cordial glass, with engraved and pressed straight-sided bowl on a fine columnar opaque-twist stem, and domed foot, 7 in	L	22	0

Decanters

Early Masonic decanter of early bottle shape, with kick-in base and single collar around neck, which is engraved with a star and diamond band, the body finely wheel-engraved with a complete frieze of various Masonic insignia, 8 in	L	125	0

		£	s
Pair of ships decanters with mushroom stoppers, the pyramidal bodies cut with a band of small flutes round the base, petal cutting on the shoulders, and graduated quadruple collars round the necks, 8½ in	L	110	0
Set of four cut-glass decanters by Apsley Pellatt with globular bodies and tapered necks, cut with two rows of ovals and petal cutting, star-cut bases and minaret stoppers, 13¼ in	L	48	0
Set of three spirit decanters, thinly blown, the bodies with gilt labels inscribed 'Brandy', 'Hollands', 'Rum', the necks with triple-milled collars, surmounted by vesica stoppers bearing the appropriate initials, 7⅛ in	L	48	0
Pair of massive cut decanters, the globular bodies above waisted bases, star cut, decorated around the centres with broad bands of alternate strawberry hobnails and oval panels, mushroom stopper, 8½ in	L	42	0
Pair of cut ships' decanters, with mushroom stoppers, the conical bodies with prismatic cutting almost to the necks, and with star-cut bases, 8¾ in	L	34	0
Pair of shouldered decanters with heart-shaped stoppers, engraved in Adam style and festoons and ribbon ties, still showing signs of the original gilding, 11 in	L	28	0
Pair of decanters with mushroom stoppers, decorated with pendant leaf cutting beneath triple collars and above a short band of flutes, 9 in	L	25	0
Pair of eighteenth-century decanters with ringed necks	WE	15	0

Goblets

		£	s
Goblet with lipped straight-sided bowl, on a hollow many-knopped baluster stem, containing a large tear and terminating in a conical foot with narrow fold, 9⅞ in	L	55	0
A pink-twist goblet with large plain ogee bowl on a tall opaque-white pink-tinged twist, supported on a conical foot, 8¼ in	L	32	0
Set of six engraved goblets with flared funnel bowls, decorated with branches of fruiting vine and supported on faceted stems and circular feet, 6½ in	L	28	0
Goblet, the ovoid bowl finely engraved with human masks from which are pendant festoons and swags of fruit and flowers, the interior with a hidden rose, supported on a massive facet-cut stem and wide conical foot, 10 in	L	26	0
Goblet, the drawn-trumpet bowl supported on a plain stem containing an elongated heart-shaped tear and terminating in a folded foot, 9¾ in	L	16	0

Honey Jars

		£	s
Pair of honey jars and covers of vase shape, ornamented with petal cutting, printies and shallow diamonds, supported on short stems and terraced square bases, 12 in	L	42	0
Honey jar and cover, of urn shape, boldly cut with a band of convex diamonds, petal-cutting and broad flutes on a short stem and square base, 11½ in	L	20	0
Honey jar and cover, the body cut all over with shallow convex diamonds, the cover with bands of similar orna-			

£   s

ment between shallow-cut panels and with faceted finial,
supported on a short stem and square star-cut base, 12 in   L   14   0

Rummers

Early rummer, the globular bowl 'nipt diamond waies'
around the base resting on a vermicular collar above a
hollow cylindrical stem decorated with six bold raspberry
prunts in relief and terminating in a high conical folded
foot, 10¼ in, *circa* 1685   L   780   0

Set of eight rummers, the upper half of the ogee bowls engraved with dot and star motifs, supported on circular
knops above short stems and square lemon-squeezer
bases, 5⅛ in   L   48   0

Set of six rummers with octagonal cut stems   M   7   5

Three knop-stem rummers   SE   4 10

Sweetmeats

Cut sweetmeat, the double-ogee bowl with vesica cutting
below a scalloped rim, supported on a faceted centre-
knopped stem and domed and scalloped foot ornamented
with printies, 8¼ in   L   25   0

Sweetmeat glass, the shallow double-ogee bowl with flat
pincered rim, supported on an opaque-twist stem and
radically moulded foot, 2¾ in   L   19   0

Sweetmeat with double ogee bowl above a plain stem with
central swelling knop, supported on a small domed foot,
5⅝ in   L   15   0

Wineglasses—Airtwist

Set of seven engraved wine glasses with bell bowls, on air-
twist stems and conical feet, the rims engraved with a
wreath of fruiting vine, 6⅝ in   L   85   0

Set of six wine glasses with bell bowls, slightly flared and
supported on columnar air-twist stems terminating in
conical feet, 6¾ in   L   48   0

Pair of wine glasses with bell bowls, on air-twist stems with
frilled collars, supported on conical feet, 6¼ in   L   38   0

Engraved wine glass, the bucket bowl unusually engraved with
a rose spray on one side and lily-of-the-valley on the reverse, on a centre-knopped air-twist stem, terminating
in a conical foot, 6⅛ in   L   26   0

Wine glass, the trumpet bowl with solid base inset in a
shoulder knopped air-twist stem, terminating in a conical
foot, 6½ in   L   20   0

Wine glass with small, straight-sided bowl, on a shoulder-
knopped air-twist stem of good quality, terminating in a
spherical knop above a conical foot, 6½ in   L   18   0

Wine Glasses—Baluster

Wine glass, the deep bowl supported on a wide baluster terminating in a ball knop and folded foot, 7½ in   L   58   0

Wine glass, the deep funnel bowl supported on a stem com-
posed of a baluster over a ball knop, and terminating in
a folded conical foot, 4¾ in   L   45   0

Wine Glasses—Jacobite

Pair of engraved wine glasses with double-ogee bowls, de-

£   s

corated with Jacobite emblems of rose, carnation and
honeysuckle divided by fruiting branches of pears, apples
and grapes on swelling knopped stems and conical feet,
6¼ in   L   48   0
Pair of Jacobite wine glasses, the straight-sided bowls engraved with a six-petalled rose and a bud and supported
on double-knopped air-twist stems and conical feet, 6¼ in   L   42   0
Set of three Jacobite wine glasses, the straight-sided bowls
engraved with sunflowers and supported on plain stems
and conical feet, 6½ in   L   40   0
Jacobite wine glass with straight-sided bowl, on a fine cable
air-twist stem encircled by a mercurial corkscrew, the bowl
unusually engraved with a daffodil, with rose leaves and
stems, the reverse with a moth-like butterfly, 5¾ in   L   36   0
Pair of engraved Jacobite wine glasses with straight-sided
bowls on facet-cut stems, the bowls engraved with Jacobite
emblems, including a rose, single bud, bees and also birds
in flight and forget-me-nots, 6 in   L   24   0
Jacobite wine glass, the bowl engraved with a sunflower, sig-
nifying the decay of the movement, the reverse with a
moth, supported on a stem containing two entwined tapes
enclosed by filigree ribbons, conical foot, 6 in   L   15   0

Wine Glasses—Opaque-twist
Eight wine glasses with a variety of ogee bowls on different
opaque-twist stems, terminating in circular feet, 5⅝ in to
6 in   L   54   0
Six wine glasses with bell bowls, on different types of
opaque-twist stems, terminating in conical feet, 6⅜ in   L   28   0
Wine glass with ovoid bowl, attractively engraved with a
band of fruiting vine, supported on an unusual triple
series opaque-twist stem, terminating in a conical foot,
6½ in   L   18   0

Wine Glasses—Plain-stemmed
Six wine glasses, all with similar drawn-trumpet bowls and
plain stems, terminating in plain conical feet, 6⅛ to 7⅛ in   L   54   0
Wine glass with flared bell bowl, resting on a triple collar
above a pure baluster stem, terminating in a wide conical
foot, 7⅛ in   L   40   0
Set of five wine glasses with drawn-trumpet bowls, and plain
stems, the bowls engraved with fruiting vine trees, sup-
ported on conical feet, 6⅛ in   L   35   0
An engraved wine glass, the bell bowl with a border of fruiting vine, supported on a baluster stem terminating in a
conical foot, 6⅝ in   L   35   0

COLOURED GLASS
Blue Glass
Set of three Bristol blue decanters and stoppers labelled in
gilt—'Brandy', 'Rum', 'Hollands'; height 8½ in   SE   32   0
Set of six blue glass finger bowls of cup shape, entirely
plain, the glass of rich tone, 4¾ in diam   L   32   0
Bristol blue decanter and six glasses   WE   18   0

		£	s
Set of four Bristol blue glass finger bowls	M	4	0
Bristol blue glass roller	WE	1	10

Cameo Glass

Cameo vase of conical shape with slightly flared neck, the yellow frosted body overlaid and carved in white, with sprays of flowering roses, the reverse and neck with small sprigs of leaves, 16 in	L	175	0
Small glass vase of ovoid shape, with flared rim, overlaid in white on a wine-red ground and cut with a design of ferns and grasses, 4½ in	L	90	0
Scent bottle of globular shape, the translucent-red body overlaid in white and cut with a design of flowering hawthorn beneath a border of florettes, silver screw stopper, 5 in. Mark—'Thomas Webb and Sons'	L	95	0

SMALL ORNAMENTAL ANTIQUES

Miniatures

Bust portrait of a lady wearing white bonnet and blue dress, painted on ivory, 1½ in by 1¼ in, Cairngorm back, gold frame	N	19	0
Bust portrait of a gentleman wearing dark coat and white cravat (painted on ivory), 2¾ in by 2¼ in. The back compartment containing a lock of hair, and seed pearl decoration, gold frame	N	17	0
Three-quarter length portrait of Lady Hamilton (painted on ivory) after Gainsborough, 3¼ in by 2½ in. Tortoiseshell frame	N	15	0
Bust portrait of a gentleman wearing dark coat and white cravat (painted on ivory), 2¾ in by 2 in, the back compartment containing a lock of hair, and seed pearl decoration, gold frame	N	14	0
Bust portrait of a gentleman (painted on ivory), 2¾ by 2¼ in, signed 'R.M.K.' gilt frame, in velvet-lined case	N	9	0
Bust portrait of a lady (painted on ivory), 4 in by 3 in, gilt frame, in velvet-lined case	N	8	0
Bust portrait of a lady (painted on ivory), 2½ in by 2 in, gilt frame, in velvet-lined case	N	8	0
Oval portrait of a girl with her hair in ringlets, in red leather case	SE	6	10
Victorian lady in blue dress, holding a book, James Holmes, 1844	SE	5	10
Bust portrait of a gentleman wearing a wig and pink coat, 3¼ in by 2¾ in	N	5	10
Bust portrait of a gentleman wearing blue coat and white cravat, 3⅜ in by 2¾ in	N	4	10
Bust portrait of a military gentleman, 2 in circular, ebonized frame	N	3	15

Paperweights

Baccarat blue carpet-ground weight inscribed 'B 1848', the ground of dark blue and white florettes into which are sunk a variety of geometric canes and also corrugated

		£	s
canes containing silhouettes in white of an ibex and a swan and in black of a deer and a dog, 2⅝ in diam	L	520	0
St Louis pink carpet-ground weight with five clusters of predominantly pale green canes sunk in a carpet of pink corrugations, in the centre a red-lined white star-shaped florette encircled by green corrugations, 3¼ in	L	360	0
Baccarat scattered millefiori weight, dated 'B 1848', the upset muslin ground containing blue and red threads and set with a variety of canes, including silhouettes of an elephant, horse and swan, 2¾ in	L	115	0
Baccarat mushroom weight, the tuft set in clear glass and formed of a close group of various millefiori canes, including stars, pastry-moulds and whorls, enclosed by an opaque-white gauze encircled by a blue spiral strand, star-cut base, 3 in	L	75	0
St Louis posy weight formed of five red, pink and yellow florettes, set amidst serrated green leaves, the tall dome cut with a cluster of printies at the top and large windows at the sides, 3⅛ in diam	L	60	0
St Louis amber-flash posy weight, cut all over with graduated facets, the posy composed of four florettes and serrated green leaves, the base only covered, 2⅛ in	L	48	0
Baccarat patterned-millefiori weight with two interlaced garlands of predominantly red and white canes, enclosing a rosette formed of a turquoise honeycomb cane encircled by blue and white star clusters, in clear glass, 2⅞ in	L	22	0
Bacchus millefiori weight with a concentric arrangement of canes in an unusual palette of liver, blue, green, red and white, 3⅛ in	L	14	0

Snuff Boxes

George III 18-carat gold snuff box, London 1809	SE	150	0
Eighteenth-century Continental silver-gilt snuff box with engraved lid, 1⅞ in	SE	10	0
Eighteenth-century Continental octagonal snuff box decorated with figures and animals in landscapes. English hall marks for 1891, 2⅛ in	SE	7	10
Early Georgian oblong engine-turned snuff box, 2⅝ in	SE	8	10
Eighteenth-century circular tortoiseshell snuff box with portraits of Louis XIV and Marie Therese, 2¼ in	SE	8	0
Eighteenth-century Spanish coin circular snuff box, 1779	SE	5	0
Copper coin circular snuff box, 1797, 1½ in	SE	3	0
Nineteenth-century gilt painted *papier mâché* snuff box, 3⅛ in	SE	2	0

Tea Caddies

Walnut three-compartment tea caddy	M	9	0
Tortoiseshell tea caddy with mother-of-pearl inlay, 7 in	N	7	10
Rosewood tea caddy with two compartments and glass blending bowl	WE	7	10
Inlaid satinwood tea caddy, 5¼ in	N	6	10
Sheraton square mahogany tea caddy	M	6	10
Victorian *papier mâché* tea caddy	WE	5	5
Mahogany tea caddy with original cut-glass liner and on ball feet	SE	5	0
Tortoiseshell tea caddy, 6½ in	N	4	15

		£	s
Regency rosewood sarcophagus-shape tea caddy, with two interior caddies and mixing bowl	WE	4	15
Inlaid maplewood tea caddy with urn motif	SE	4	0
Sheraton mahogany and satinwood banded tea caddy with three interior divisions, 11 in	WE	3	0
Small mahogany and inlaid tea caddy on ball feet	WE	3	0
Victorian inlaid walnut tea caddy with domed top	WE	2	10

Workboxes

		£	s
Small satinwood shaped-top needlework box	M	17	0
Sheraton mahogany round-topped workbox	M	8	10
Octagonal rosewood sewing box with ring handles	WE	6	0
Victorian sewing cabinet	WE	6	0
Lacquered workbox	M	2	10
Inlaid walnut workbox with interior fittings, 9½ in	N		18

Writing Desks

		£	s
Mahogany brass-bound writing desk	SE	5	15
Walnut writing compactum	WE	2	15
Walnut writing box with slope, hinged compartment and brass bands	WE	2	0

INDEX

(Figures in italics refer to pages on which saleroom prices are quoted.)